IMAGES
of America

Rural Life in the Piedmont of South Carolina

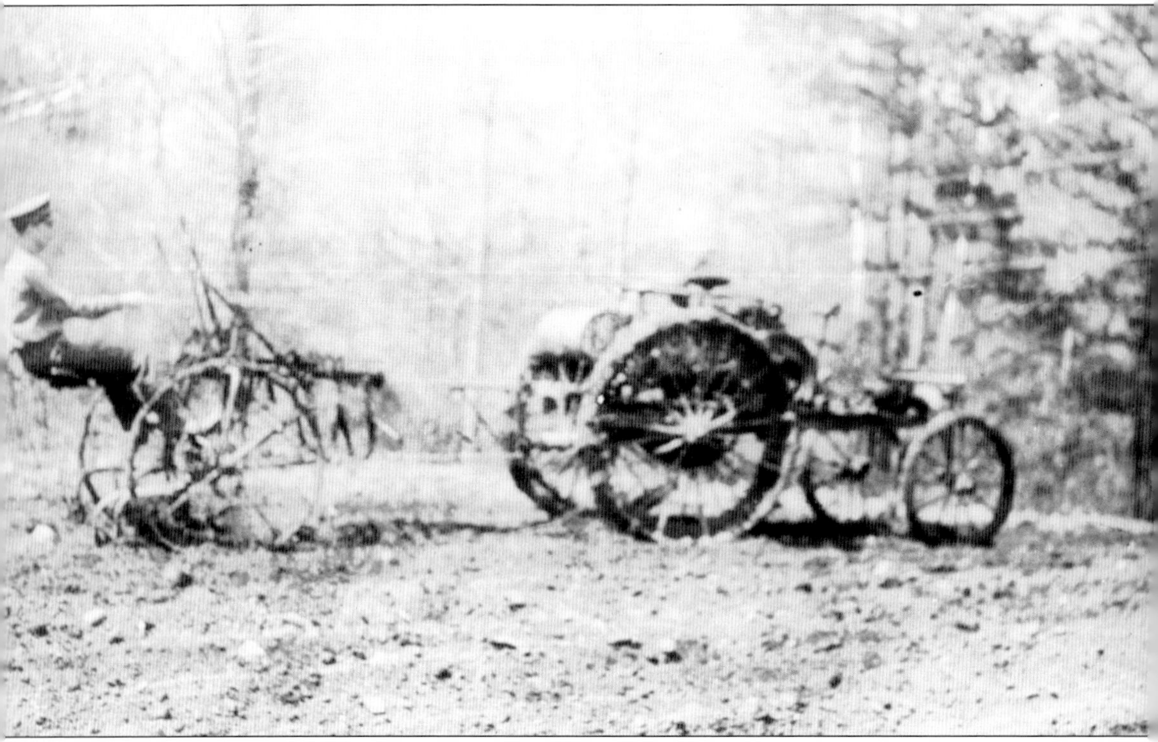

CLEMSON COLLEGE CADET WITH TRACTOR, C. 1920. In the early decades of this century, cadets helped grow food used by the college. The cadet shown here actually steered this tractor from behind.

IMAGES
of America

RURAL LIFE IN THE PIEDMONT OF SOUTH CAROLINA

Dennis S. Taylor
Clemson University Libraries

ARCADIA PUBLISHING

ISBN 978-0-7385-0198-7

Published by Arcadia Publishing
Charleston, South Carolina

Printed in the United States of America

Library of Congress Catalog Card Number: Applied for.

For all general information contact Arcadia Publishing at:
Telephone 843-853-2070
Fax 843-853-0044
E-Mail sales@arcadiapublishing.com
For customer service and orders:
Toll-Free 1-888-313-2665

Visit us on the Internet at www.arcadiapublishing.com

Contents

ACKNOWLEDGMENTS

Special thanks go to the following people who helped make this book possible:

Mark Berry, Editor, Arcadia Publishing;
Joseph F. Boykin, Dean, Clemson University Libraries;
Michael Kohl, Head, Special Collections, Clemson University Libraries;
Linda Ferry, Clemson University Libraries;
Dan Ezell, Clemson University Cooperative Extension Service, retired;
Larry Massey, Clemson University Cooperative Extension Service, retired;
Donna Roper, Pendleton District Historical, Recreational, and Tourism Commission.

FOREWORD

The Piedmont of South Carolina has its roots in agriculture. One might find this difficult to believe given the rapid development and growth of the industrial and service sectors in the Upstate region. Accompanying the economic development of the region has been a continuous and rapid growth in the population. The landscape has changed dramatically with lakes, industries, shopping centers, resorts, and housing developments occupying land that once grew cotton, corn, tobacco, timber, and pastures for livestock as the main source of income for families. This book has an excellent pictorial history of the diversity of agriculture and families that exemplified the Piedmont region in the earlier days of development.

The Land Grant mission of Clemson University in providing research-based and unbiased education is evident in the pictures. The Clemson University Cooperative Extension Service played a major educational role in delivering the latest research information from the experiment station, which related to agriculture, home economics, community development, and 4-H to farmers and rural families. The pictures in this book were taken by county extension agents, and they show the diversity and scope of programs that helped families improve their quality of life through education. The 4-H and home economics programs, in addition to agriculture, were a prominent part of Clemson University mission in assisting youth, families, and communities.

As the Piedmont has changed so has the agriculture in the region. Clemson Extension continues to conduct educational programs in the counties to address the needs of a dynamic and growing population; examples include environmental and conservation issues, nutrition, food safety, youth, economic development, water quality, as well as agriculture and forestry. The Piedmont continues to be a unique and vibrant part of the economy of South Carolina.

Daniel B. Smith
Director
Clemson University Cooperative Extension Service
April 1999

INTRODUCTION

The Piedmont, or as it is often called, "Upcountry," lies in northwestern South Carolina. Bordering North Carolina and Georgia, the Piedmont covers almost one-third of the state or roughly 17 counties: Abbeville, Anderson, Cherokee, Chester, Edgefield, Fairfield, Greenville, Greenwood, Laurens, McCormick, Newberry, Oconee, Pickens, Saluda, Spartanburg, Union, and York.

The terrain of the Piedmont, its soil, climate, and growing season have affected life fundamentally. These attributes determined not only the kinds of crops that could be grown, but also when and how those crops were planted and harvested. Planting and harvesting, in turn, determined how and when children were educated, because schools followed the agricultural calendar. Leisure, as well, when it did occur, followed the lead of agriculture.

This rural life, then, and the activities associated with it, are depicted in the images presented herein. Captured by the photographers of the Clemson University Cooperative Extension Service for five decades, these pictures represent only a portion of the thousands of images now held by the Clemson University Libraries. The collection is rich for further mining.

Because many images lacked names of individuals, locations, and dates, I have tried to supply that information, whenever possible, using context. Otherwise, I have provided only minimal interpretation because the pictures speak eloquently for themselves.

D.S.T.
April 1999

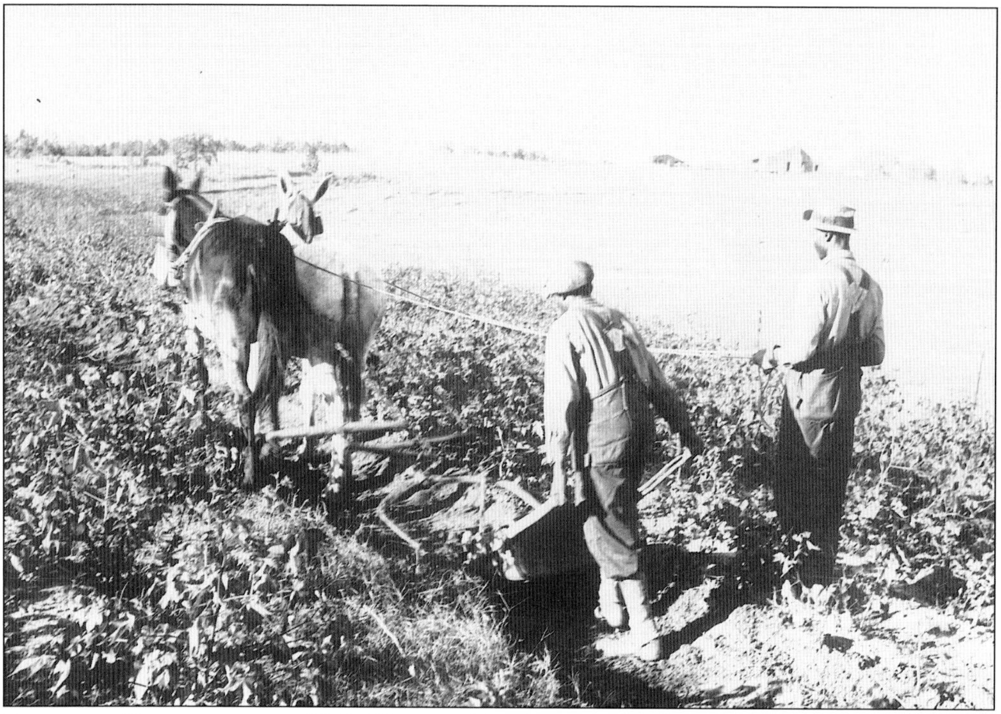

PLOWING A TERRACE ON THE W.B. KENNEDY FARM, 1938, FAIRFIELD. Terraces permitted steep, unusable land to become productive.

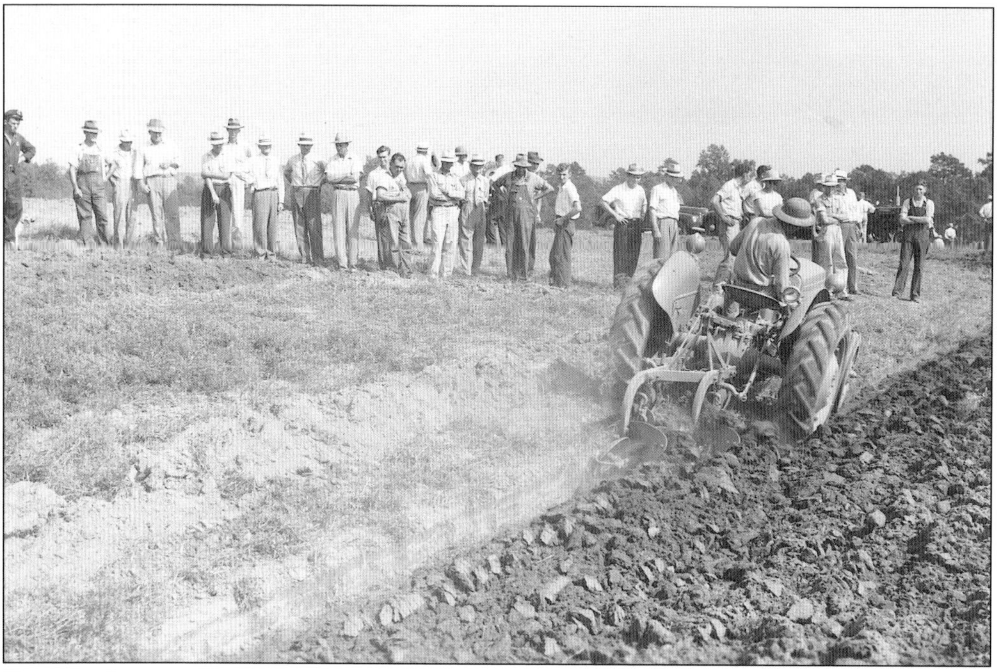

TERRACE-PLOWING DEMONSTRATION, 1948, PICKENS COUNTY.

One

The Land

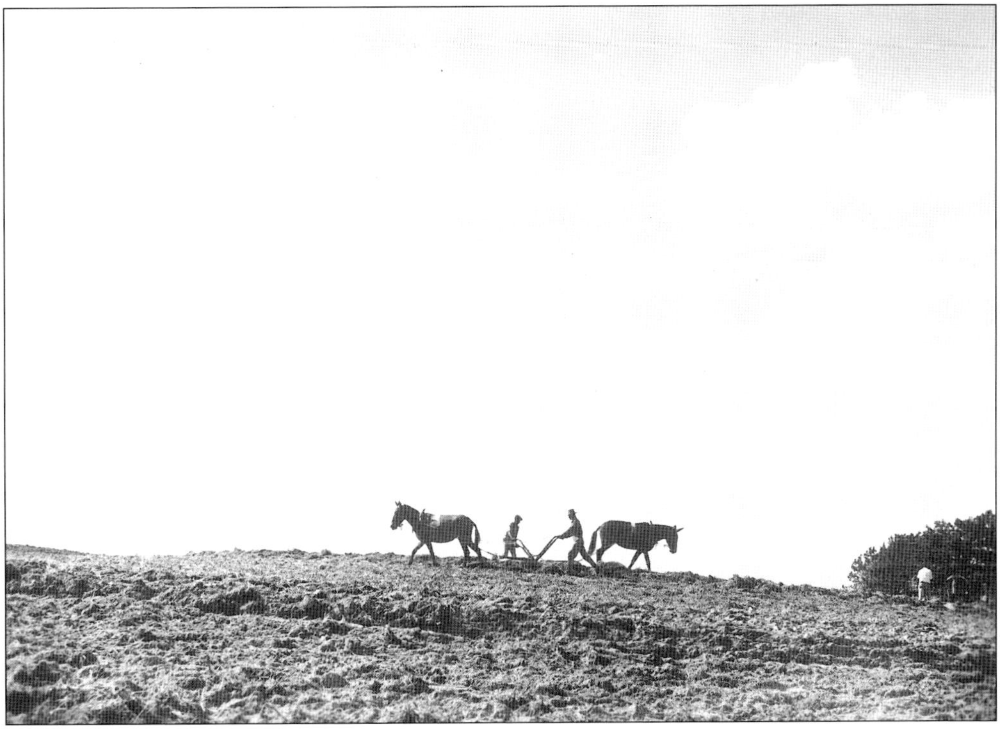

Farmers and Their Mules Plowing, 1938, Hodges. Red clay of the Piedmont proved hard to plow for even the toughest mules and strongest men.

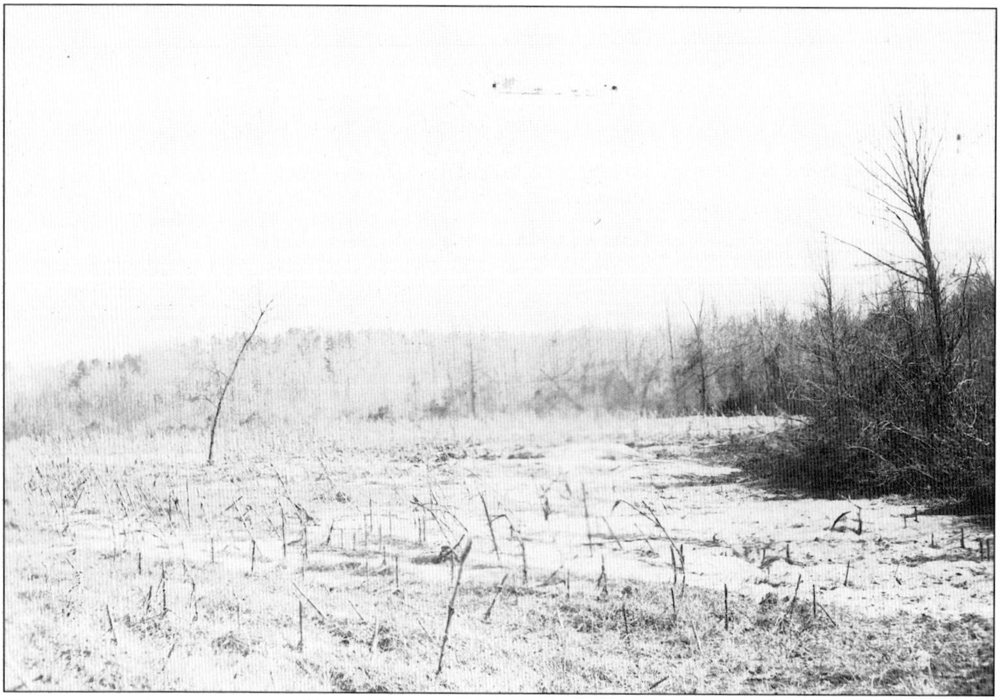

Bottomland Destroyed by Sand Deposit after a Flood, c. 1941, near Walhalla. Farmers constantly fought the forces of nature to make land productive.

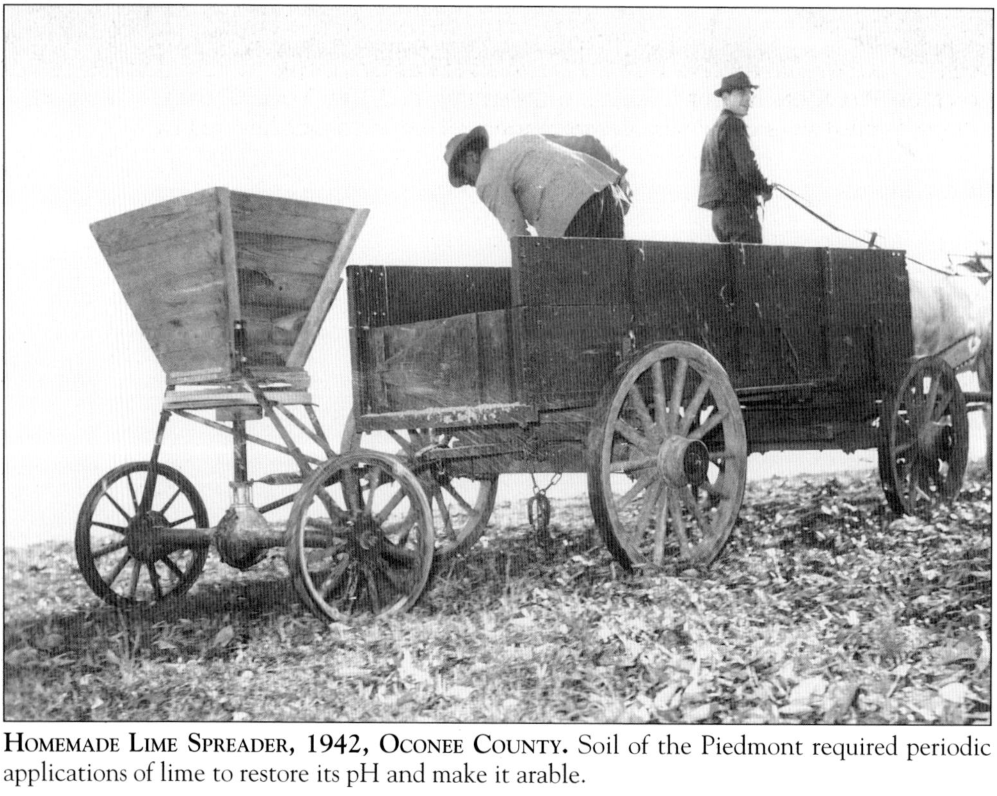

Homemade Lime Spreader, 1942, Oconee County. Soil of the Piedmont required periodic applications of lime to restore its pH and make it arable.

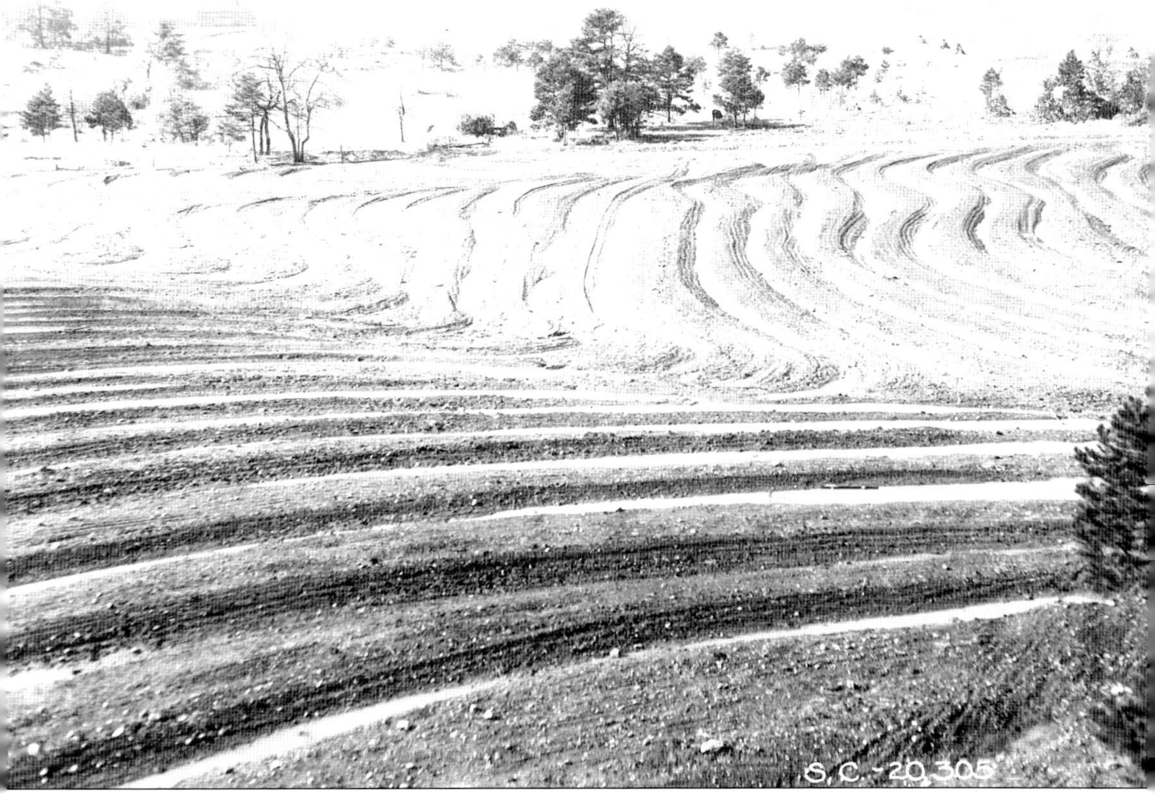

CONTOUR WORK ON PASTURE, READY FOR SEEDING, C. 1939, YORK COUNTY. The swirling patterns fulfilled an essential purpose: preventing soil erosion during heavy rains.

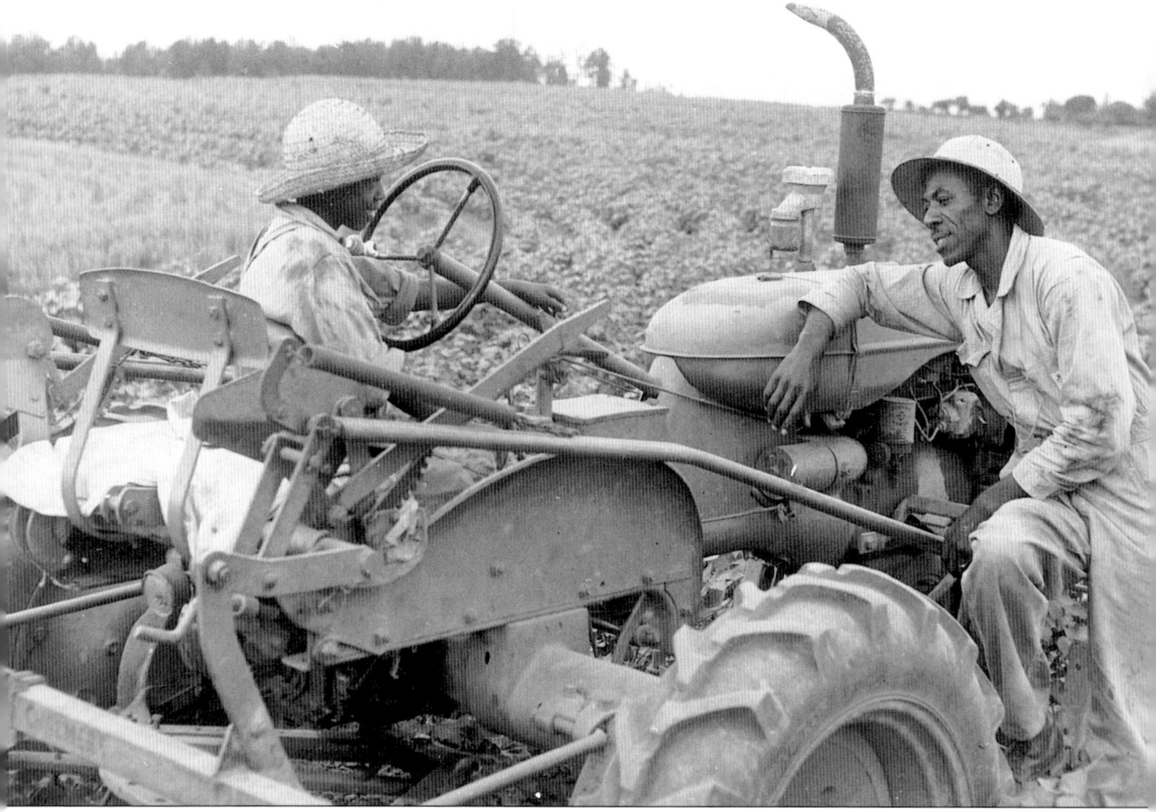
FATHER TEACHING SON TO DRIVE TRACTOR, 1947, ANDERSON.

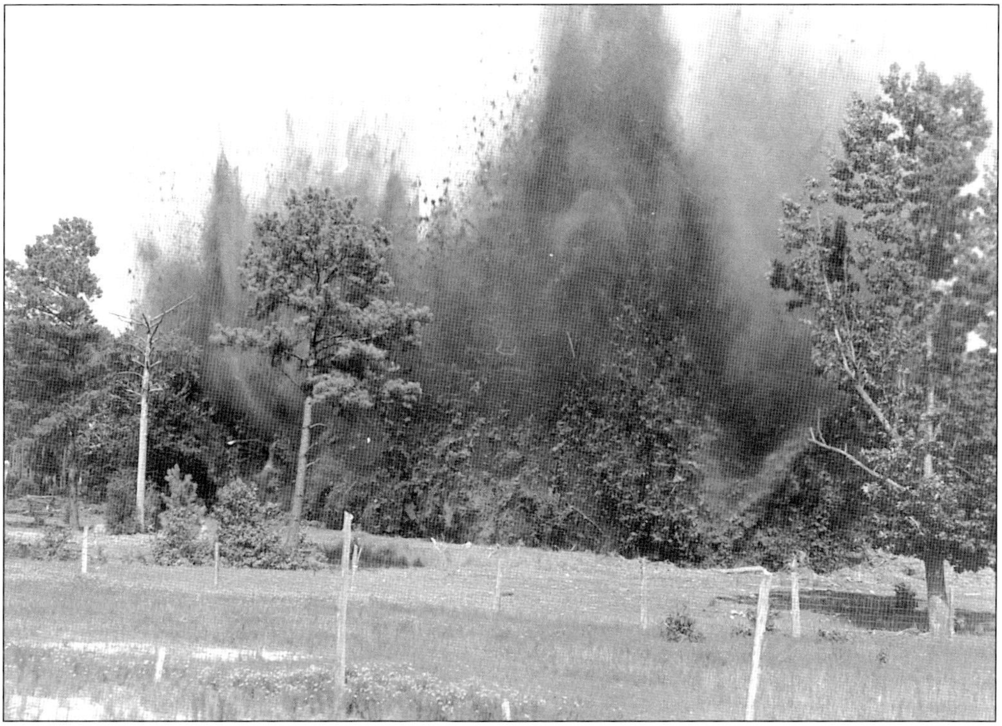

Blasting a Drainage Ditch, 1947, Pickens County. Dynamite proved superior to the backbreaking manual excavation of earth.

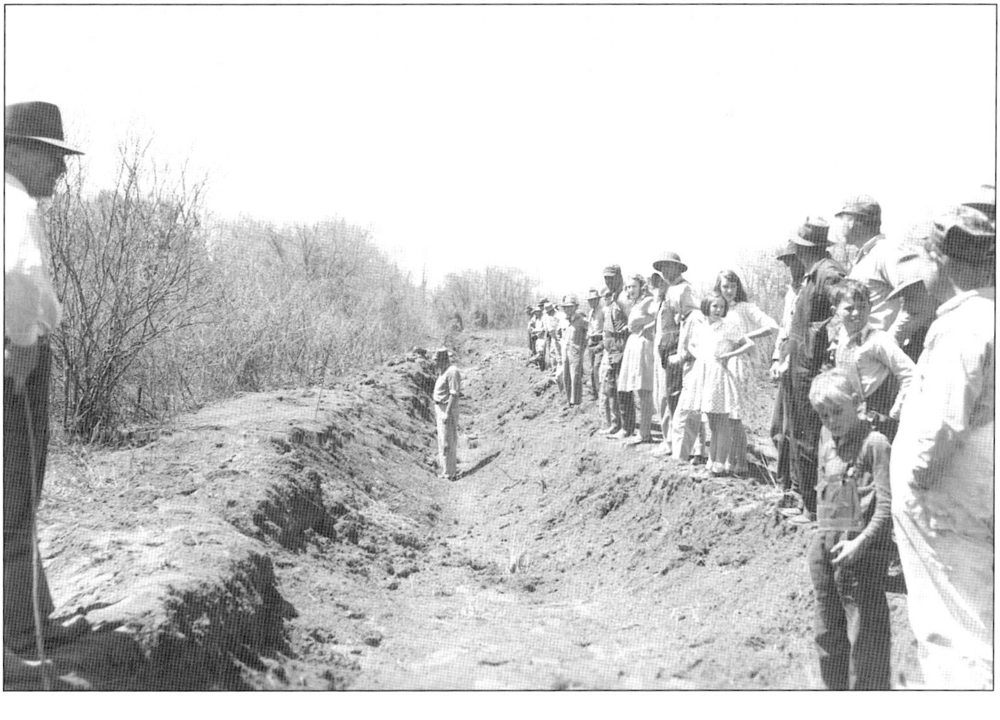

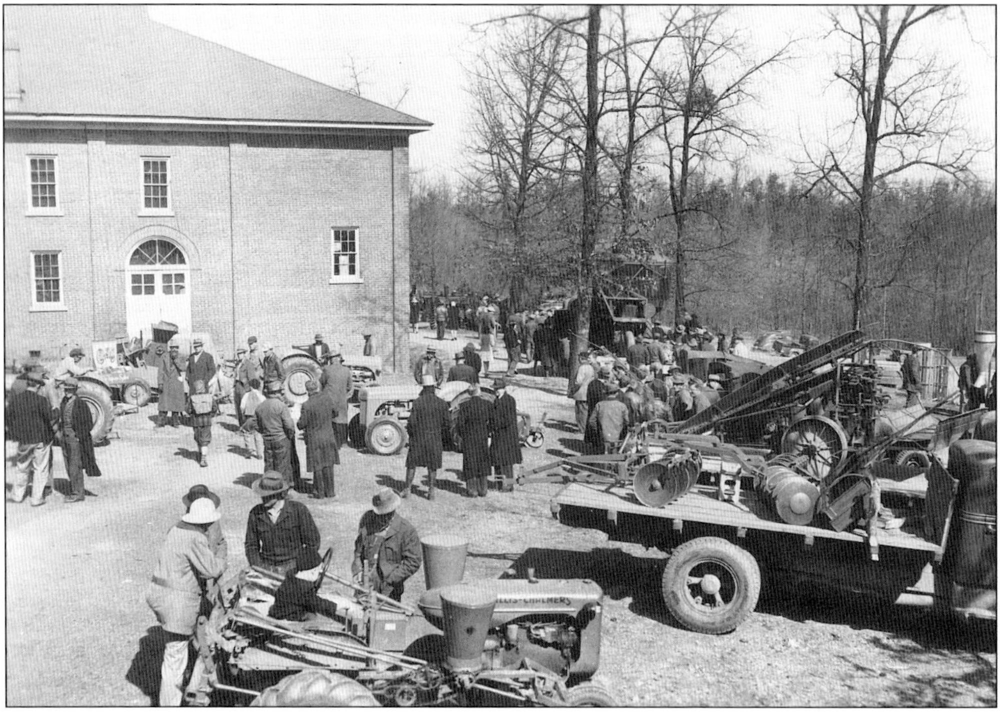

LABOR-SAVING SHOW, 1947, OCONEE COUNTY. These demonstrations showcased the latest farming implements and equipment.

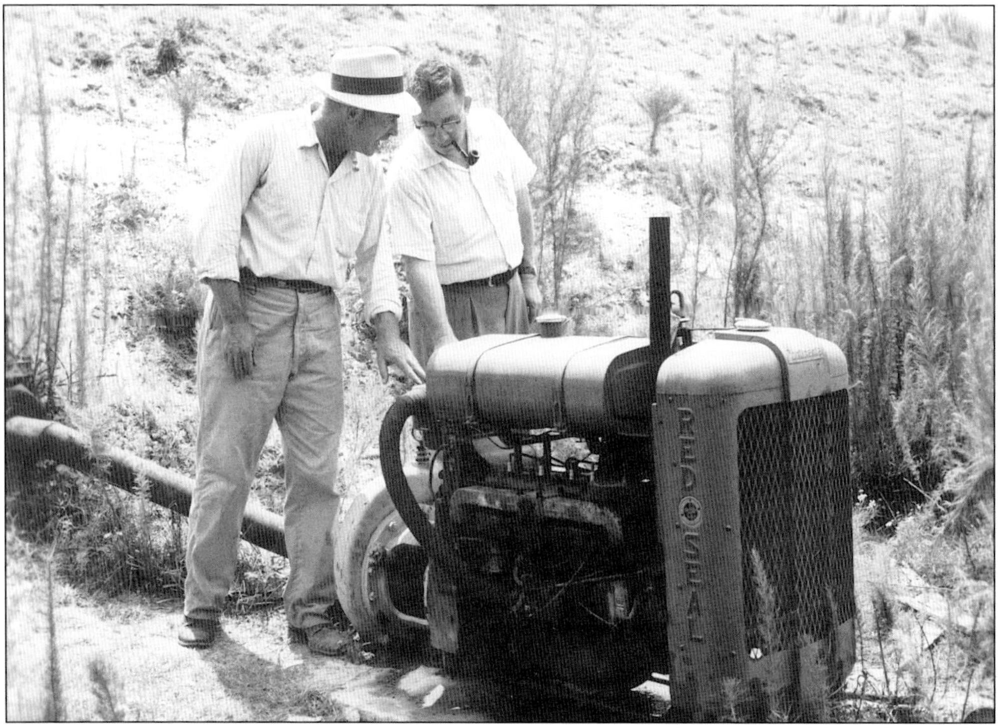

TRACTOR ENGINE USED TO POWER IRRIGATION PUMP, 1956, EDGEFIELD.

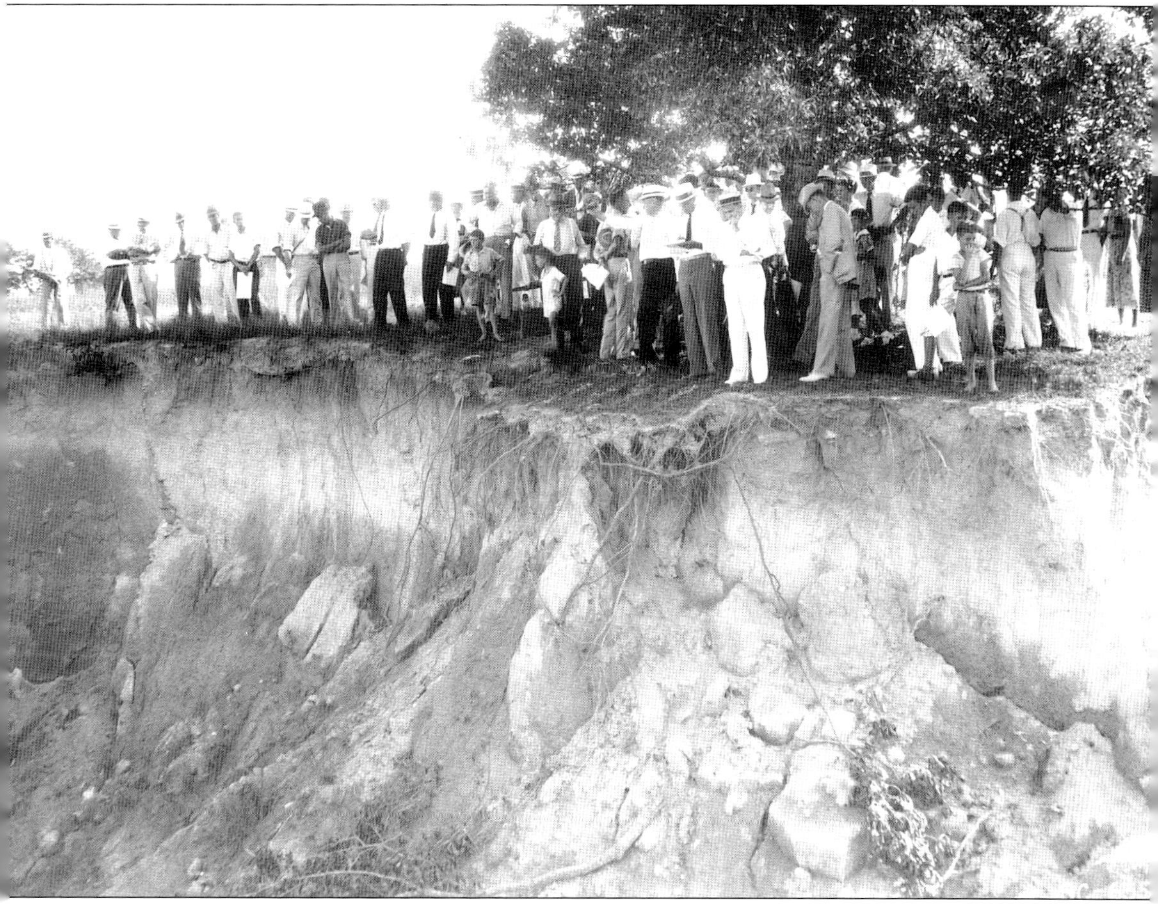

GULLY WASH, C. 1950, CHESTER COUNTY. Erosion, uncorrected, caused the loss of precious topsoil. Left untreated, a gully wash had the potential to cause loss of crops and cattle as well as human injury. Land reclamation projects were one response to the problem of erosion.

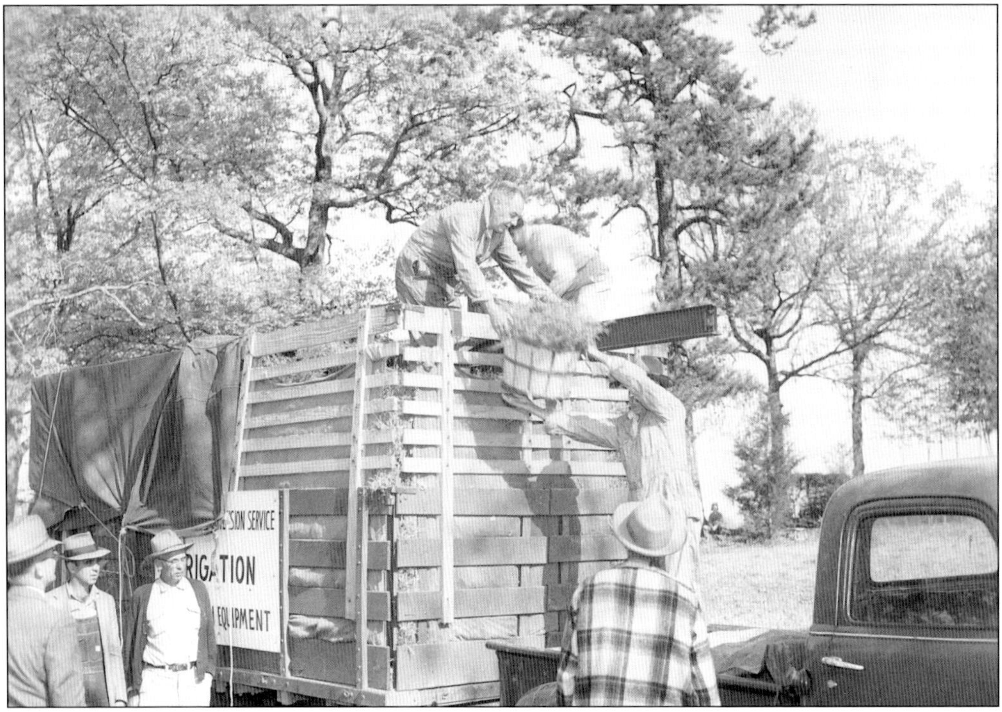

Bermuda Grass Distribution, 1950, Pickens. Many farmers planted Bermuda grass to control erosion.

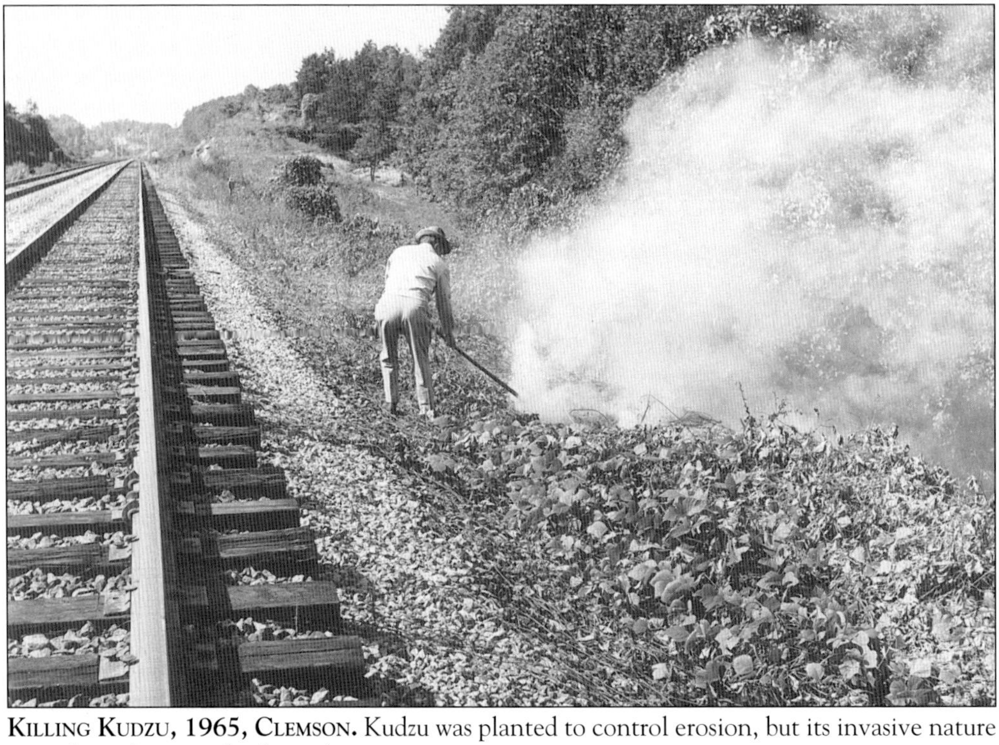

Killing Kudzu, 1965, Clemson. Kudzu was planted to control erosion, but its invasive nature caused it to become the farmer's nemesis.

Two

HOME

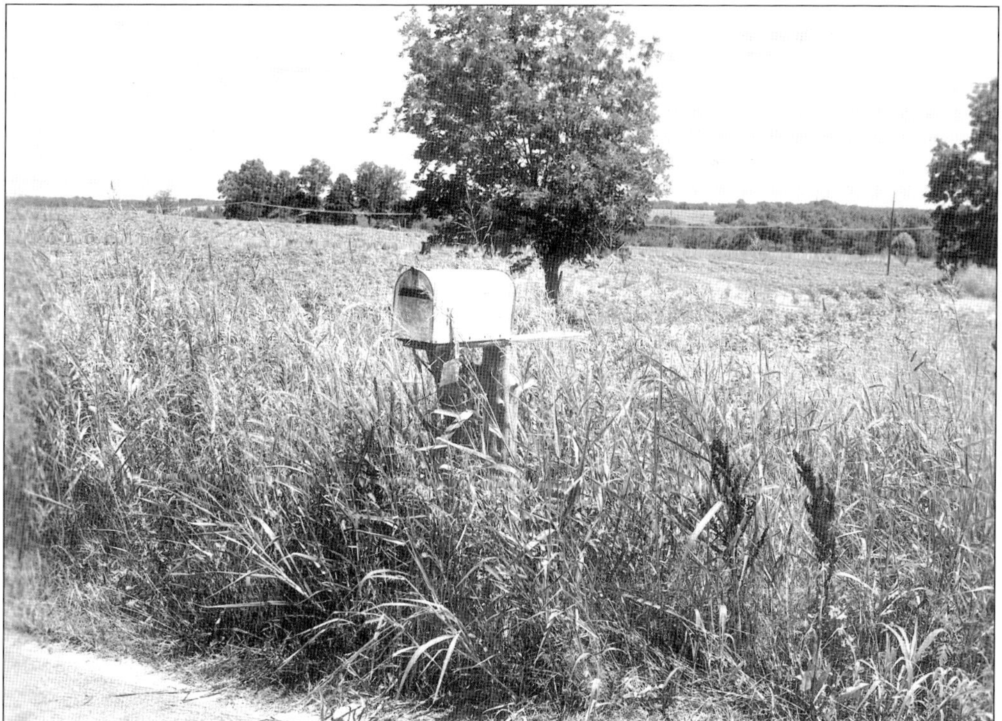

MAILBOX, C. 1940, LOCATION UNKNOWN. Mailboxes varied from farm to farm. Some bore the personal stamp of the owner, while others had no distinguishing features.

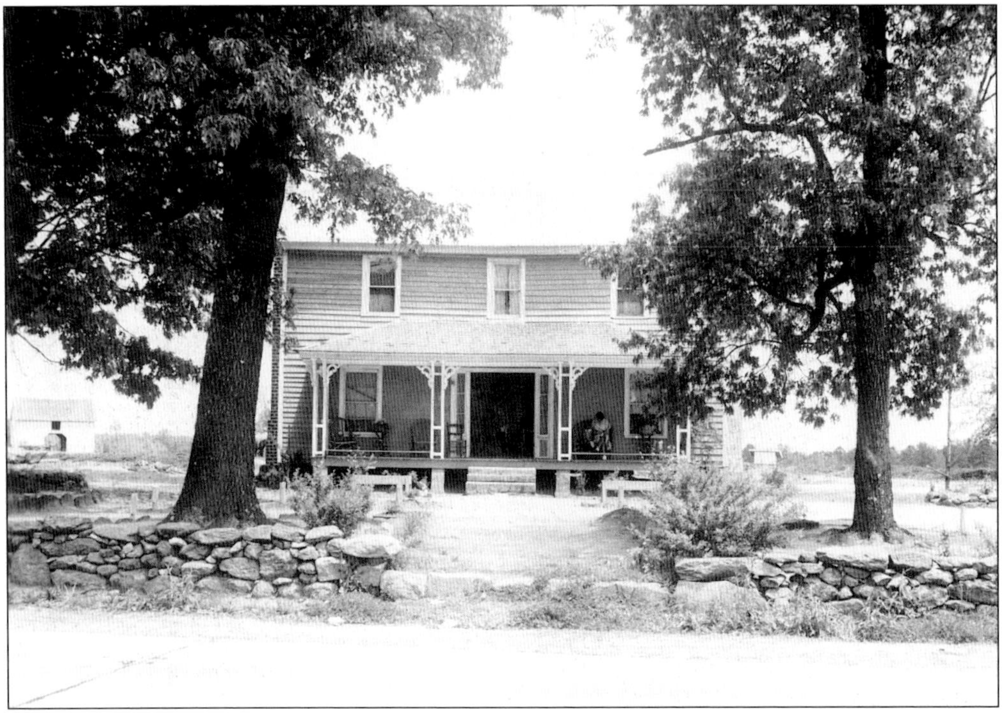

FARMHOUSE OF MARY ARNOLD, 1939, PELZER. Almost every upcountry home had a porch with a swing, or other comfortable furniture, for relaxing in the evenings.

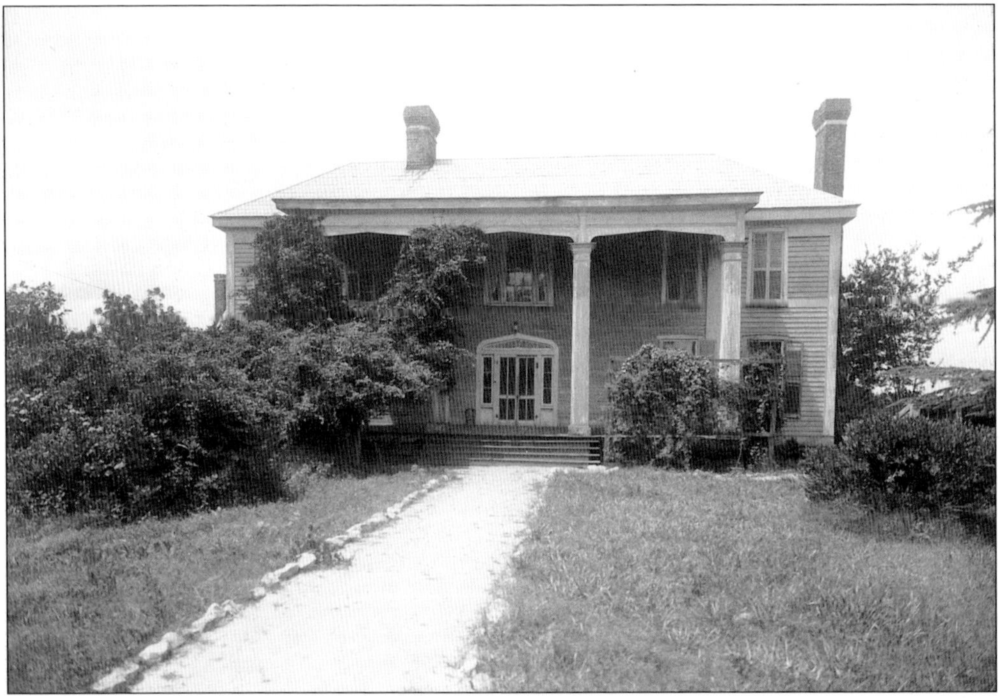

HOME OF COLONEL R.B. WATSON, RIDGE SPRING. Watson pioneered the shipping of peaches to market.

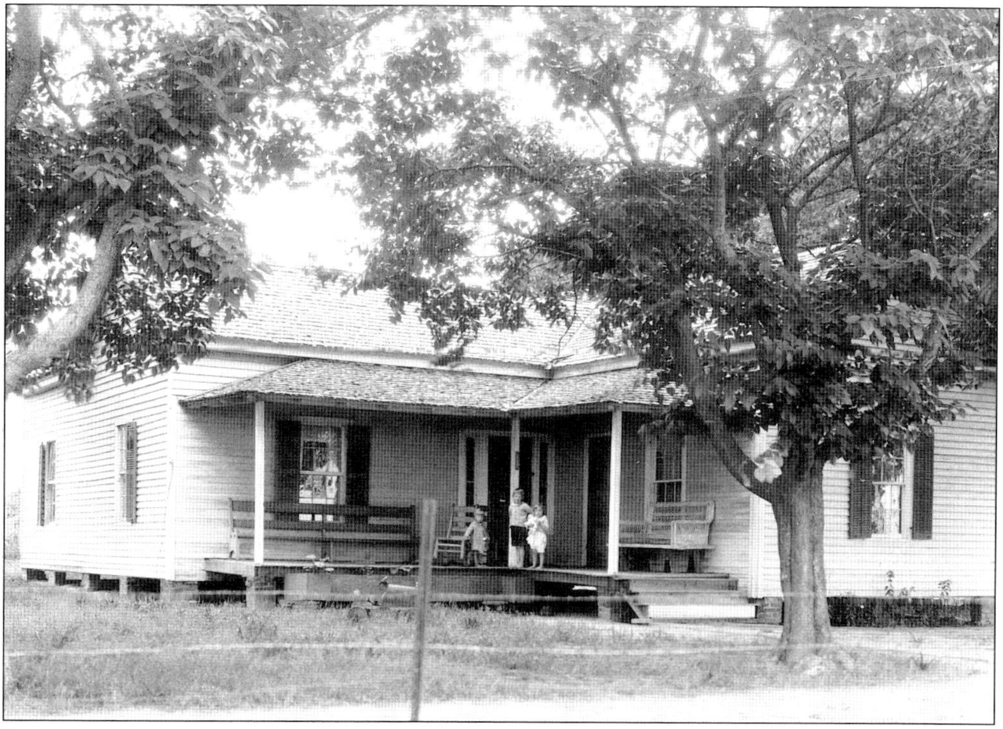

FARMHOUSE WITH L-SHAPED PORCH, C. 1935, LOCATION UNKNOWN.

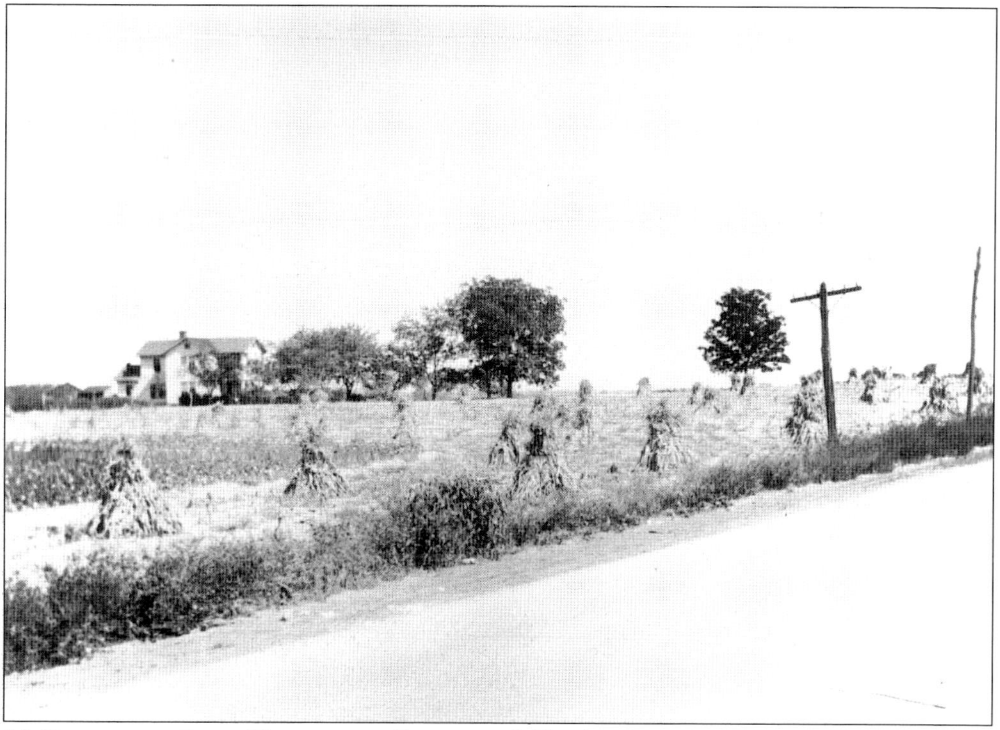

"A PROSPEROUS FARM HOME IN THE PIEDMONT." Shocks of corn, a common site on the farm, dot the landscape.

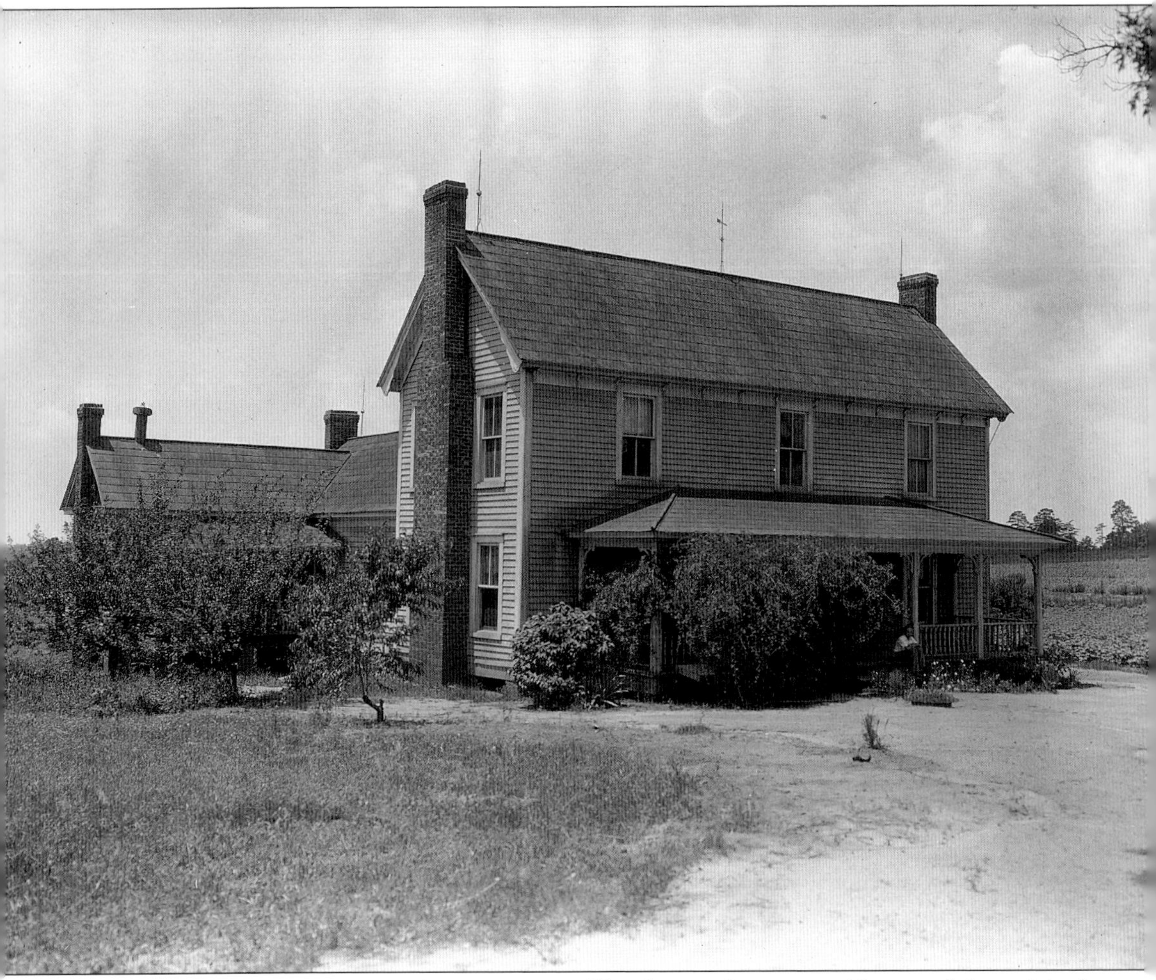

J.W. Gaston Farm, 1930s, Spartanburg. This house shows an addition of the original dwelling. Many farm houses began as a single room and were enlarged over time as the family grew.

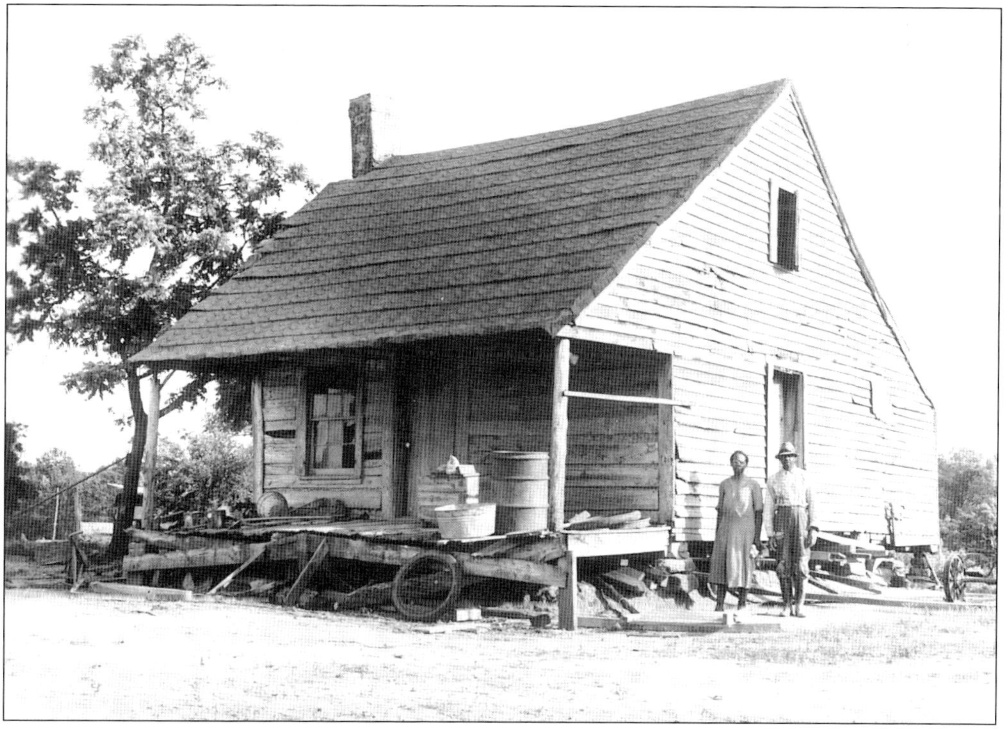

Dwelling, c. 1939, Union. The owners later moved to the house pictured below.

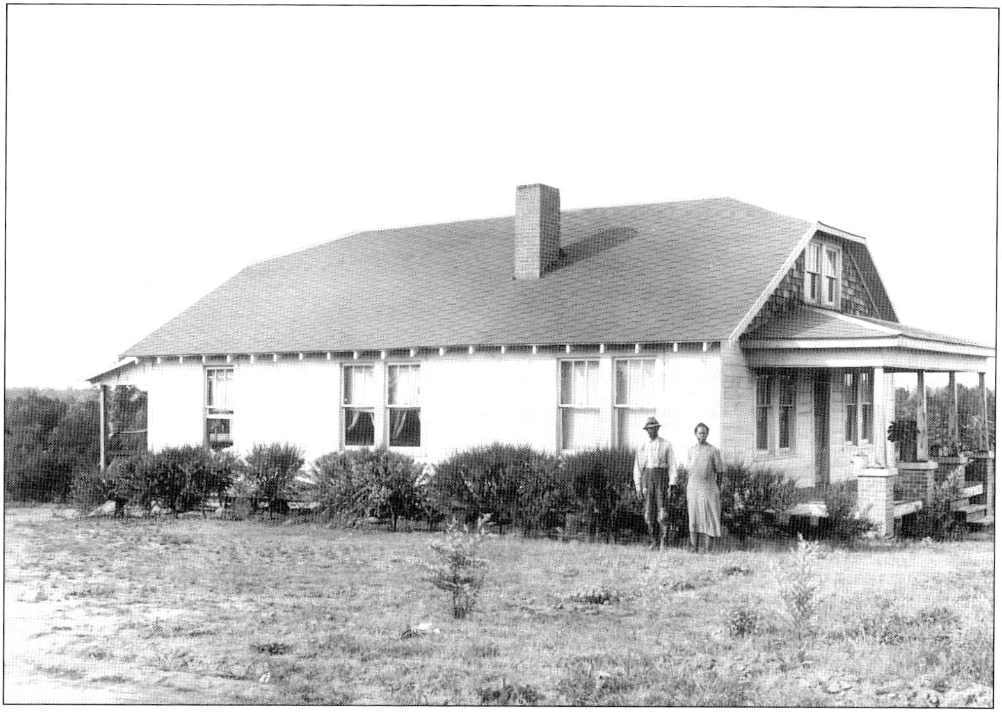

Another Dwelling Occupied by Same Owners. This house was constructed from plans available through the Extension Service.

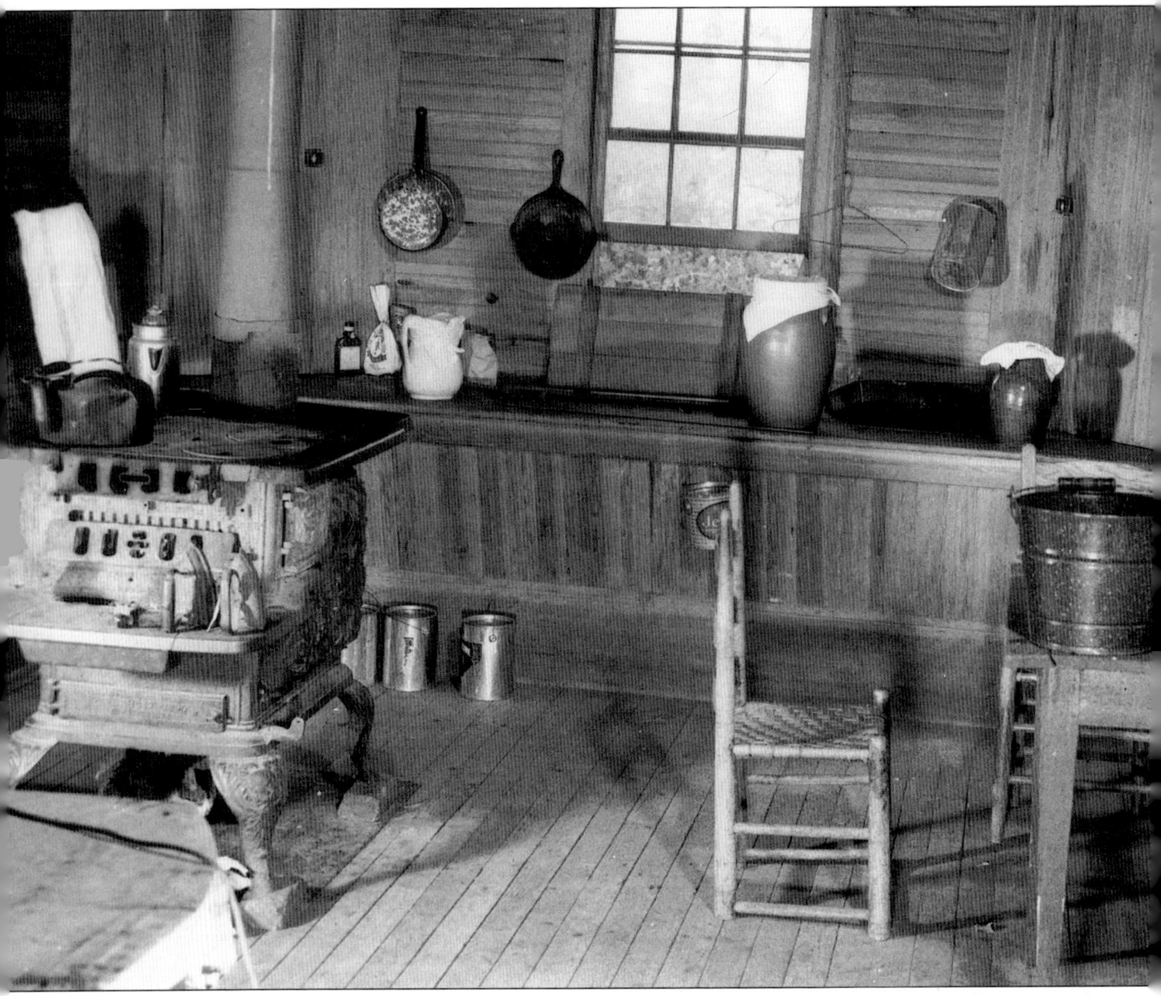

Farm Kitchen, 1939, Laurens. Early kitchens had wood-burning stoves, iceboxes, and water (carried from wells). It came as no surprise that women spent most of their lives in the kitchen.

MODERNIZED KITCHEN, C. 1951, FAIRFIELD.

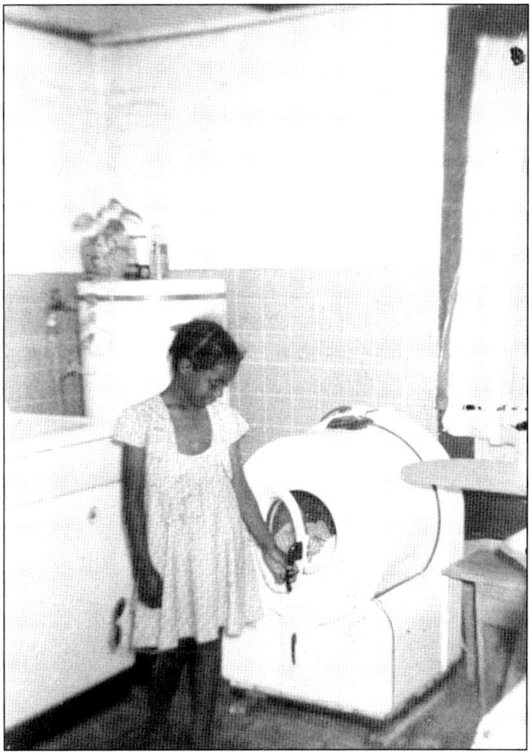

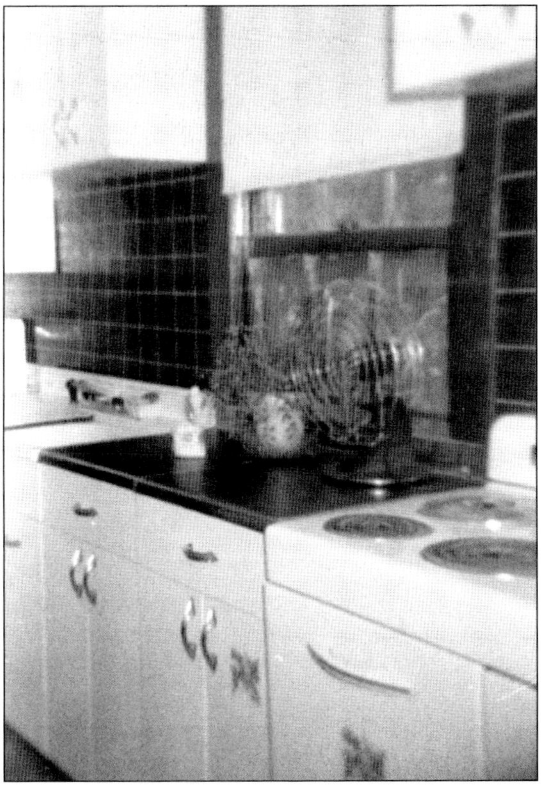

KITCHEN, 1951, FAIRFIELD. Rural electrification revolutionized methods of food preparation. Gone were the days of carrying in wood for stoves and the removal of ashes.

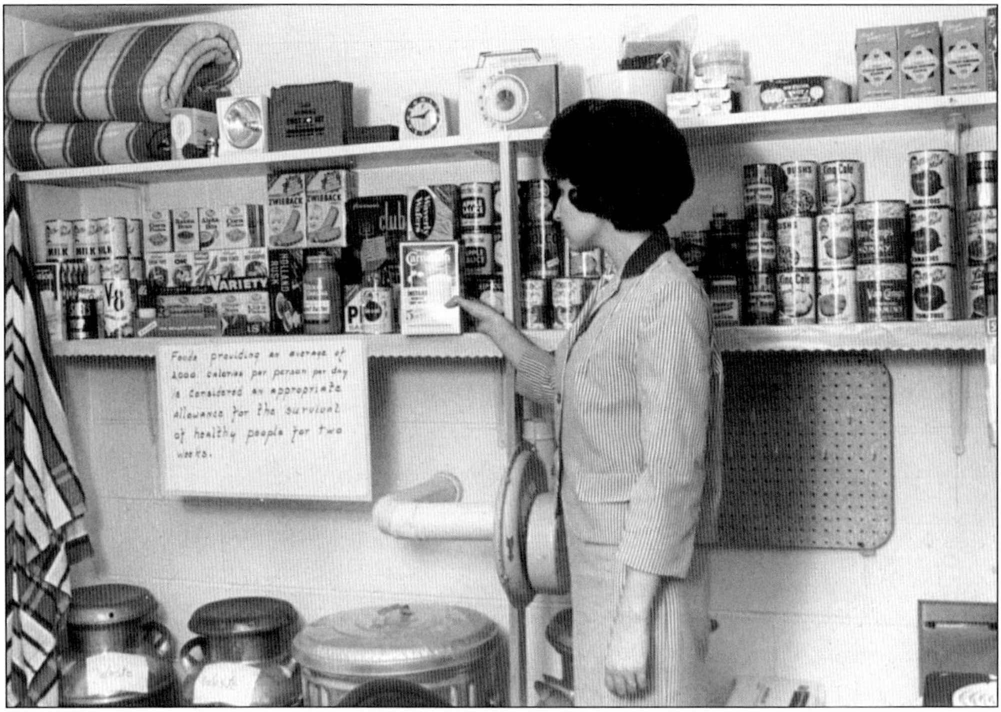

FALLOUT SHELTER, 1963, CLEMSON. The decades of the Cold War prompted citizens' fears of the use of nuclear weapons. As a response to the threat of nuclear attack, many families built their own shelters to protect themselves from radioactive fallout.

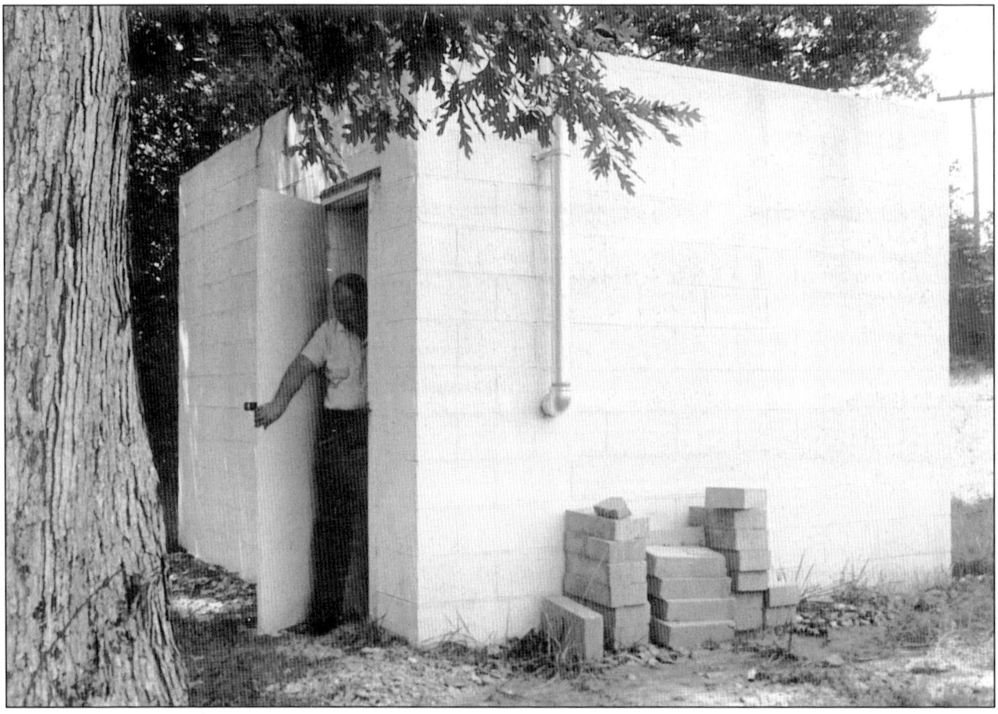

FALLOUT SHELTER (EXTERIOR VIEW), 1963, CLEMSON.

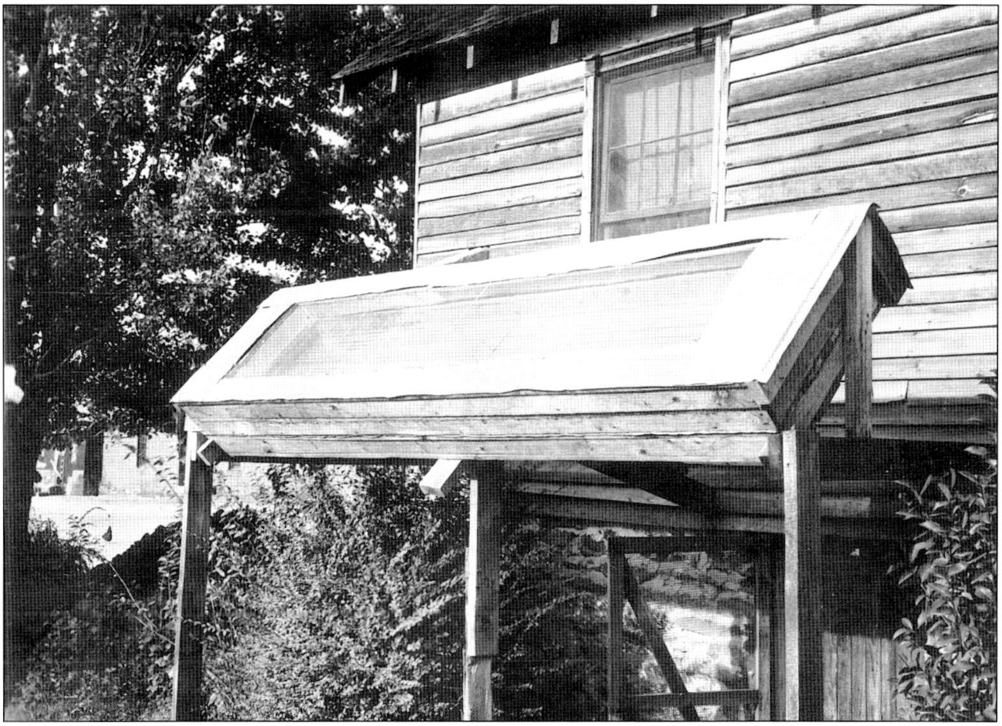

SOLAR WATER HEATER, H.B. GOSSETT FARM, 1939, GRAY COURT.

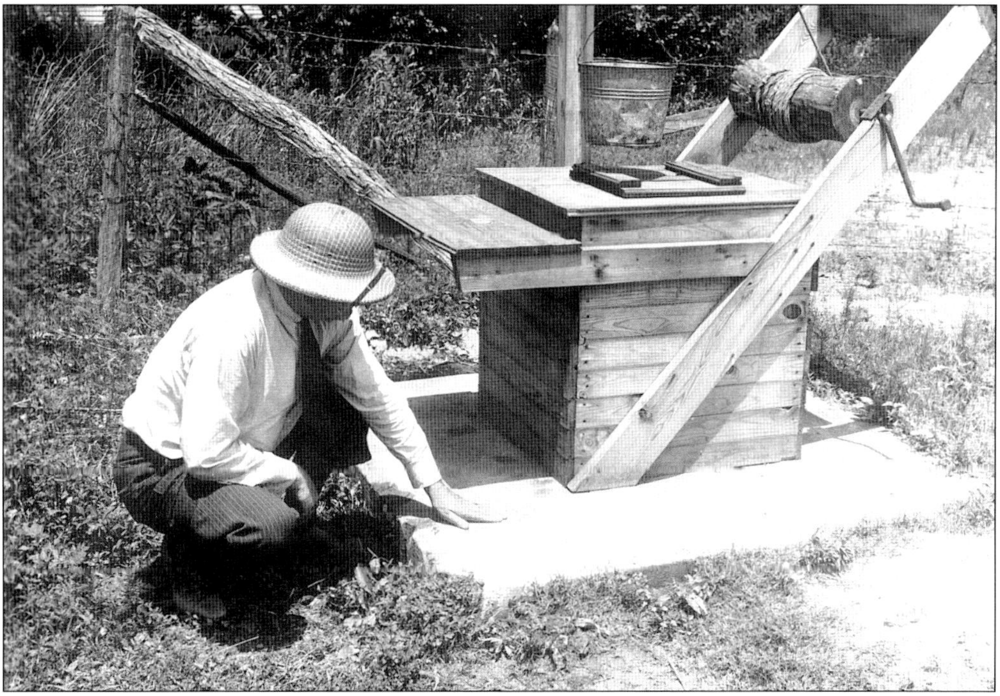

E.P. JOSEY INSPECTING WELL CURB, 1939, ANDERSON. To prevent contamination of well water, various methods (the concrete curb being one highly effective method) were used to divert runoff.

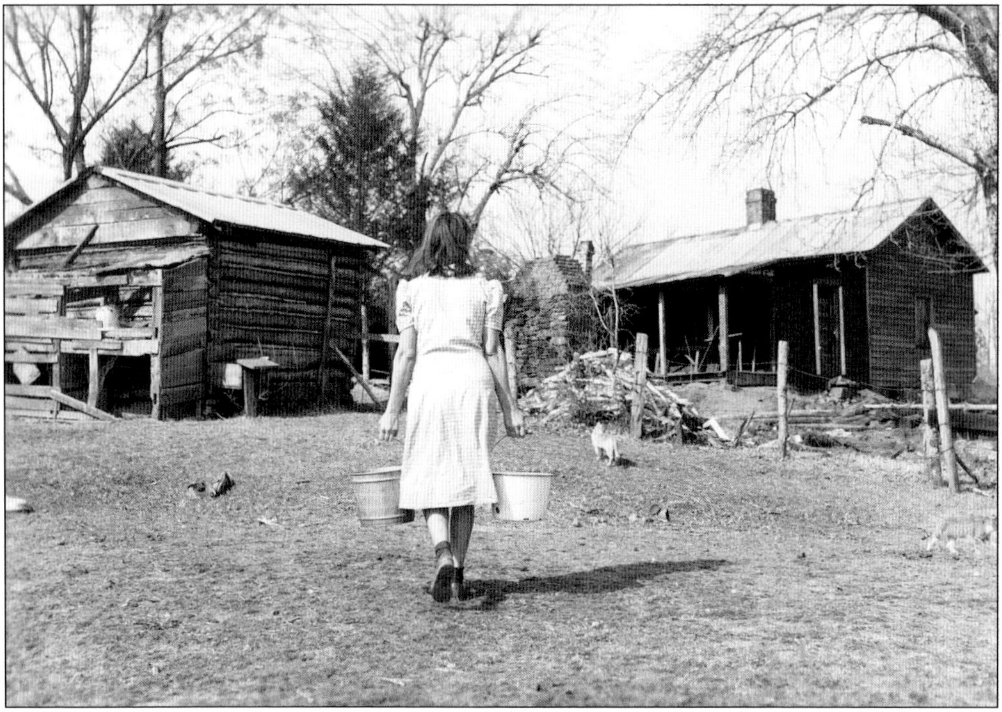

GIRL CARRYING WELL WATER, 1947, PICKENS.

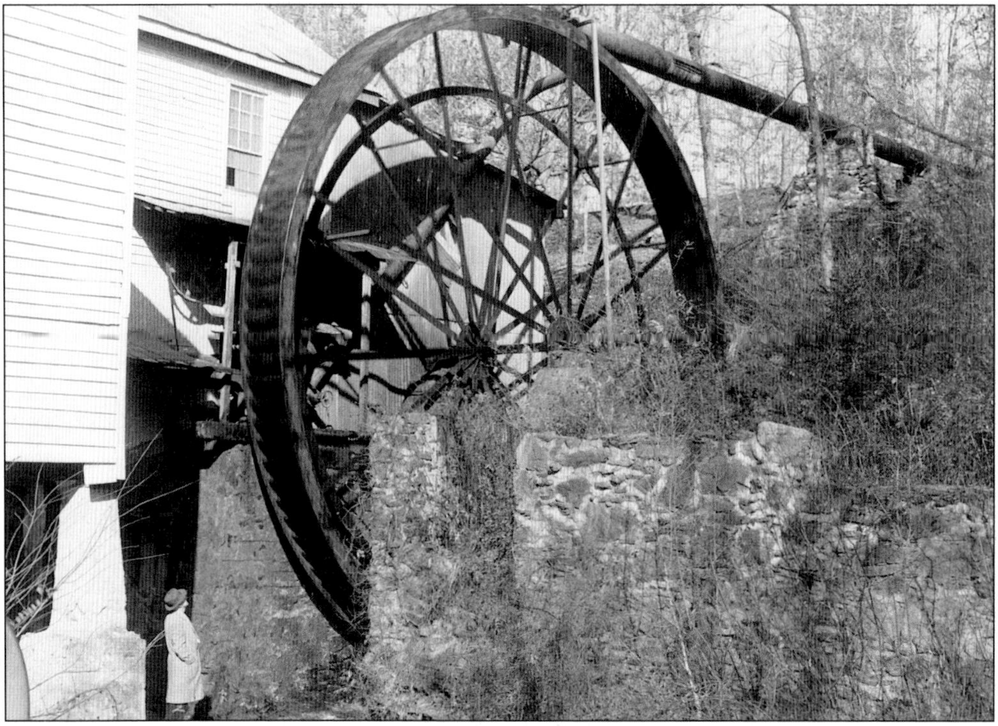

GRISTMILL, 1947, SANDY SPRINGS. Waterpower provided a major source of energy for rural areas before the advent of electricity.

Three

Crops and the Harvest

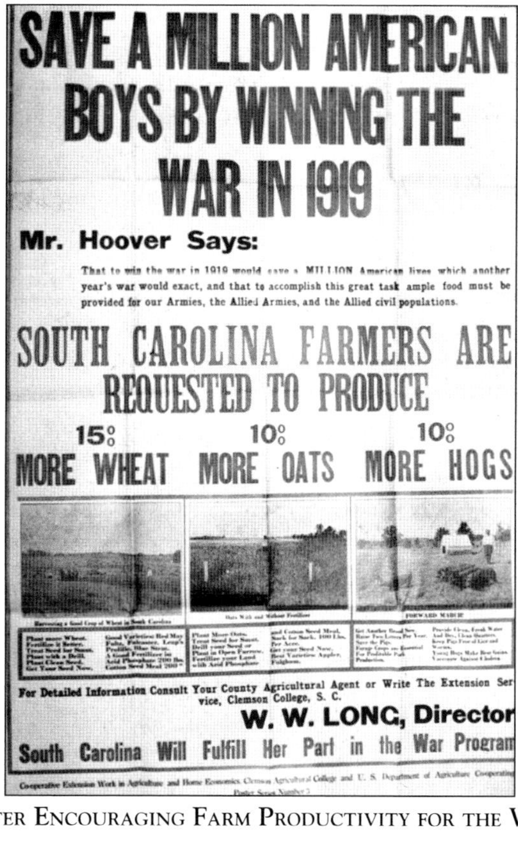

USDA Poster Encouraging Farm Productivity for the War Effort.

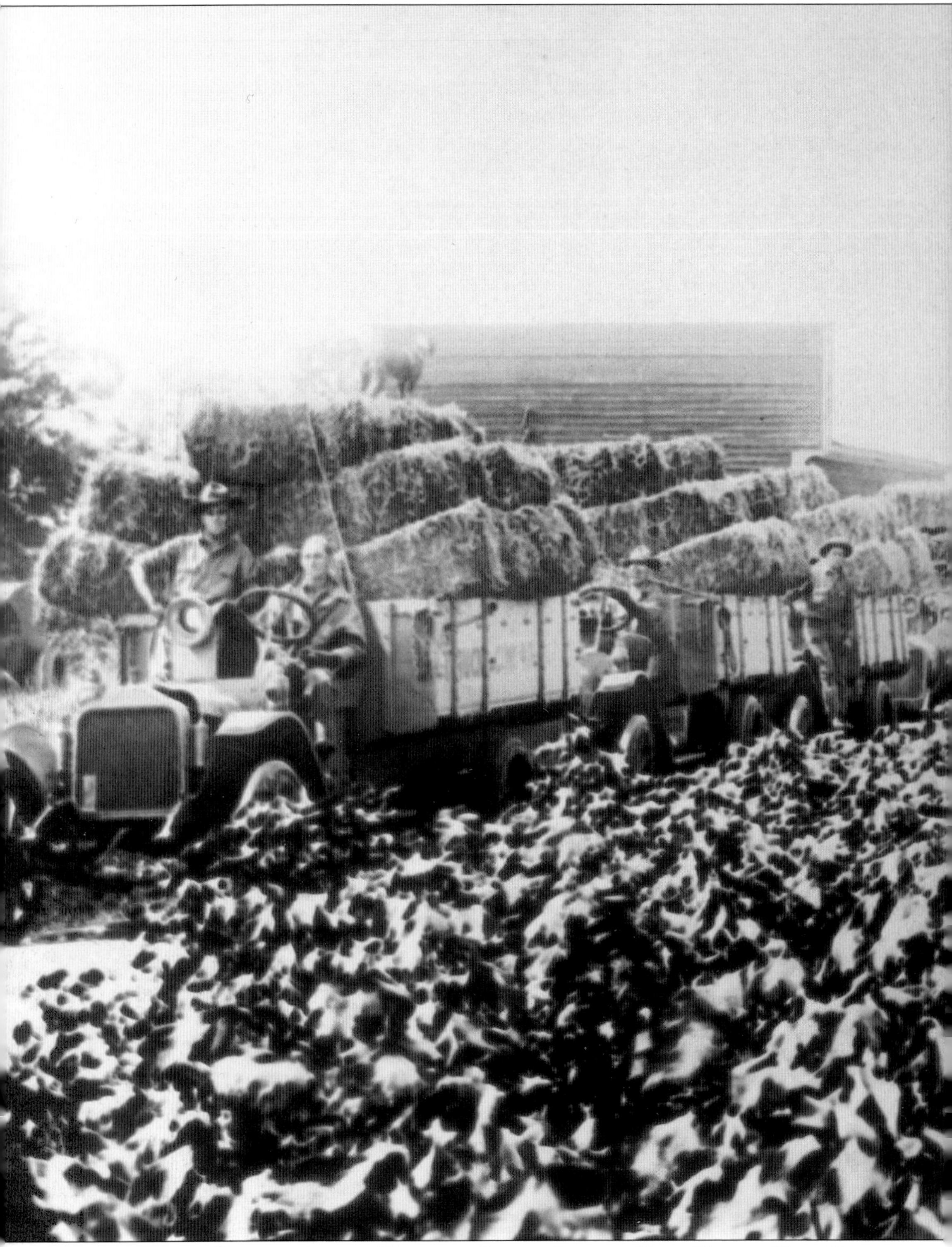

ARMY TRUCKS HAULING ALFALFA HAY FROM CHERRY FARMS IN ROCK HILL TO CAMP GREENE,

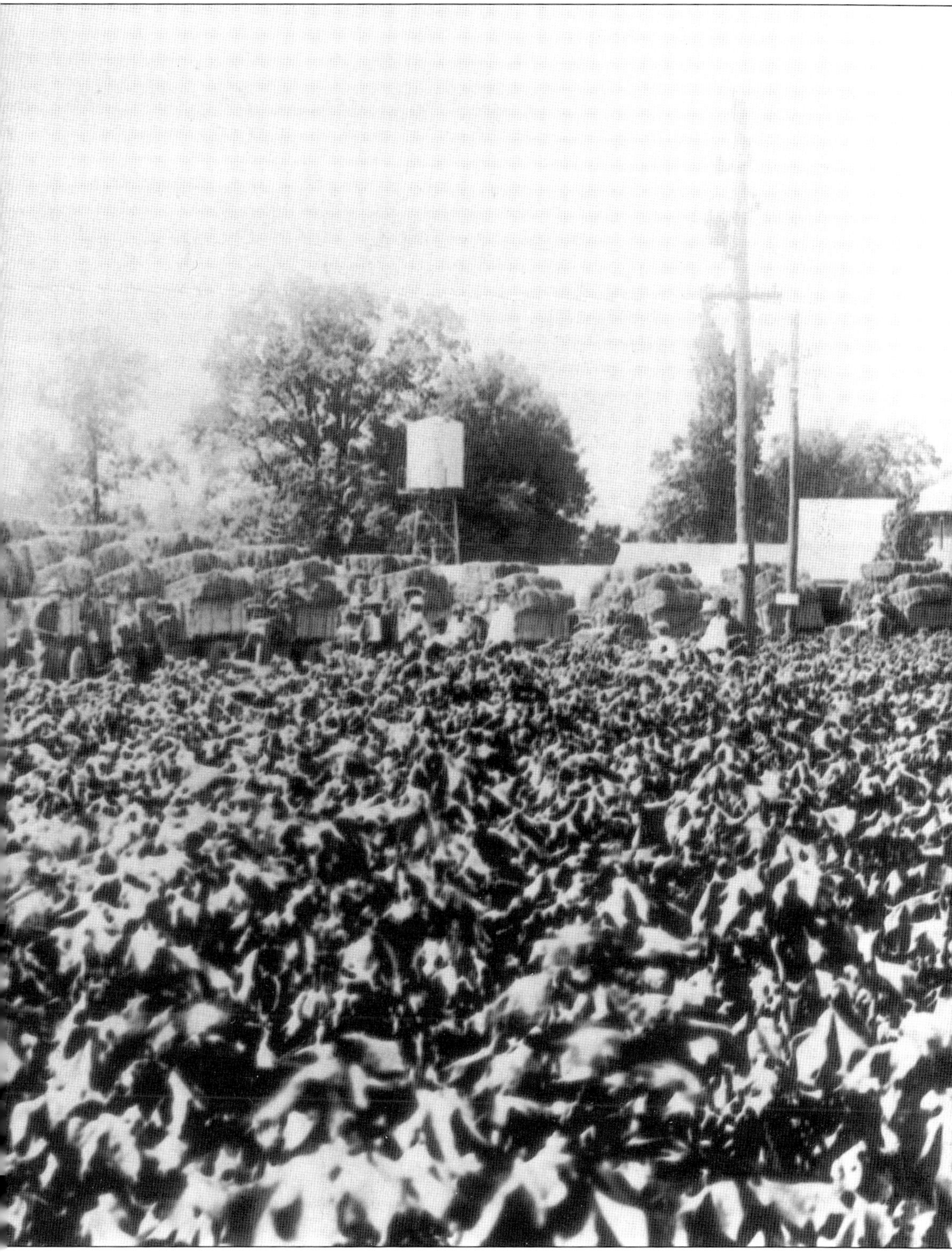

North Carolina, 1918.

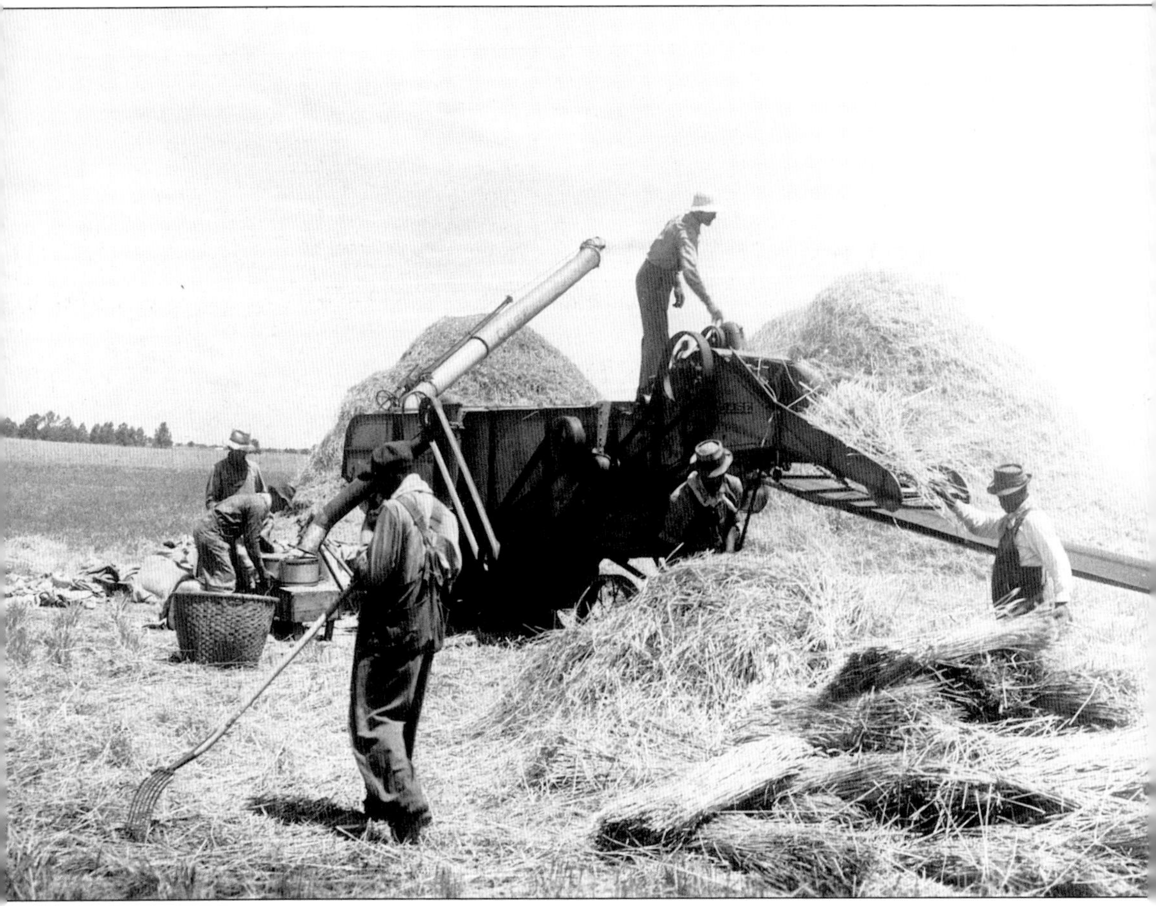

WHEAT THRESHING, 1939, ANDERSON. Separating wheat grain from chaff, which was performed manually for centuries, now required less time with the use of automated equipment.

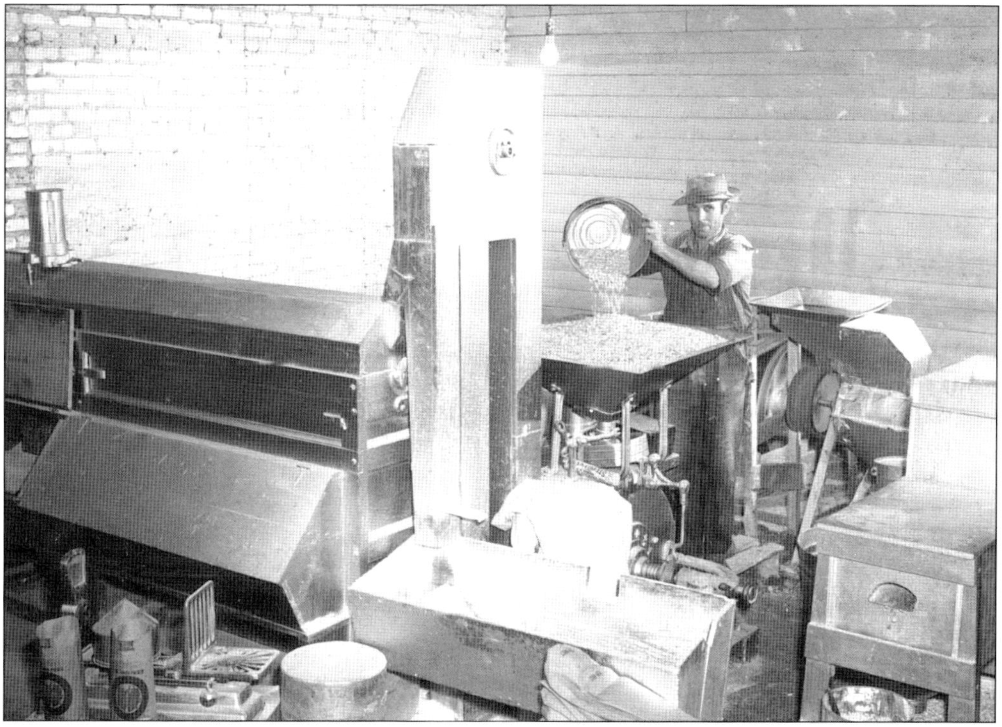

CORN MILL OF J.C. MCKINNEY, 1950, LIBERTY. Corn meal was a staple of Southern cooks.

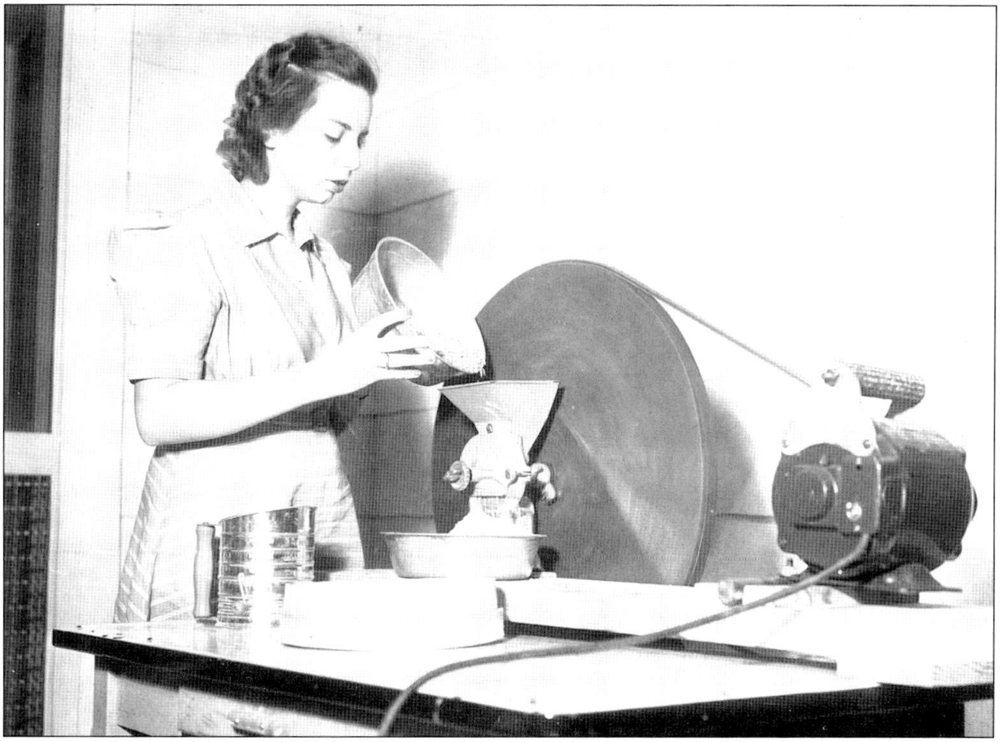

GRINDING CORN AT HOME, JO STRIBLING, 1942, PICKENS.

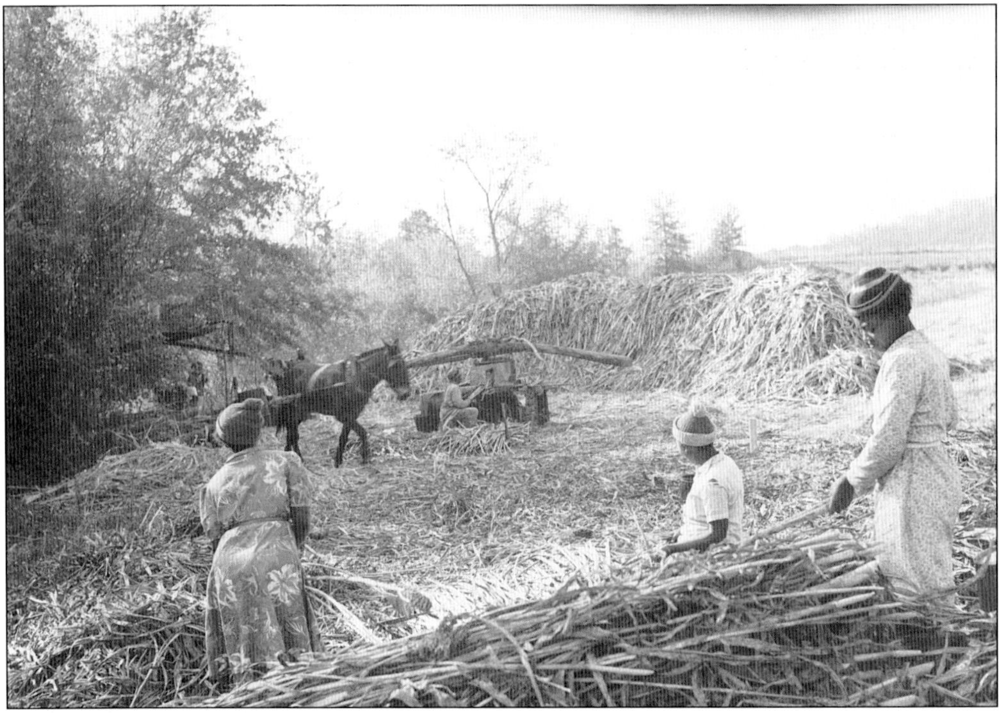

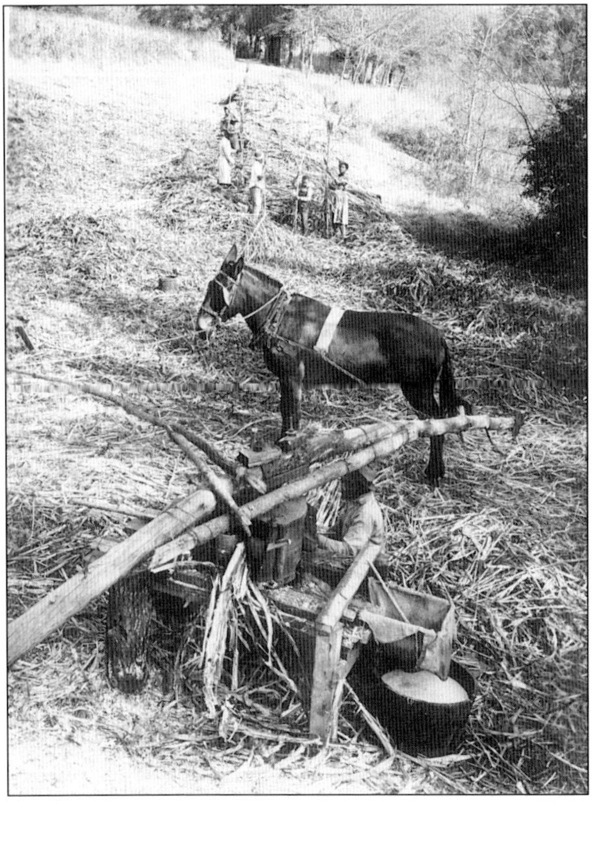

Making Sorghum Syrup, 1941, Oconee County. Several steps were involved in the syrup-making process. As seen above, cane was first cut and then stripped of its leaves. Below, stripped cane was then fed into a press (powered, as shown here, by a mule) to extract sap.

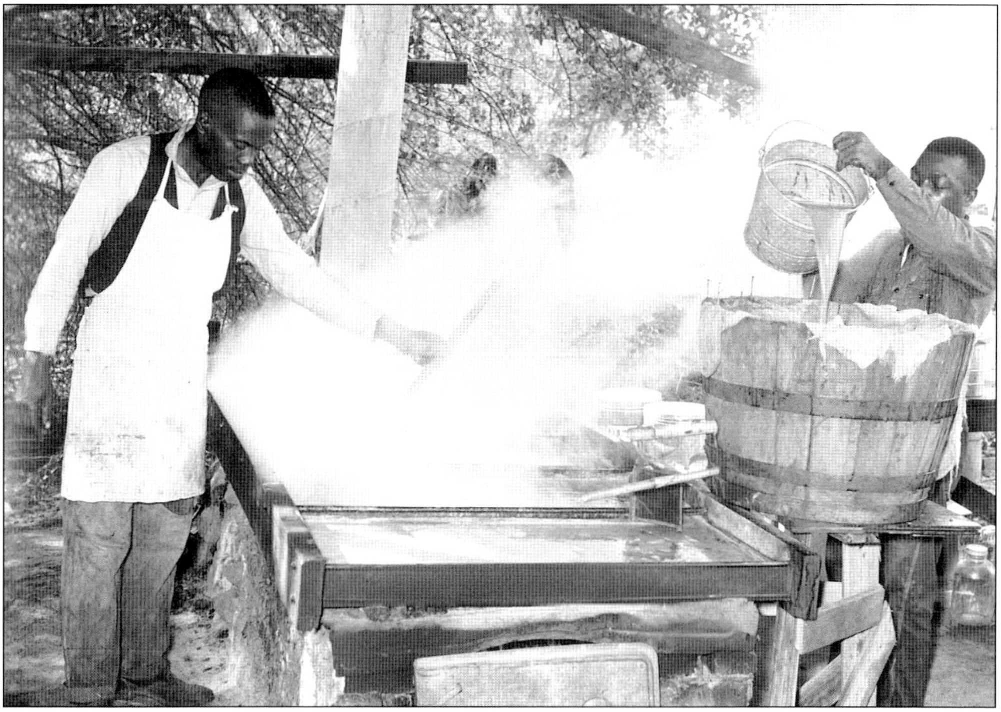

MAKING SORGHUM SYRUP, 1941, OCONEE COUNTY. Above, the sap was then boiled until the proper consistency was reached. Finally, the syrup was poured into containers (seen below). Sorghum syrup, with its acrid taste, could appear a dark or light color depending upon the type of soil in which the cane was grown.

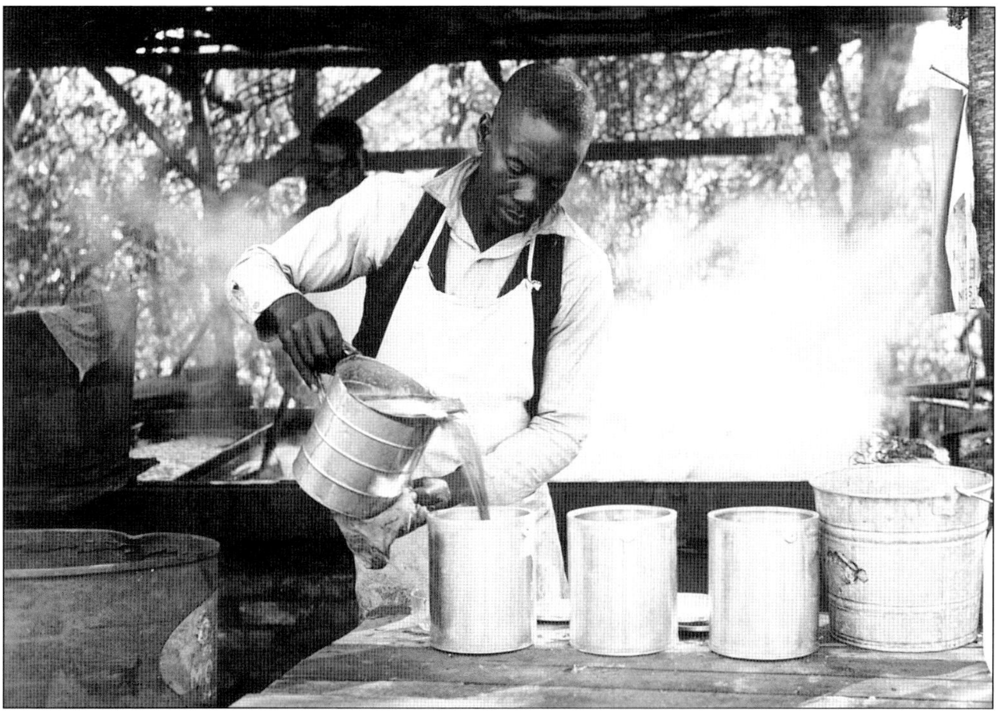

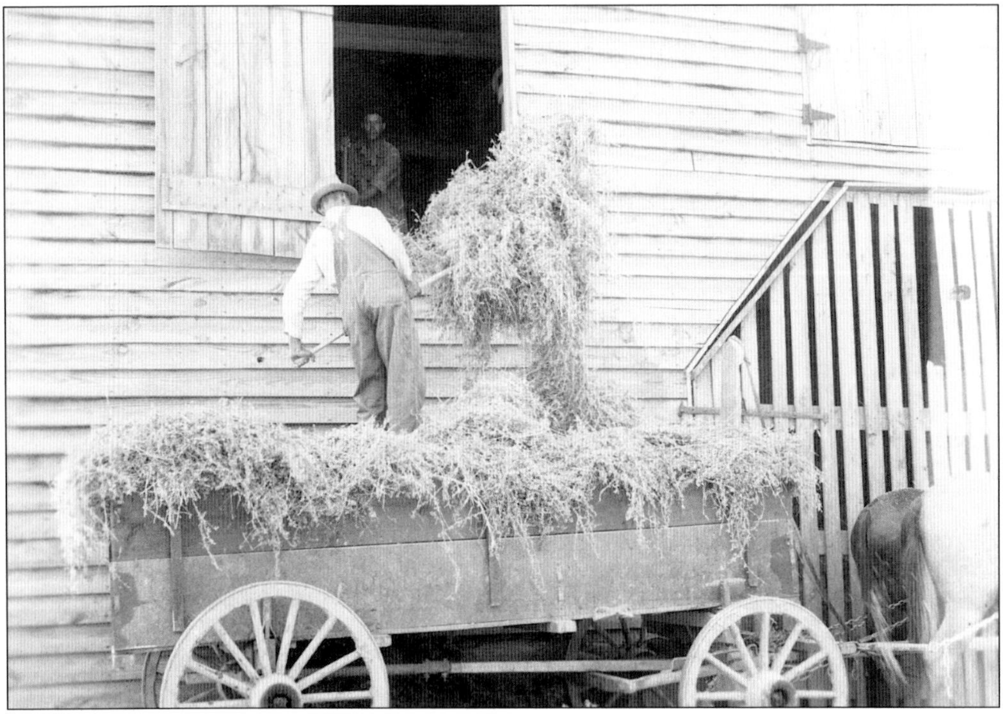

M.C. HARRISON UNLOADING HAY, 1940, FAIRFIELD.

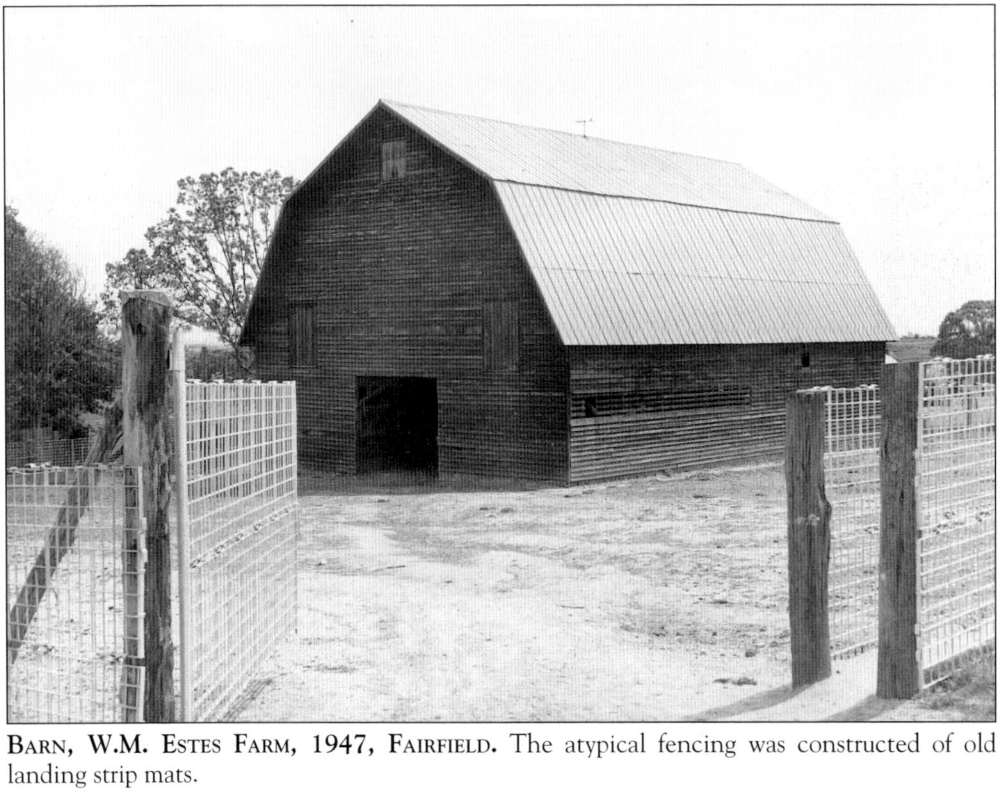

BARN, W.M. ESTES FARM, 1947, FAIRFIELD. The atypical fencing was constructed of old landing strip mats.

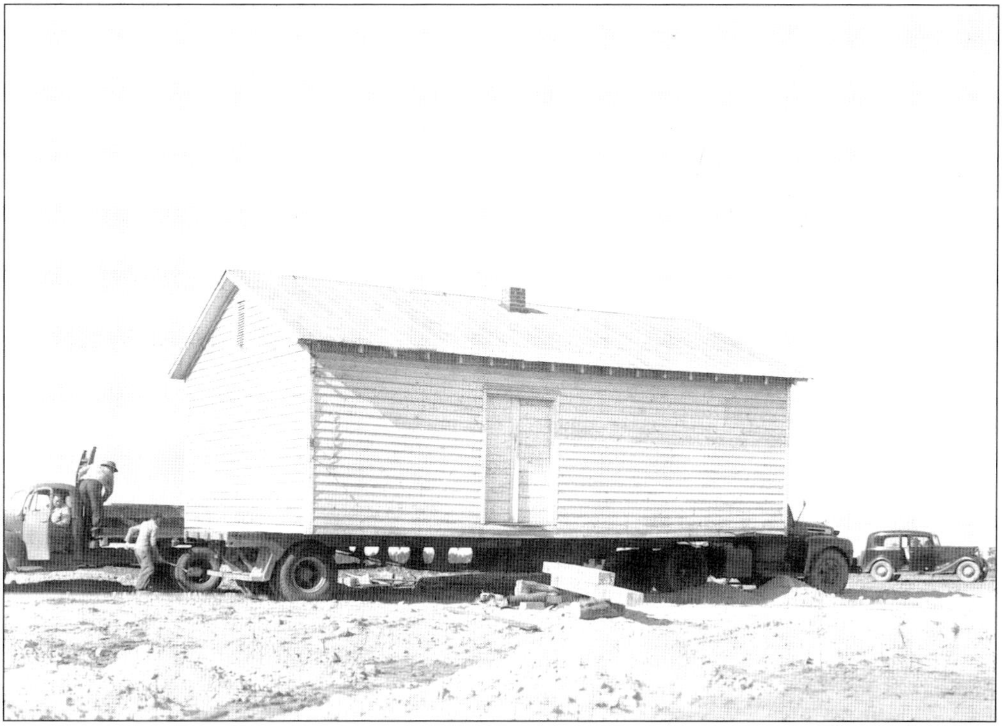

Farm Building Being Moved, 1949, Newberry. Farmers valued well-constructed buildings as much as their own dwellings.

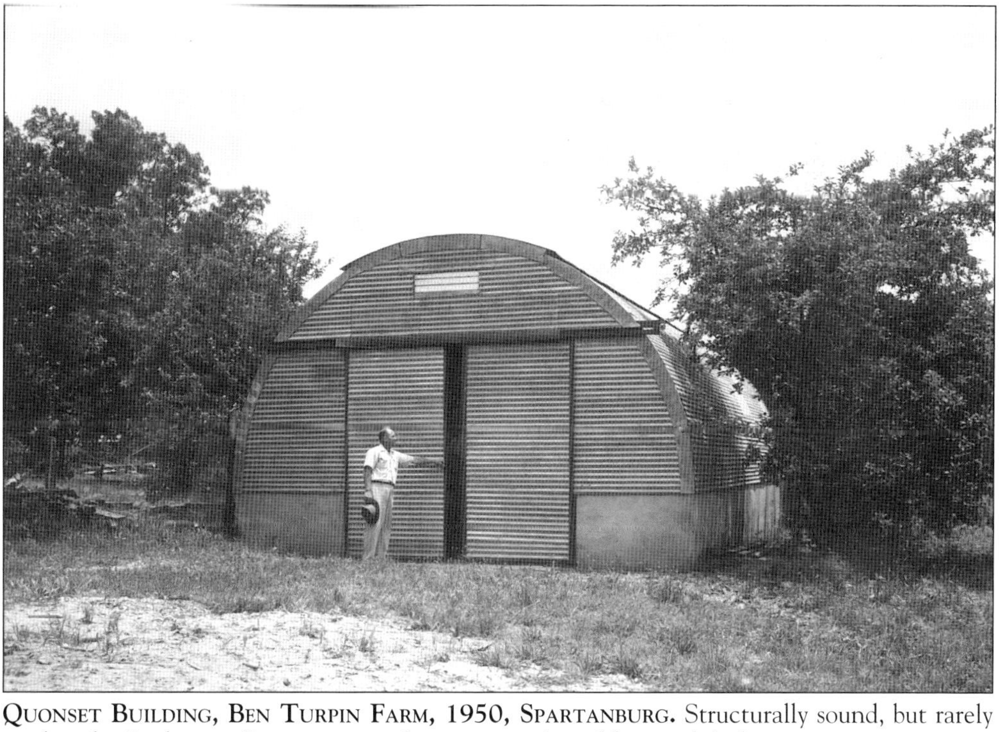

Quonset Building, Ben Turpin Farm, 1950, Spartanburg. Structurally sound, but rarely used in the Piedmont, Quonsets were forerunners of pre-fabricated shelters.

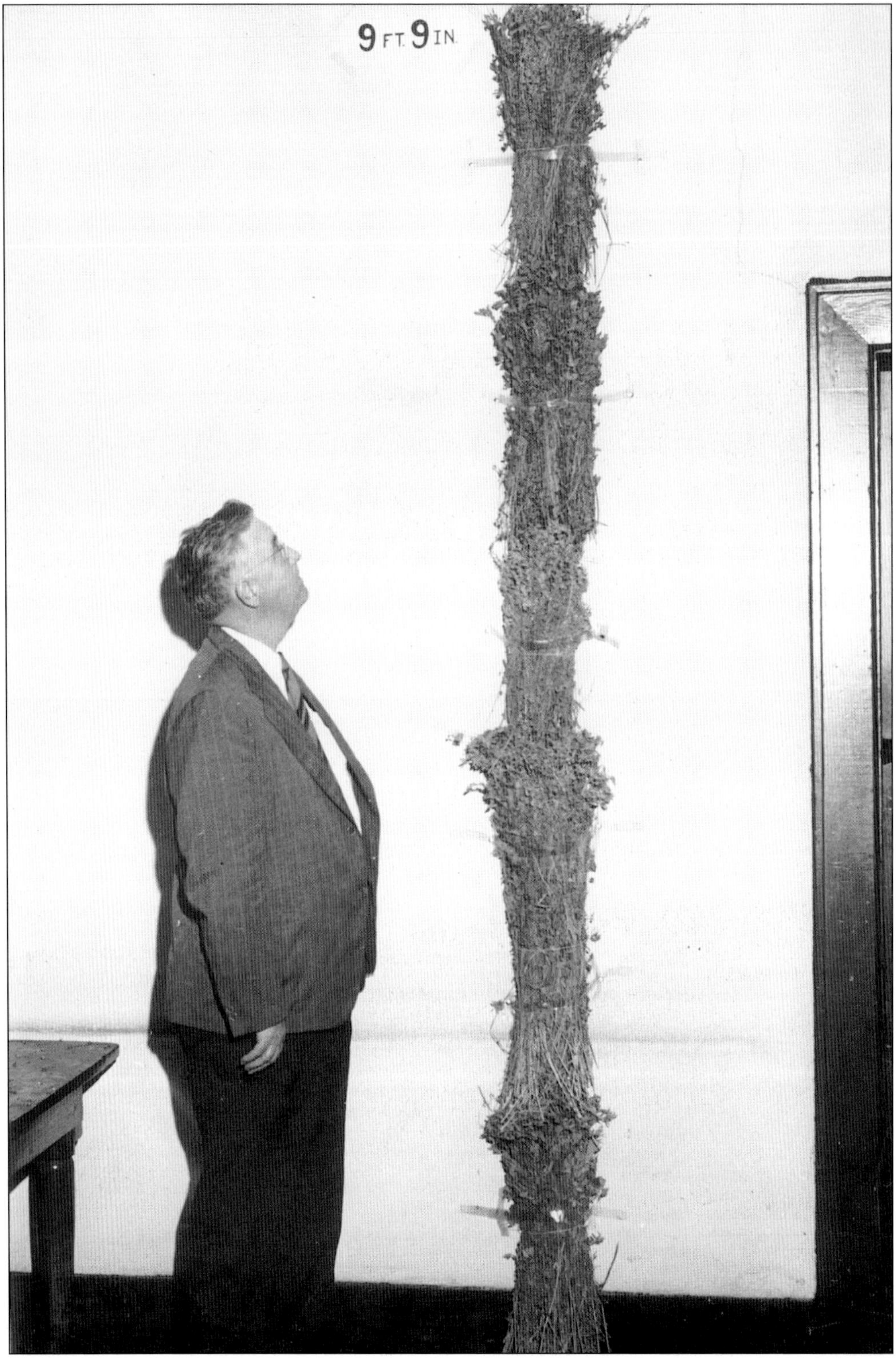

AGENT PAUL B. EZELL WITH RECORD-BREAKING ALFALFA PLANT, 1946, NEWBERRY.

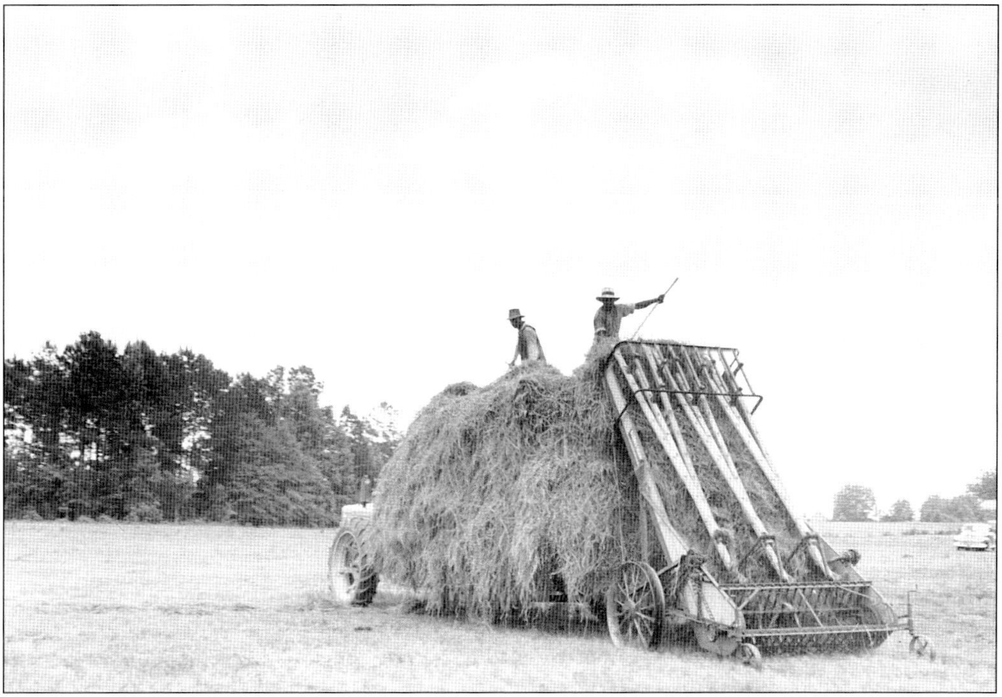

Hay Loader, 1948, Greenwood. This loader allowed hay to be gathered quickly after it was cut. If rain or dew fell on cut hay, it was likely to mold.

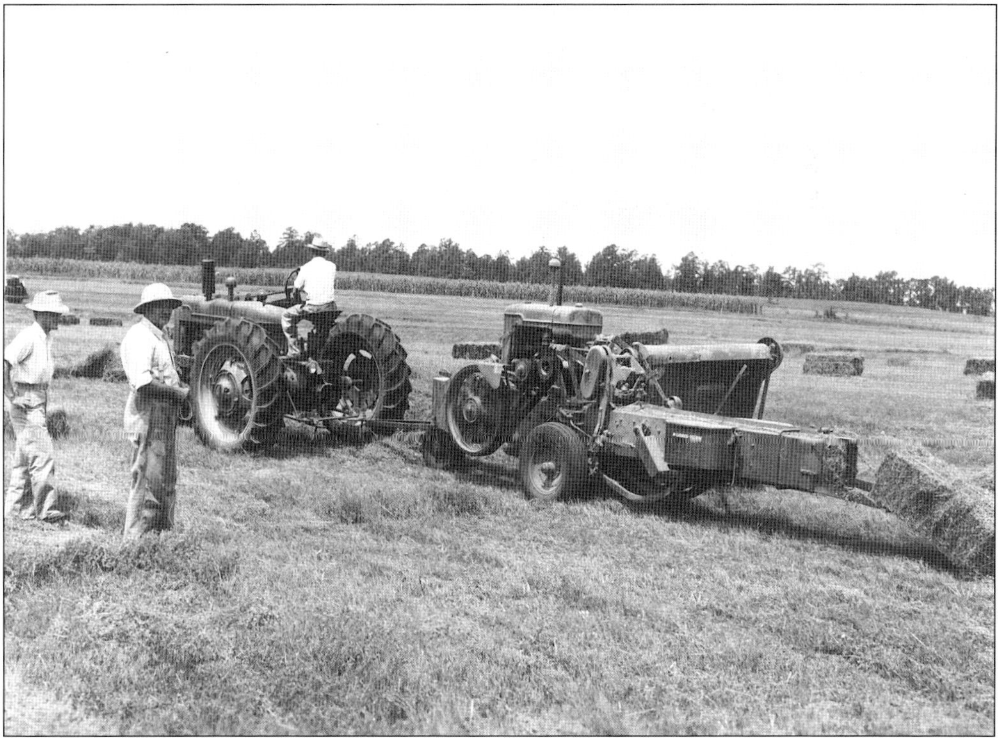

Baling Hay, 1948, Anderson.

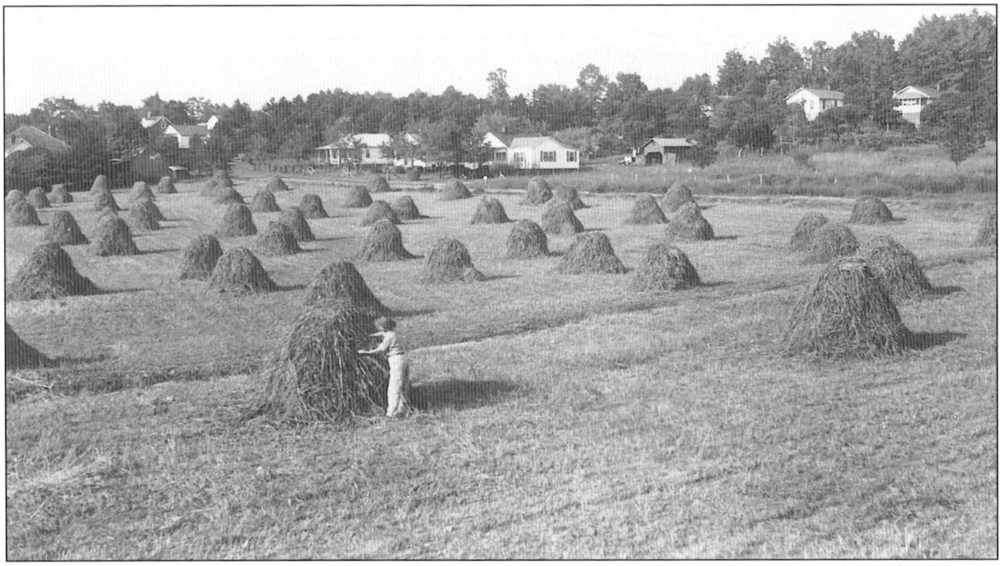

COWPEA AND SORGHUM HAY LEFT TO DRY ON RACKS, 1949, PICKENS.

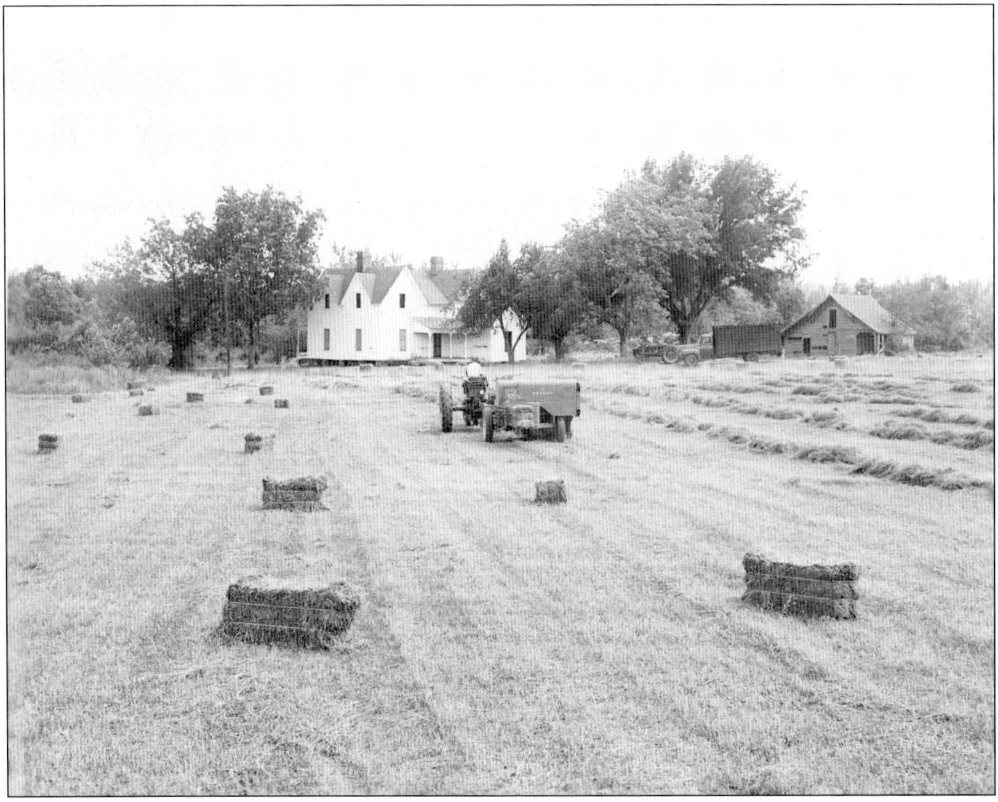

BALING HAY, 1952, ABBEVILLE. After bailing, hay was picked up and transported to barns.

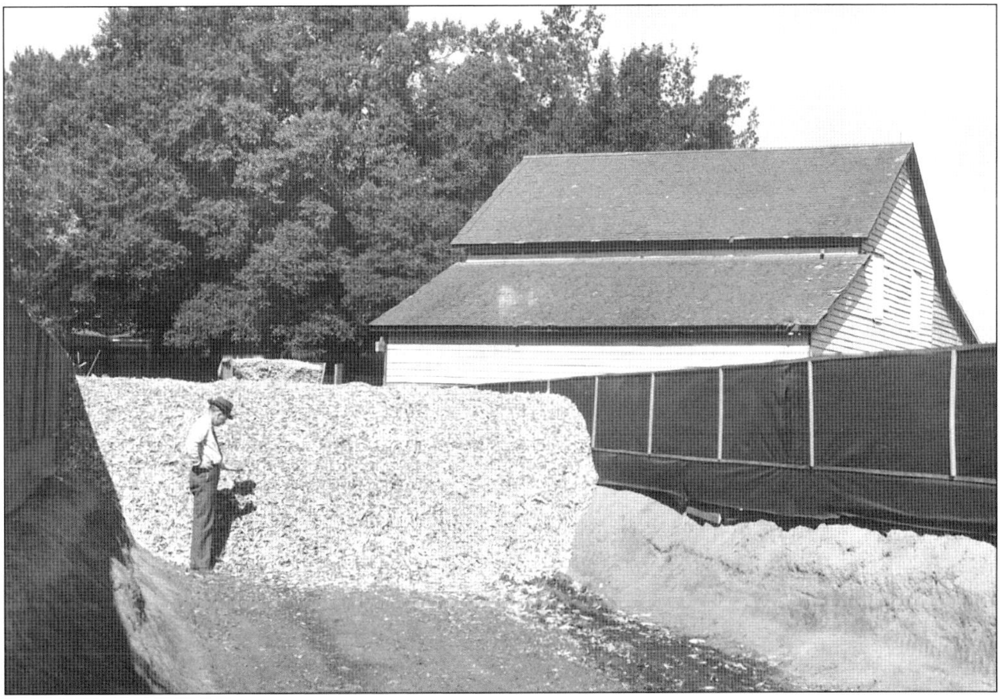

TRENCH SILO, DAVE HOLMES FARM, 1940, EDGEFIELD. This trench silo measured 150 feet long and 22 feet wide.

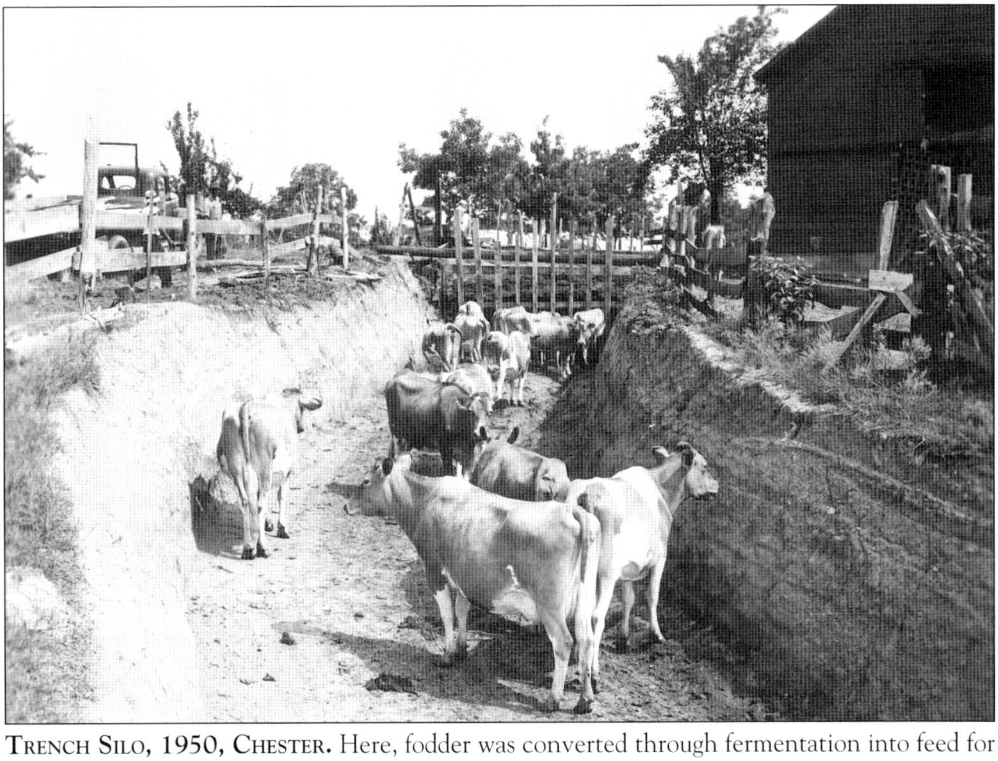

TRENCH SILO, 1950, CHESTER. Here, fodder was converted through fermentation into feed for livestock.

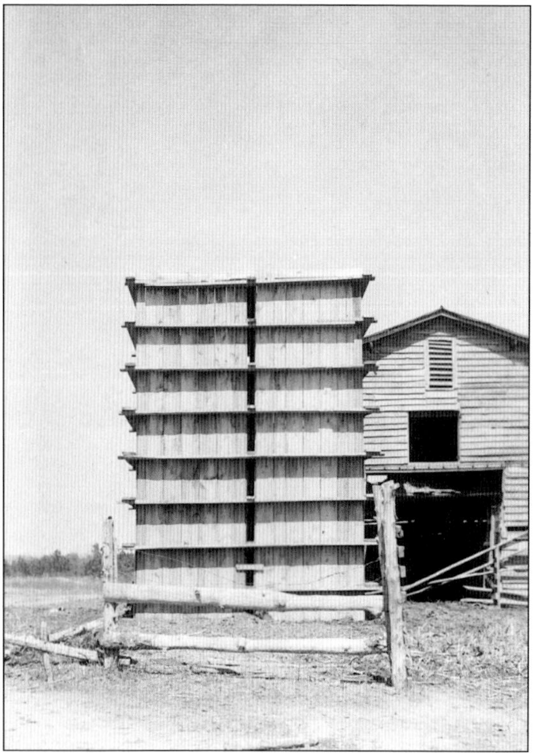

Box Silo, 1944, Chester. Box silos, one method of storing silage, were simple to construct and could easily be dismantled.

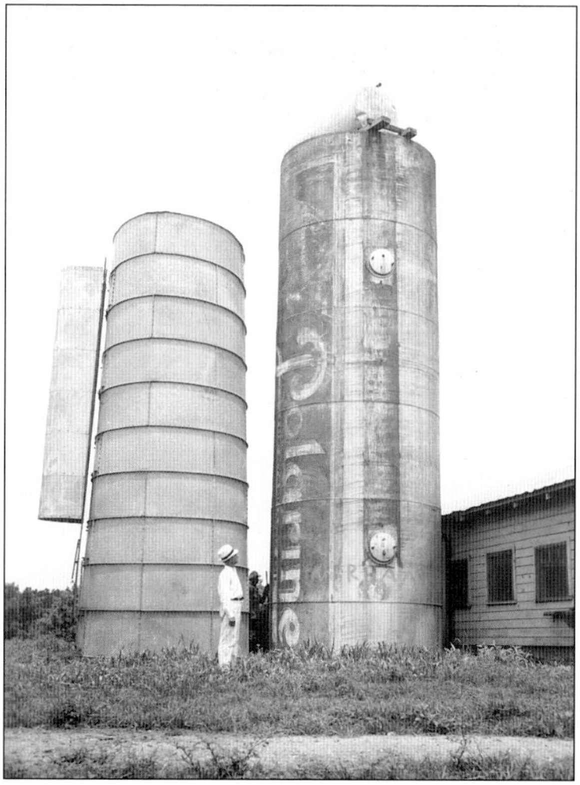

Upright Silos Made from Recycled Oil Tanks, 1939, Cherokee County.

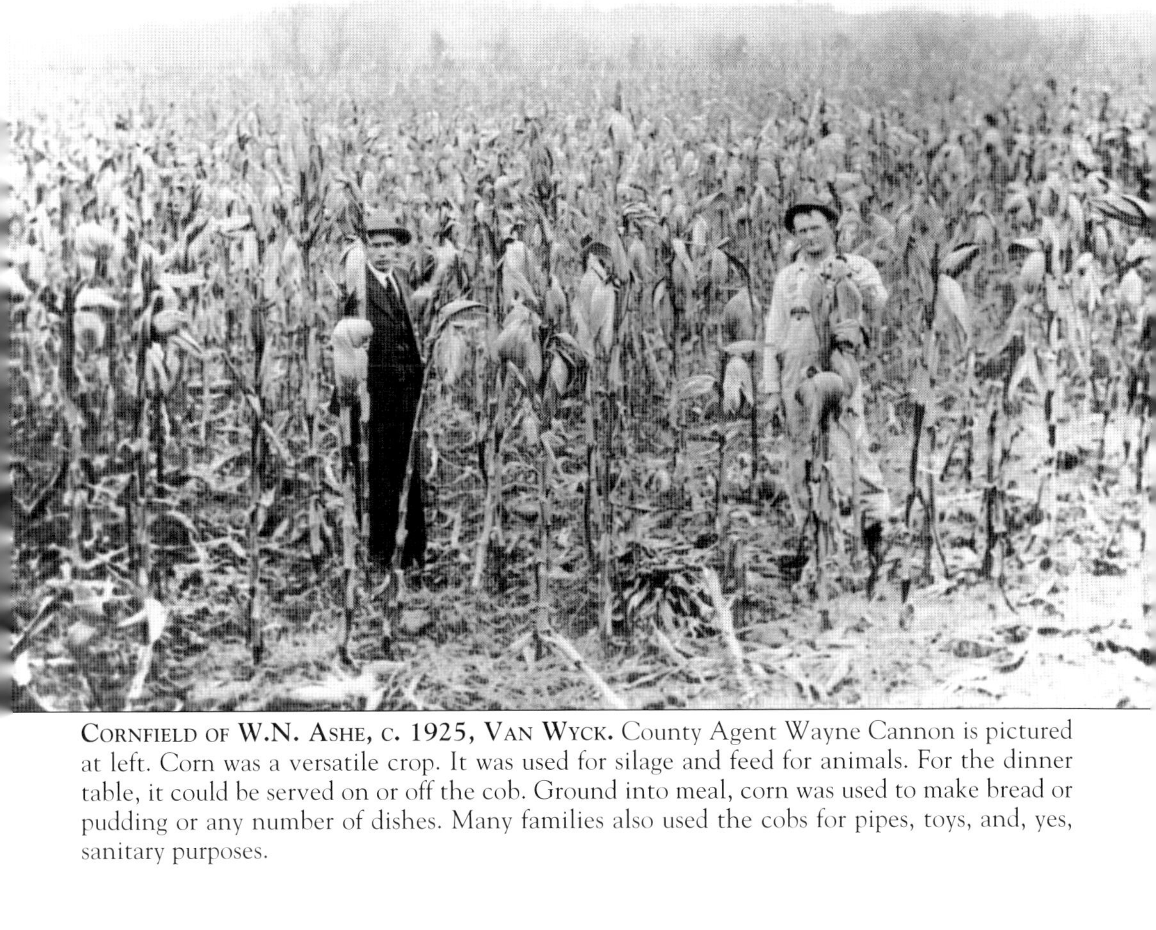

Cornfield of W.N. Ashe, c. 1925, Van Wyck. County Agent Wayne Cannon is pictured at left. Corn was a versatile crop. It was used for silage and feed for animals. For the dinner table, it could be served on or off the cob. Ground into meal, corn was used to make bread or pudding or any number of dishes. Many families also used the cobs for pipes, toys, and, yes, sanitary purposes.

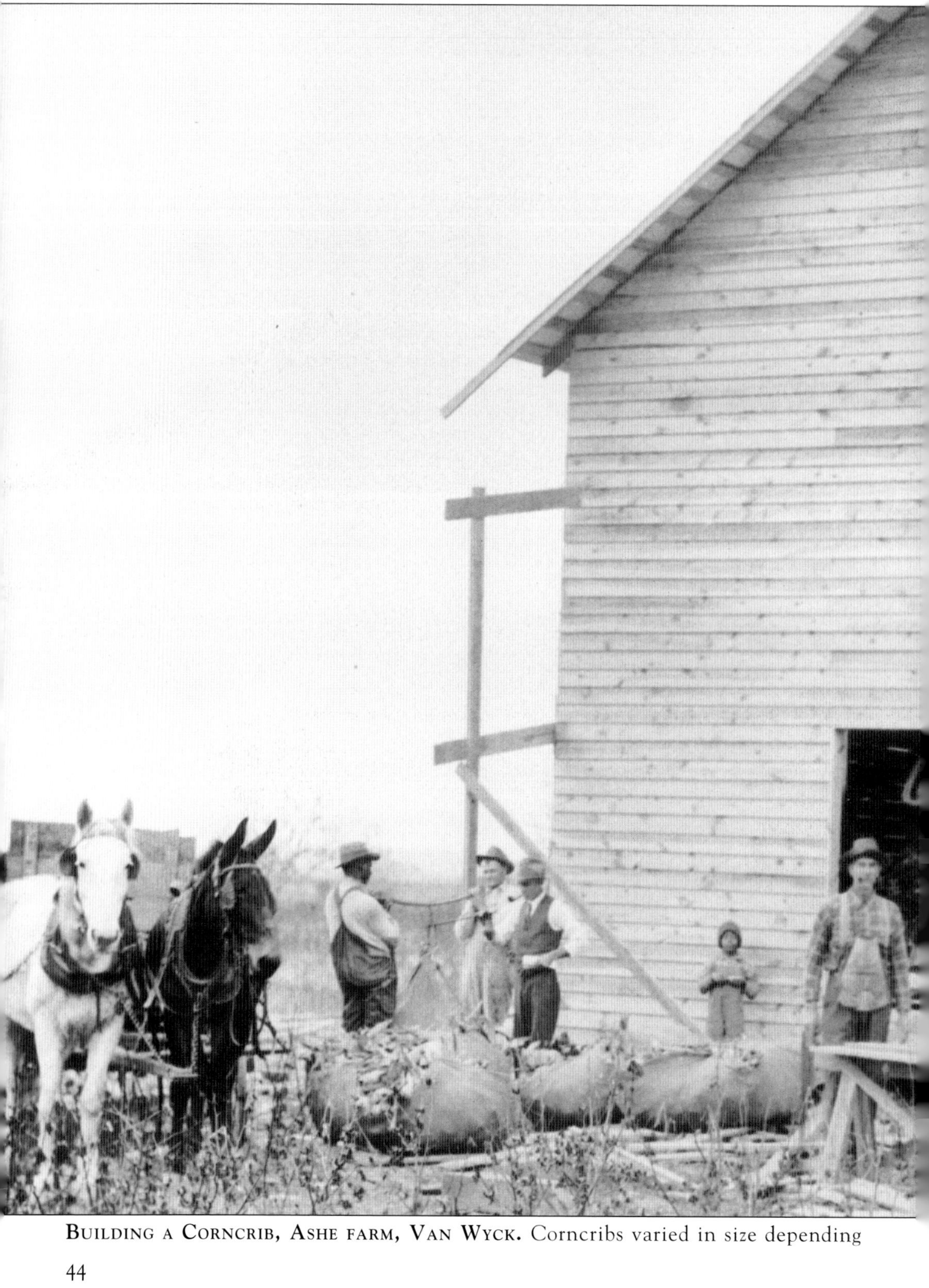

BUILDING A CORNCRIB, ASHE FARM, VAN WYCK. Corncribs varied in size depending

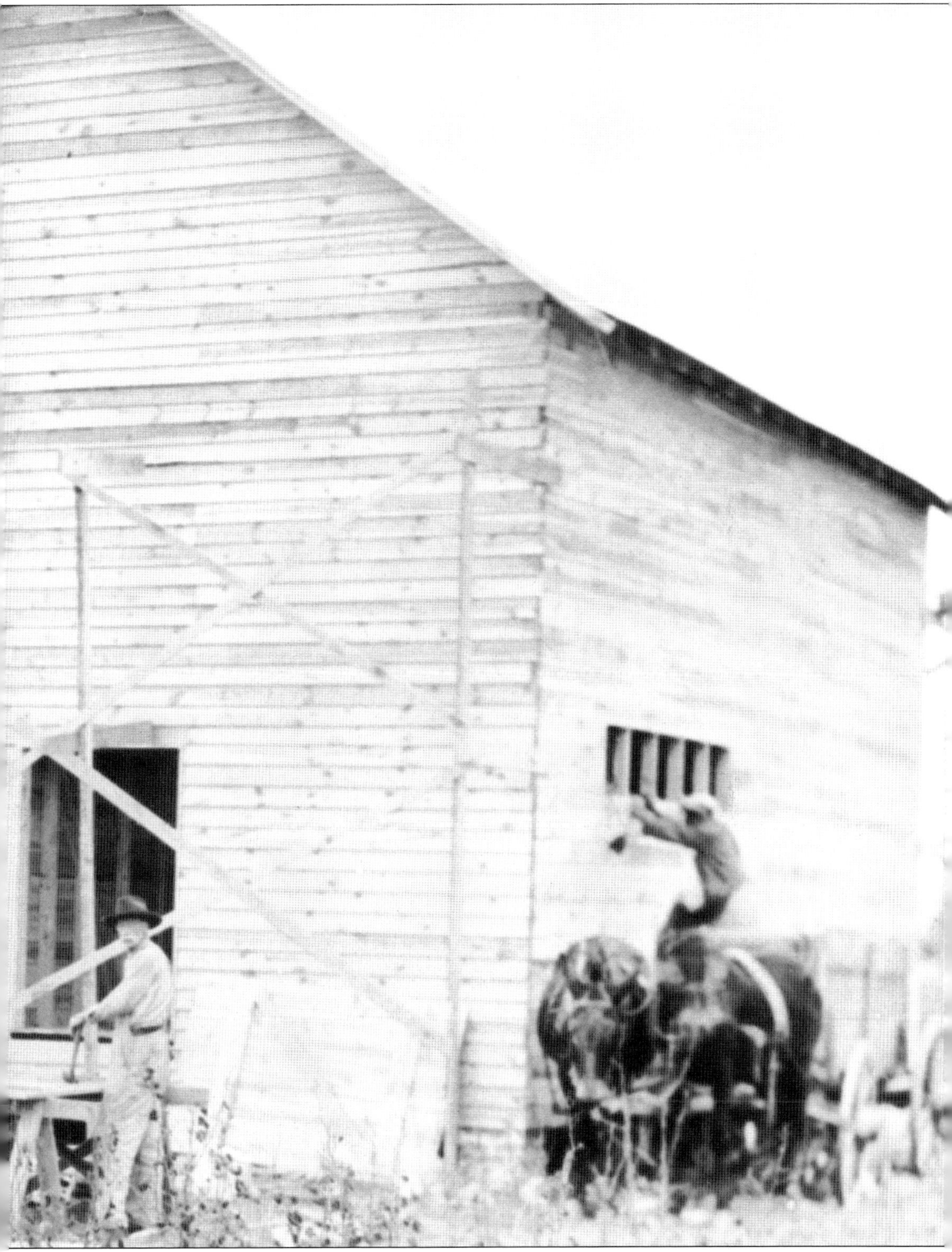

on yields.

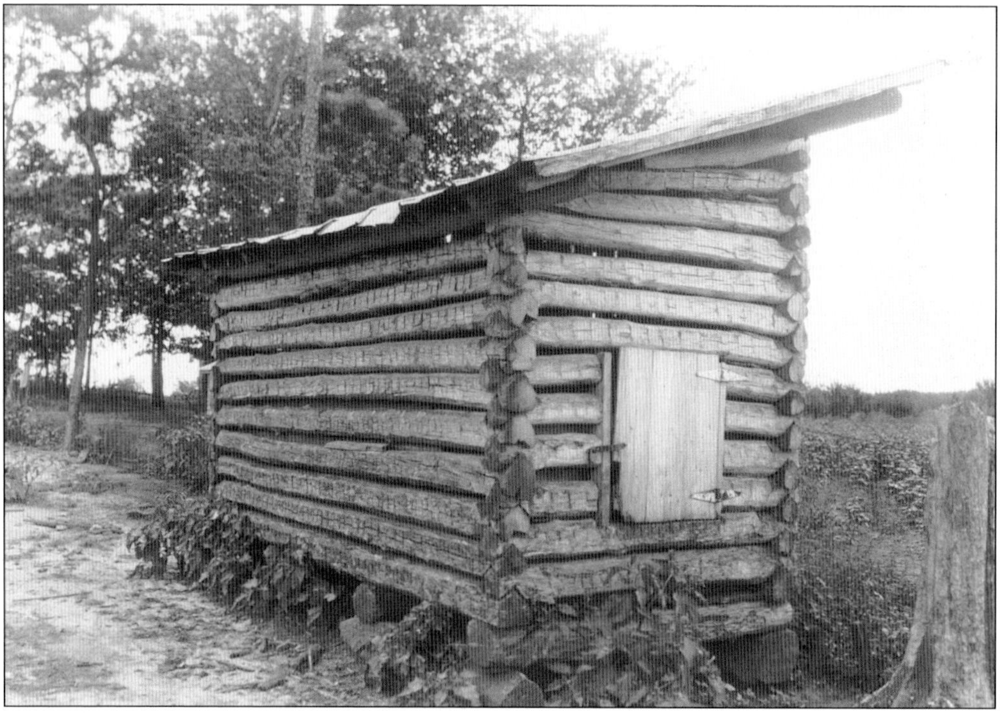

Log Crib Built by J.W. Gaston, c. 1925, Spartanburg. The information on the back of the photos says, "Gaston lived in this crib for six months."

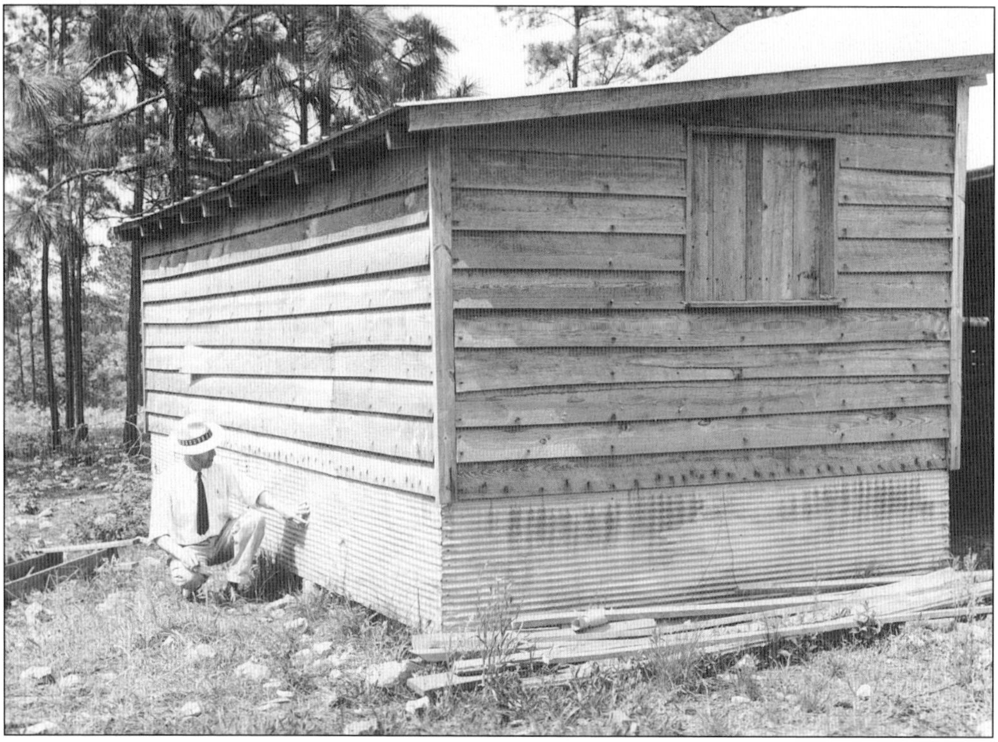

Corncrib, 1947, Fairfield. A county agent points out a barrier to rodents.

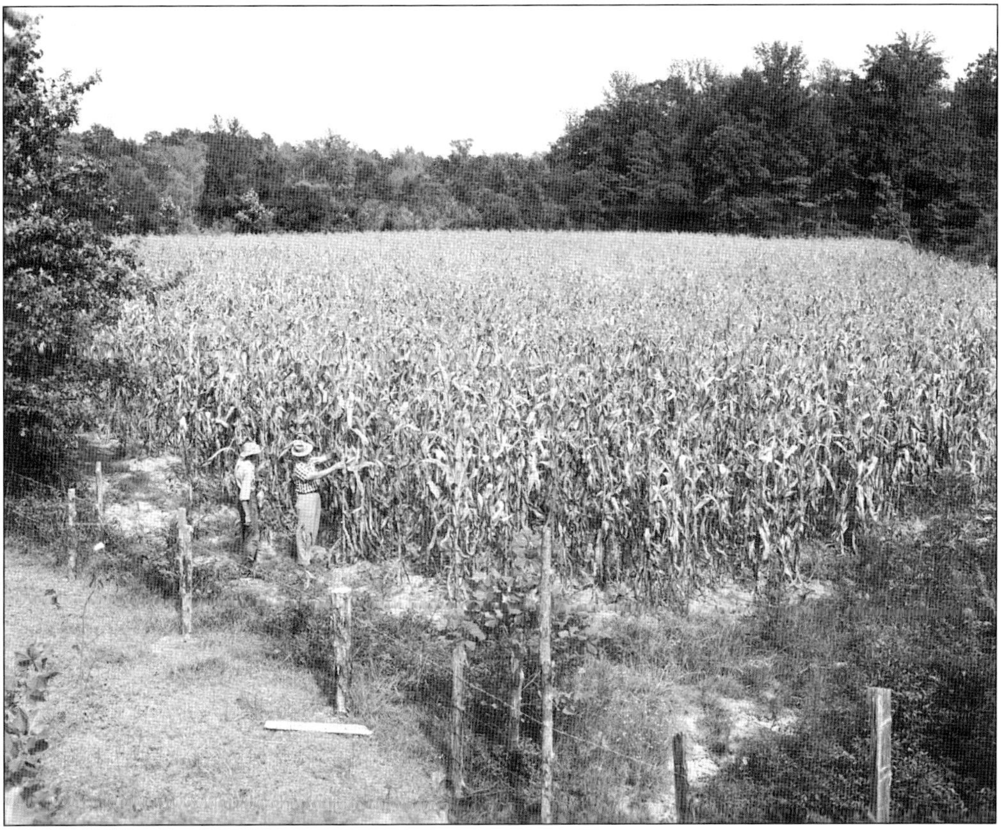

FIELD OF CORN, 1953, ABBEVILLE.

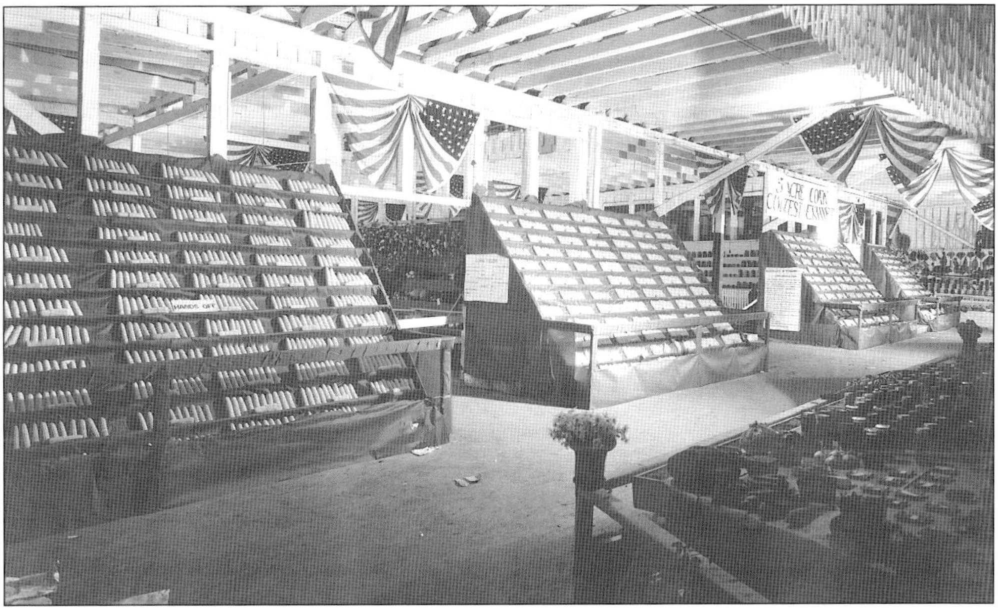

CORN CONTEST AT THE SPARTANBURG COUNTY FAIR, 1929. County fairs showcased the best that farmers produced.

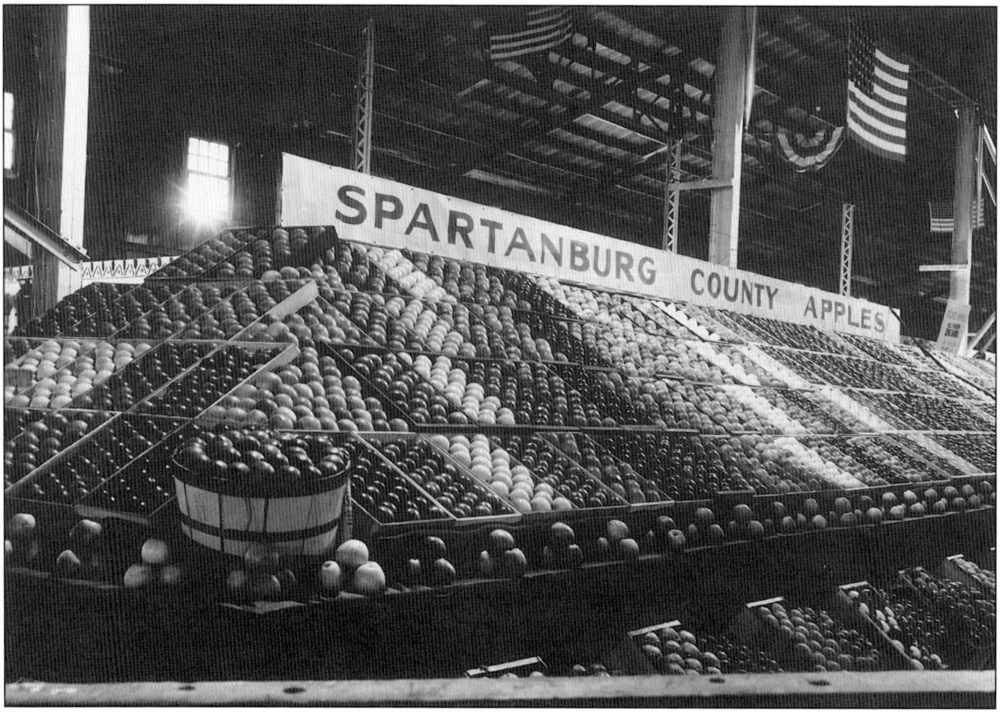

APPLE EXHIBIT AT STATE FAIR, 1940. Apple varieties included winesap, delicious, and McIntosh.

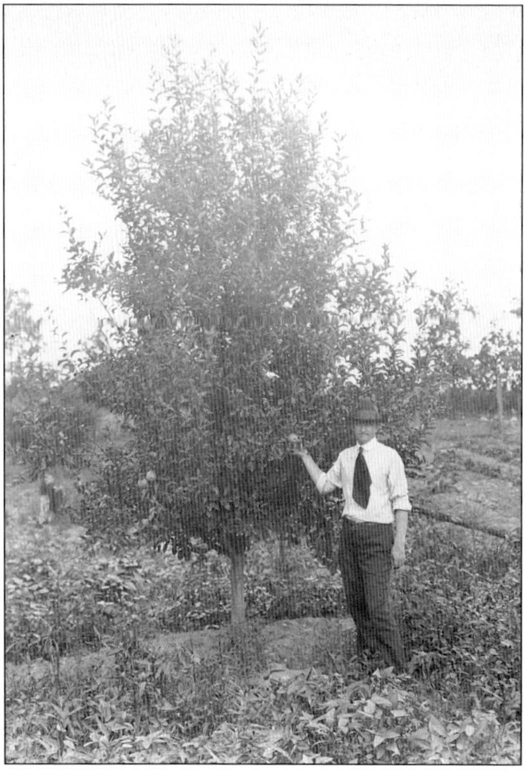

GOLDEN DELICIOUS APPLE TREE, J.V. SMITH, 1923, GREER.

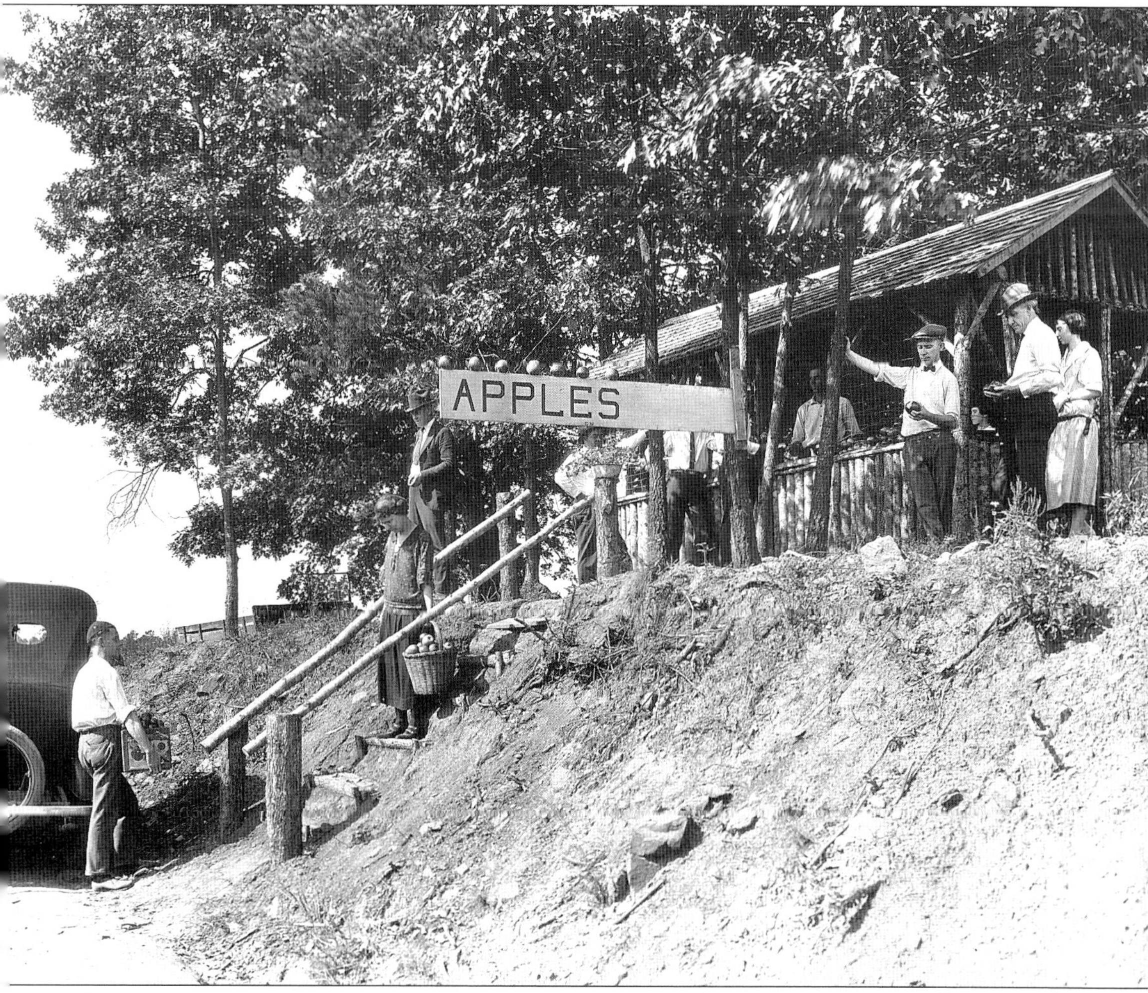

APPLE STAND, 1930s, LONG CREEK. To this day, apple stands are a common site in Long Creek. In autumn, the fragrance of ripe apples permeates the air.

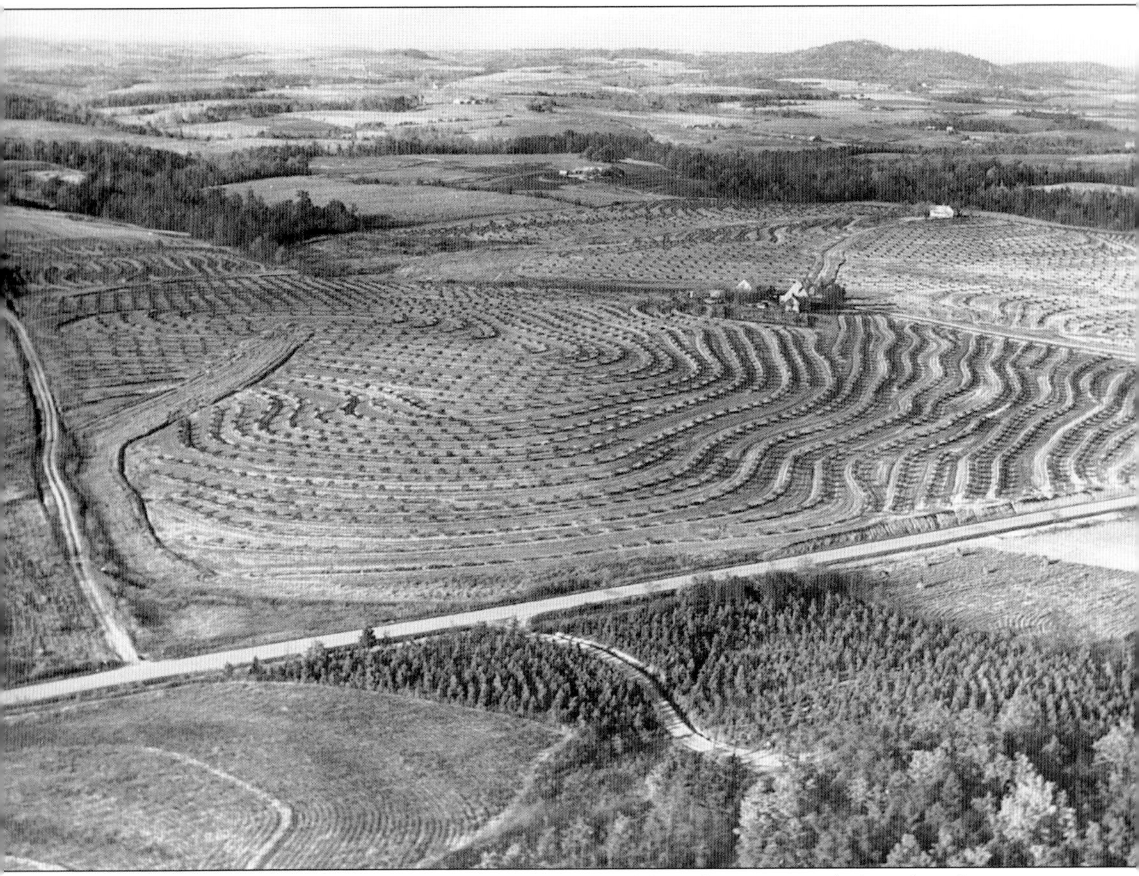

PEACH ORCHARD, 1946, CHEROKEE COUNTY. Although Georgia bears the designation "peach state," South Carolina's peaches are a major crop and, according to many, superior to Georgia's.

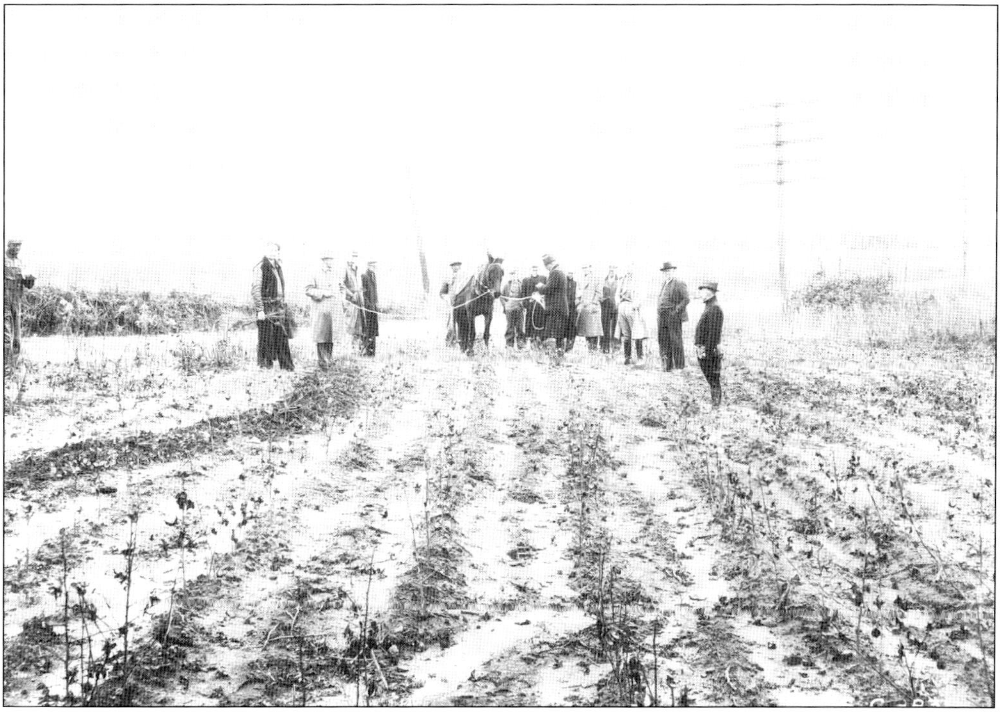

ORCHARD TO BE PLANTED IN A COTTON FIELD ON RAMSEY FARM, C. 1939, INMAN.

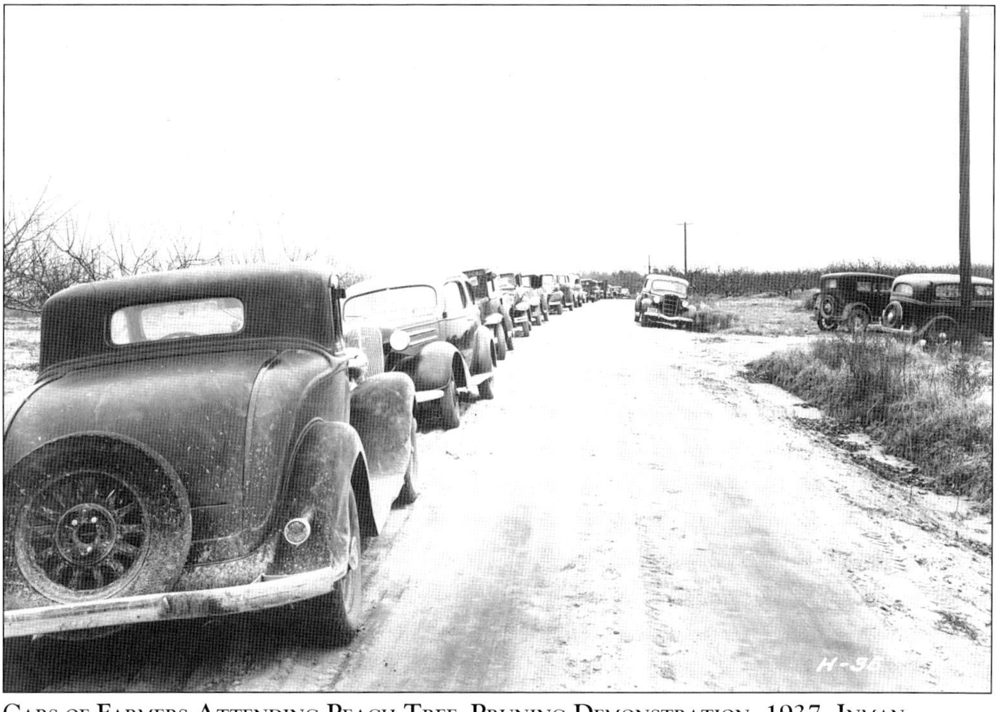

CARS OF FARMERS ATTENDING PEACH TREE–PRUNING DEMONSTRATION, 1937, INMAN.

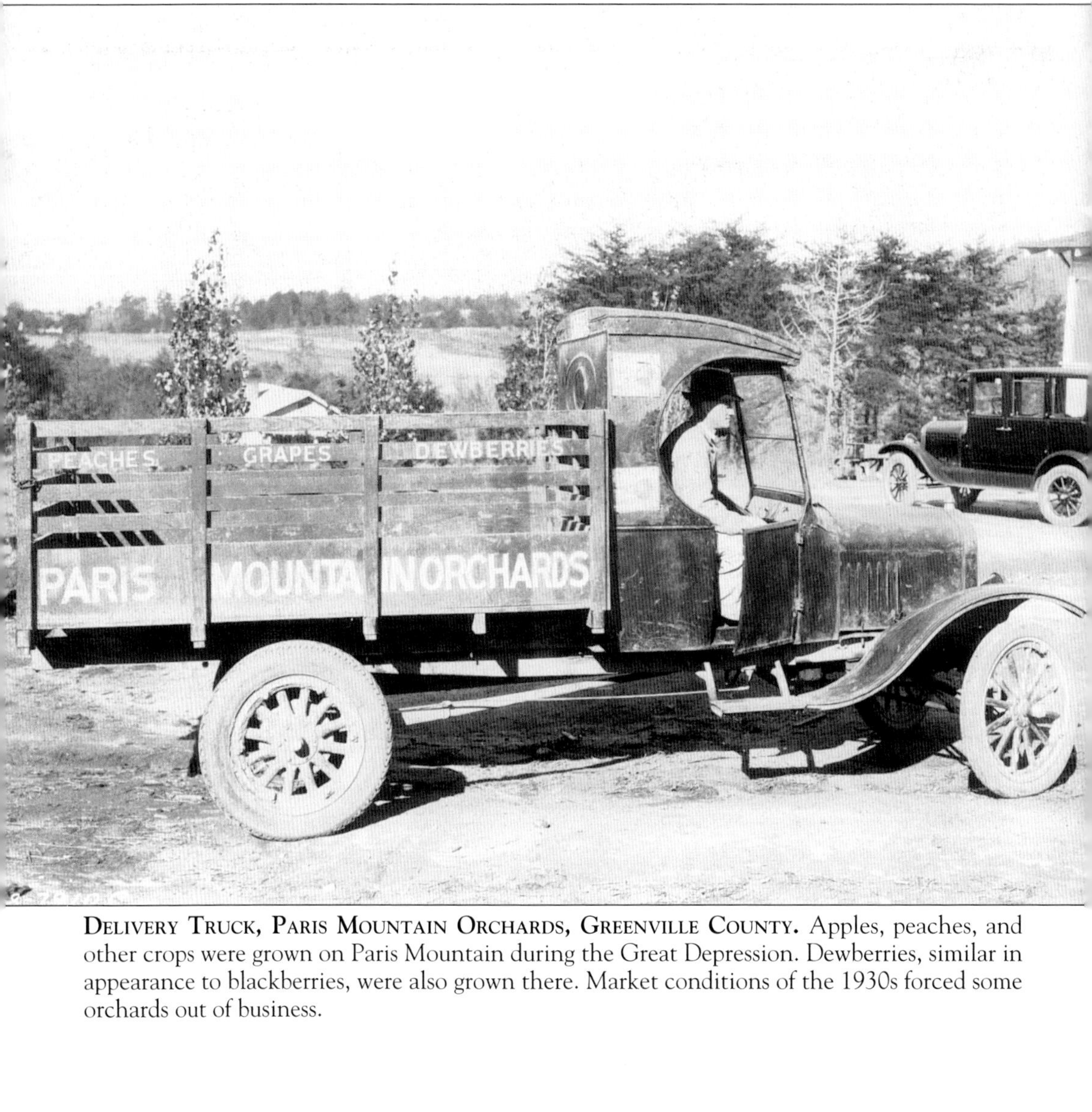

DELIVERY TRUCK, PARIS MOUNTAIN ORCHARDS, GREENVILLE COUNTY. Apples, peaches, and other crops were grown on Paris Mountain during the Great Depression. Dewberries, similar in appearance to blackberries, were also grown there. Market conditions of the 1930s forced some orchards out of business.

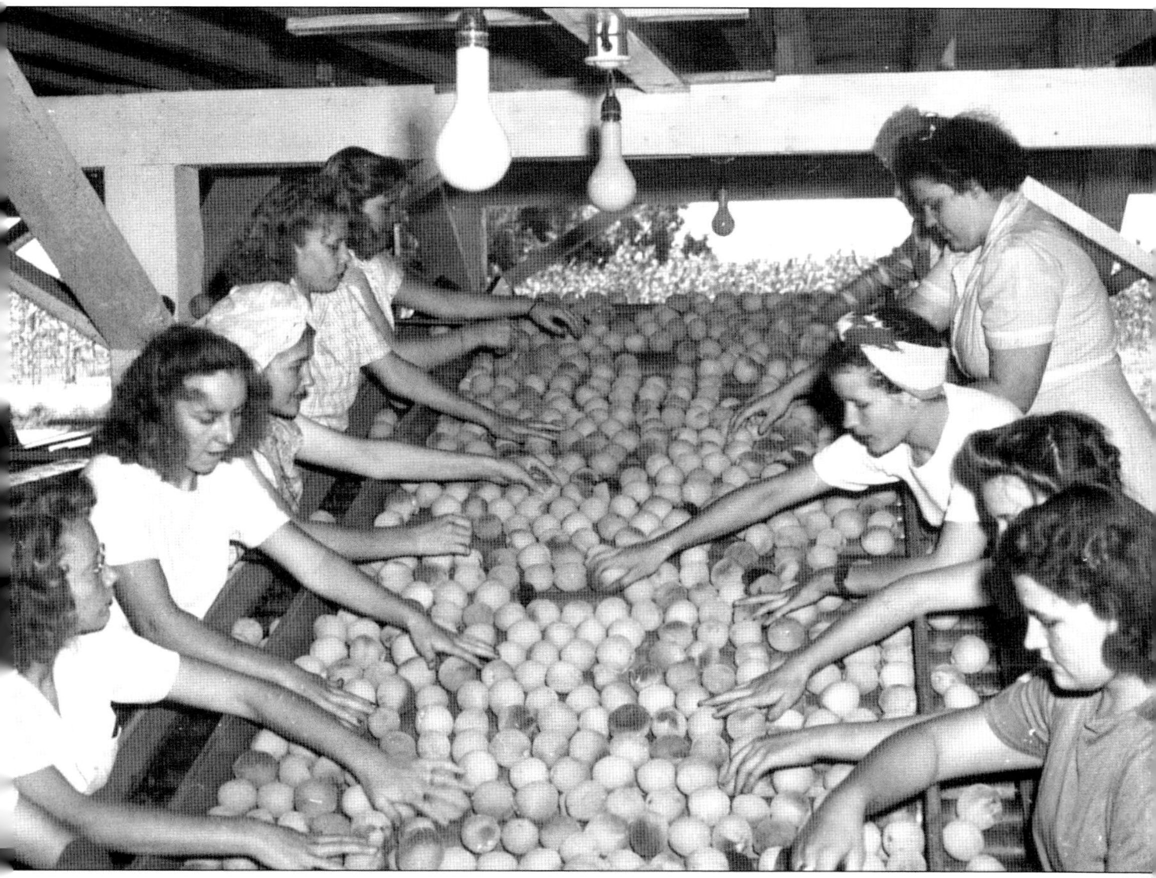

Grading Peaches, c. 1940, Spartanburg. Peach packing houses were beehives of activity. Here, women who needed to supplement family income, found jobs.

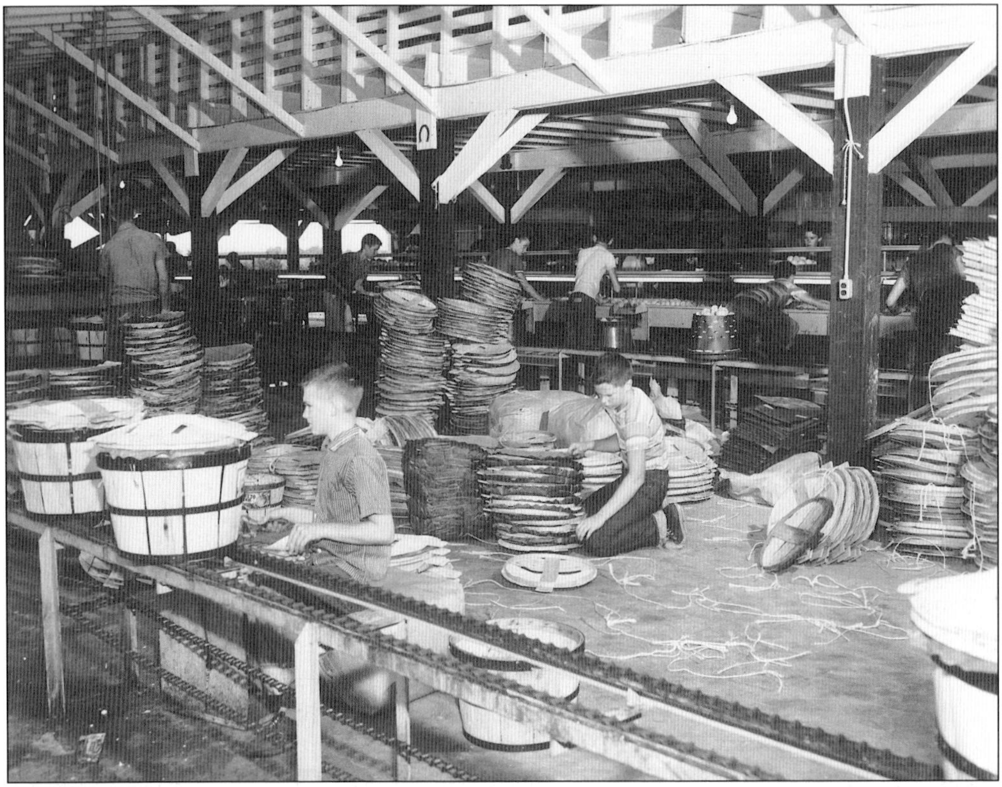

PEACH PACKING, 1950S, SPARTANBURG COUNTY. The well-made baskets also found their way into some homes as laundry hampers or even end tables.

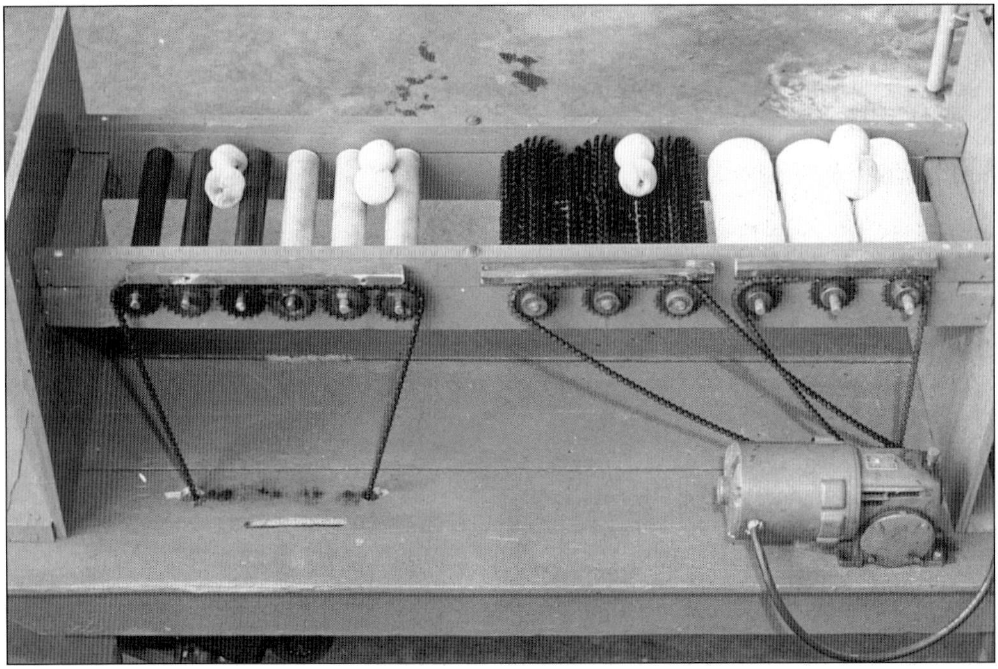

MACHINE TO TEST THE BRUISING OF PEACHES, 1968, CLEMSON.

SELECT PEACHES FROM THE GRAMLING ORCHARD, 1934.

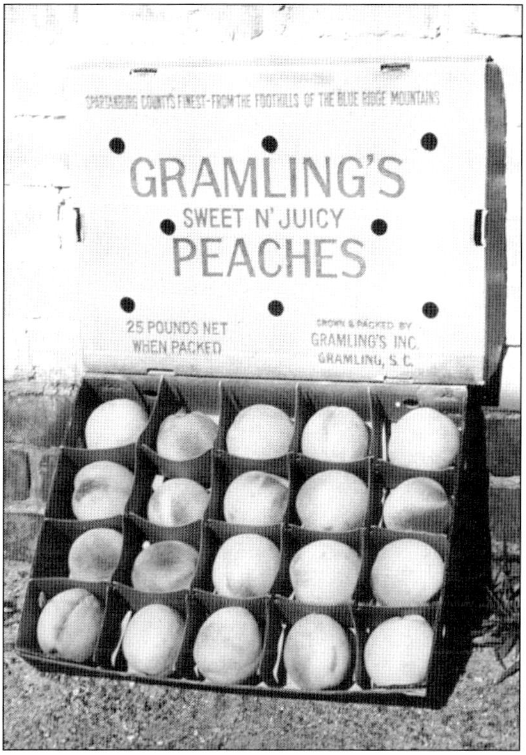

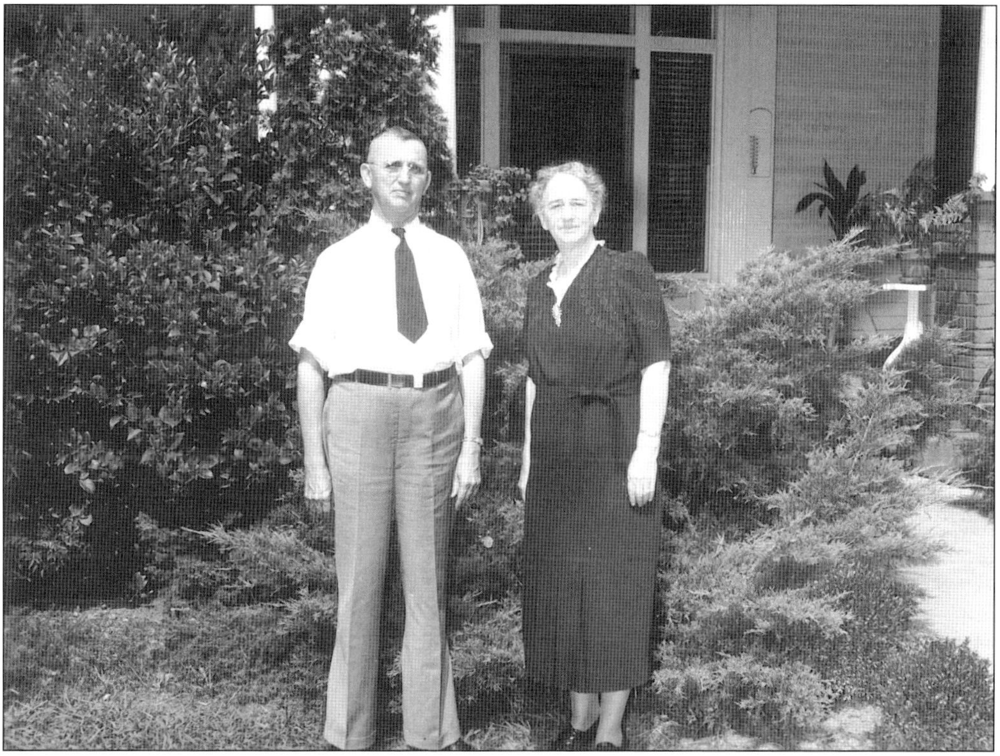

MR. AND MRS. BEN GRAMLING, 1939.

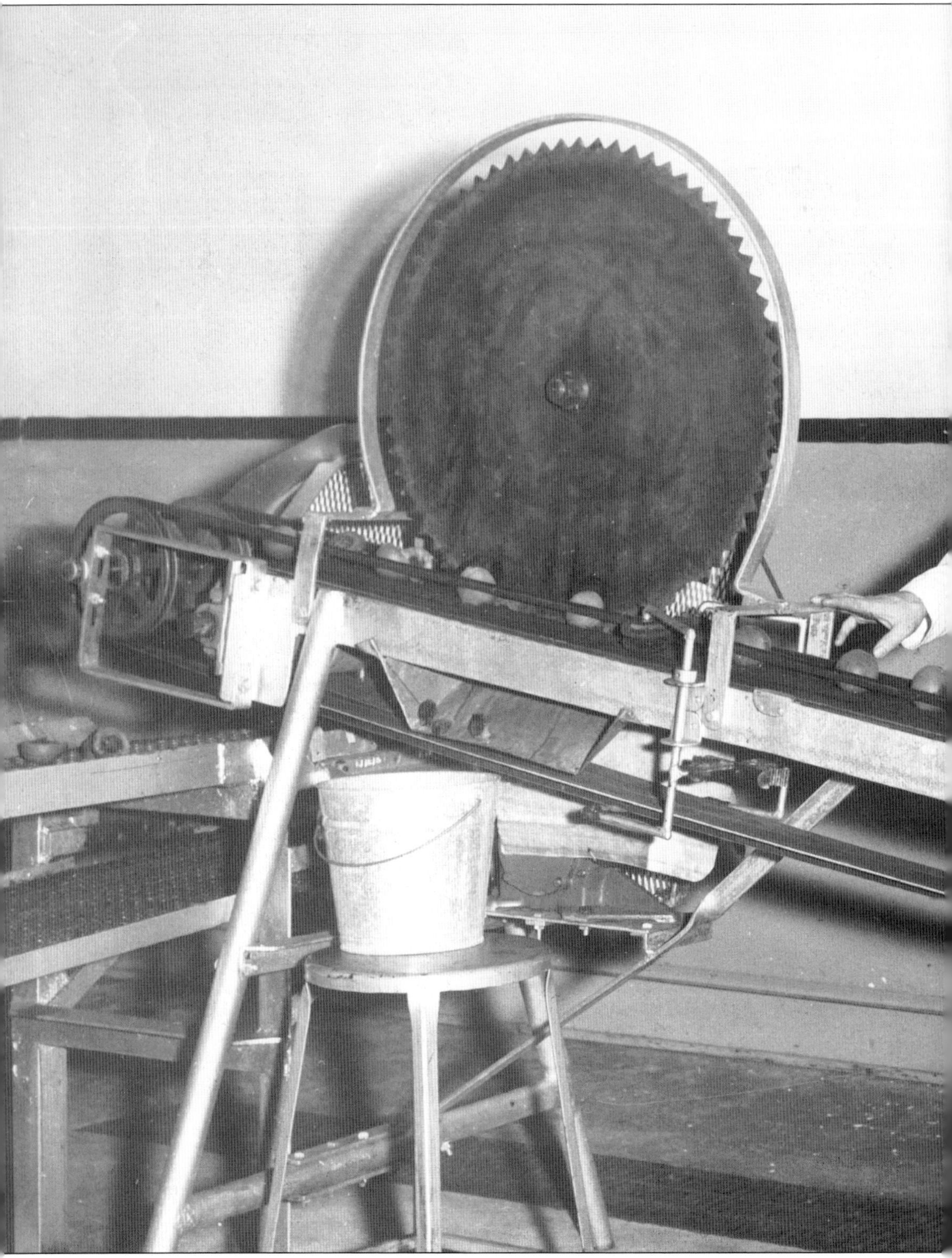

FREESTONE PEACH-PITTING MACHINE DESIGNED BY L.O. VAN BLARICOM (LEFT), C. 1950,

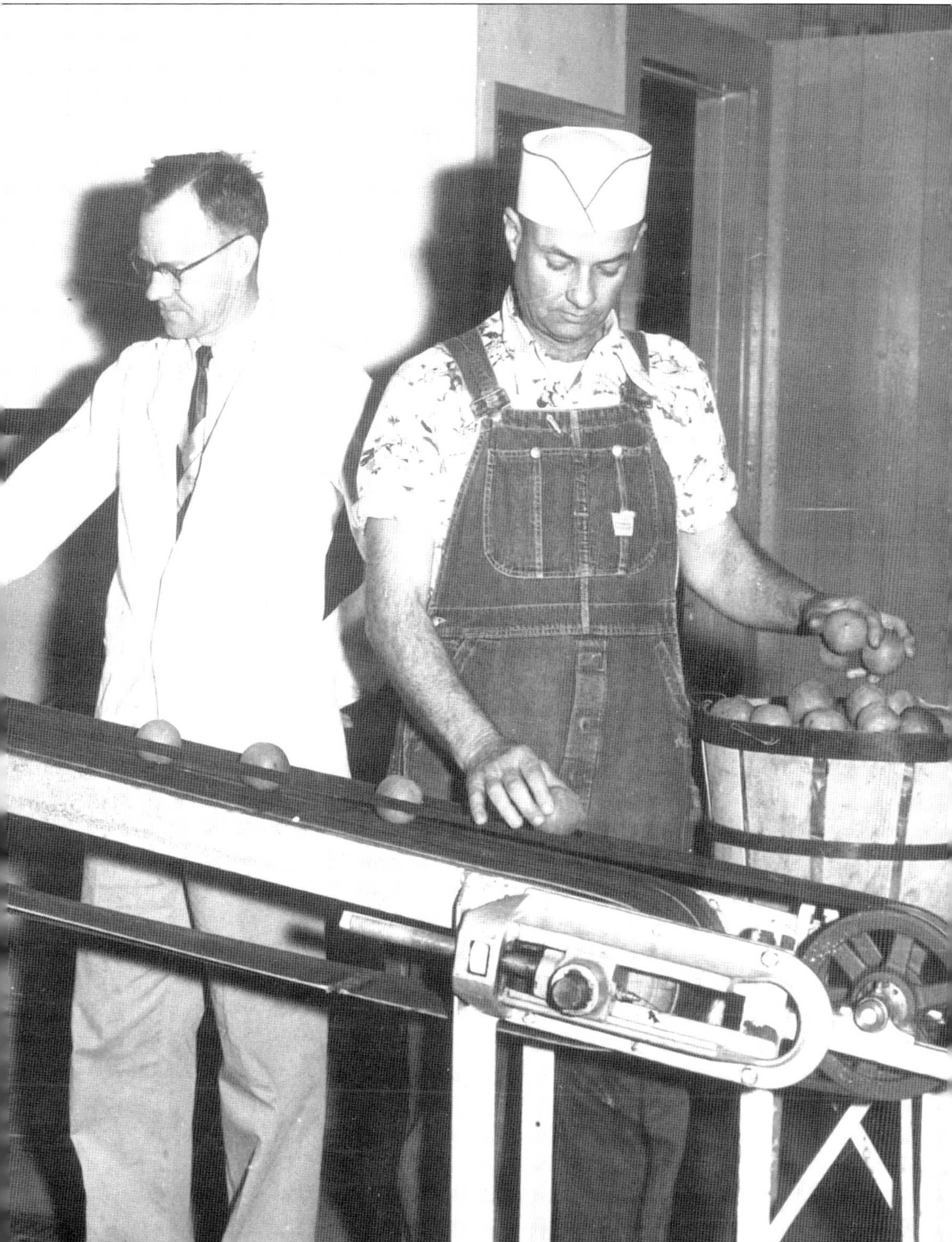

Clemson.

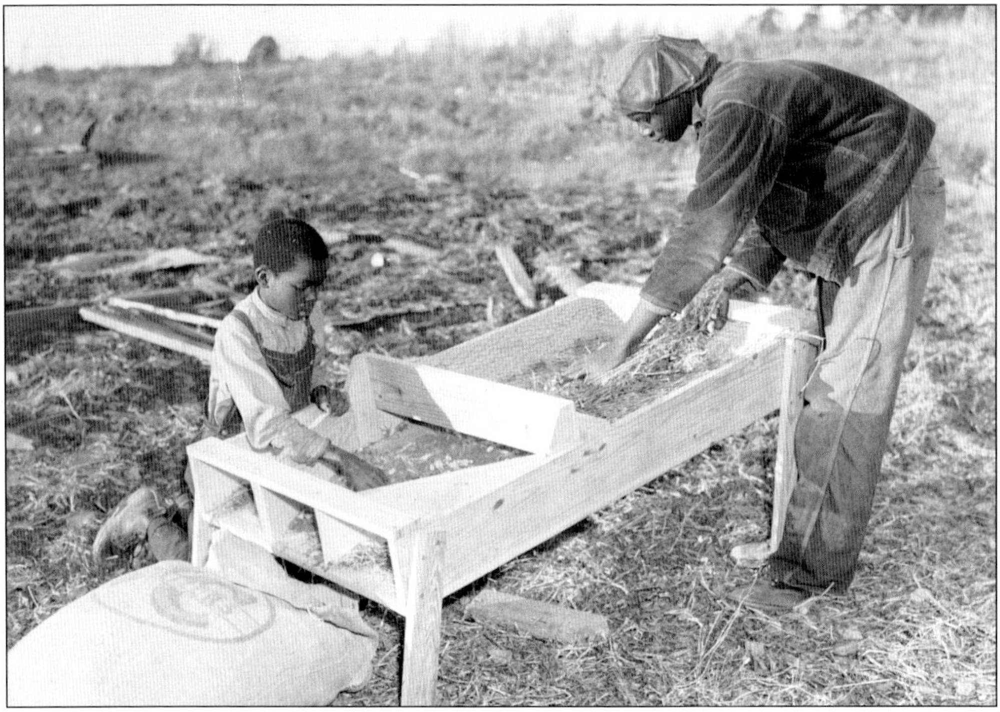

HOMEMADE PEANUT PICKER, 1942, CHESTER. Peanuts, often thought to be nuts, are actually legumes.

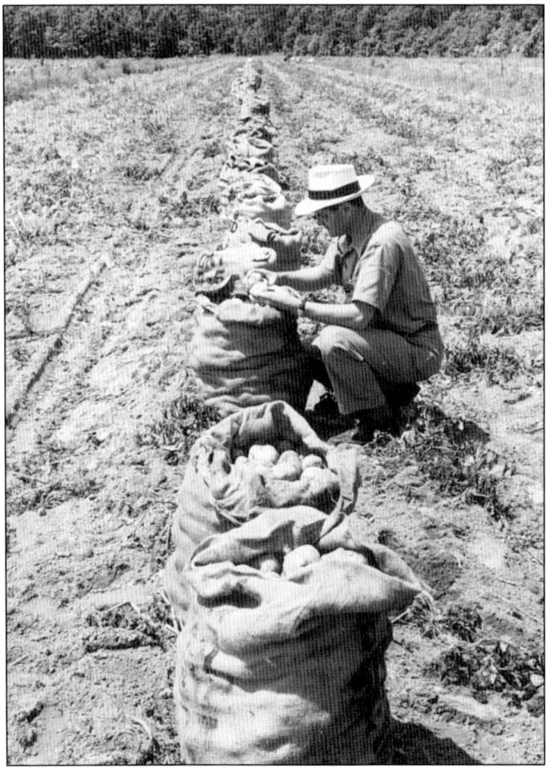

IRISH POTATO HARVEST, C. 1950, LOCATION UNKNOWN.

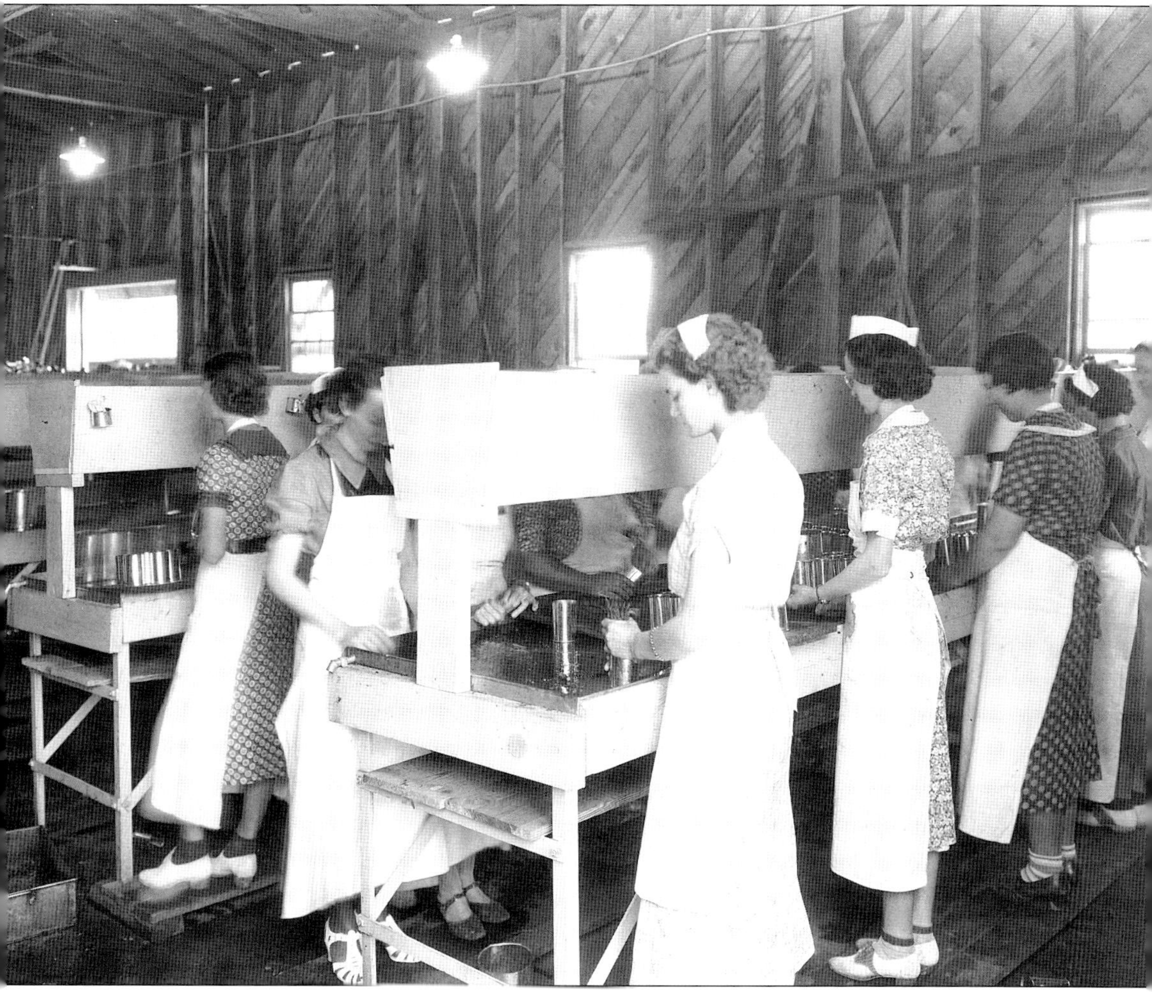

Asparagus Cannery, 1937, Johnston.

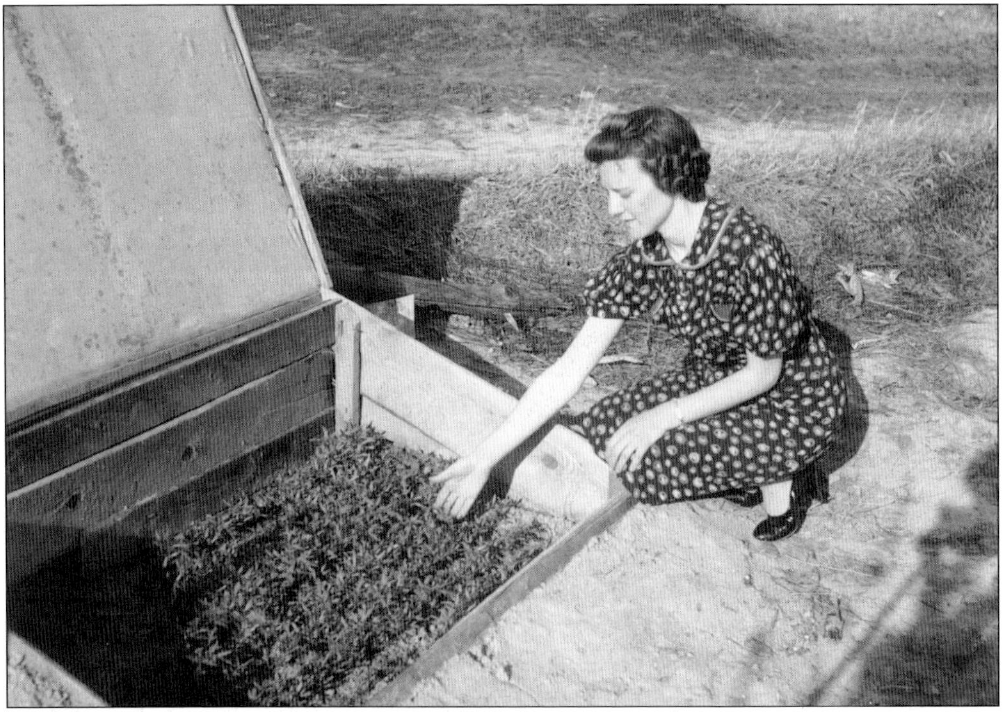

Irene Henson with Tomato Plant Hotbed, c. 1940, Lancaster.

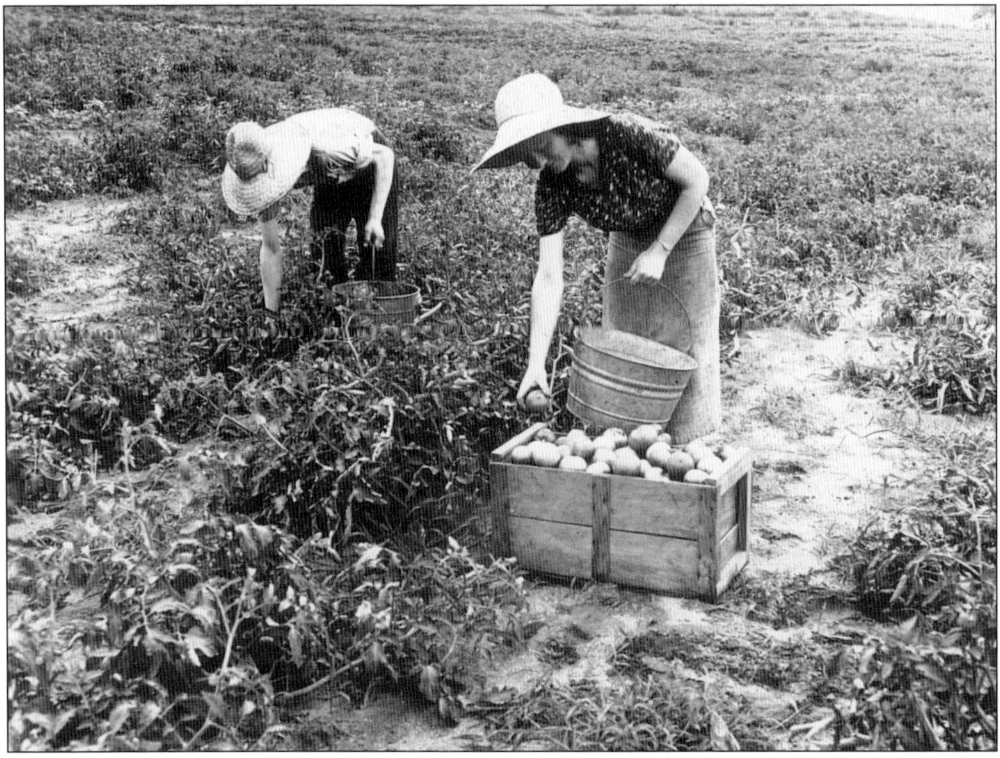

Group of 4-H Members Picking Tomatoes as Part of Project, 1939, Pickens.

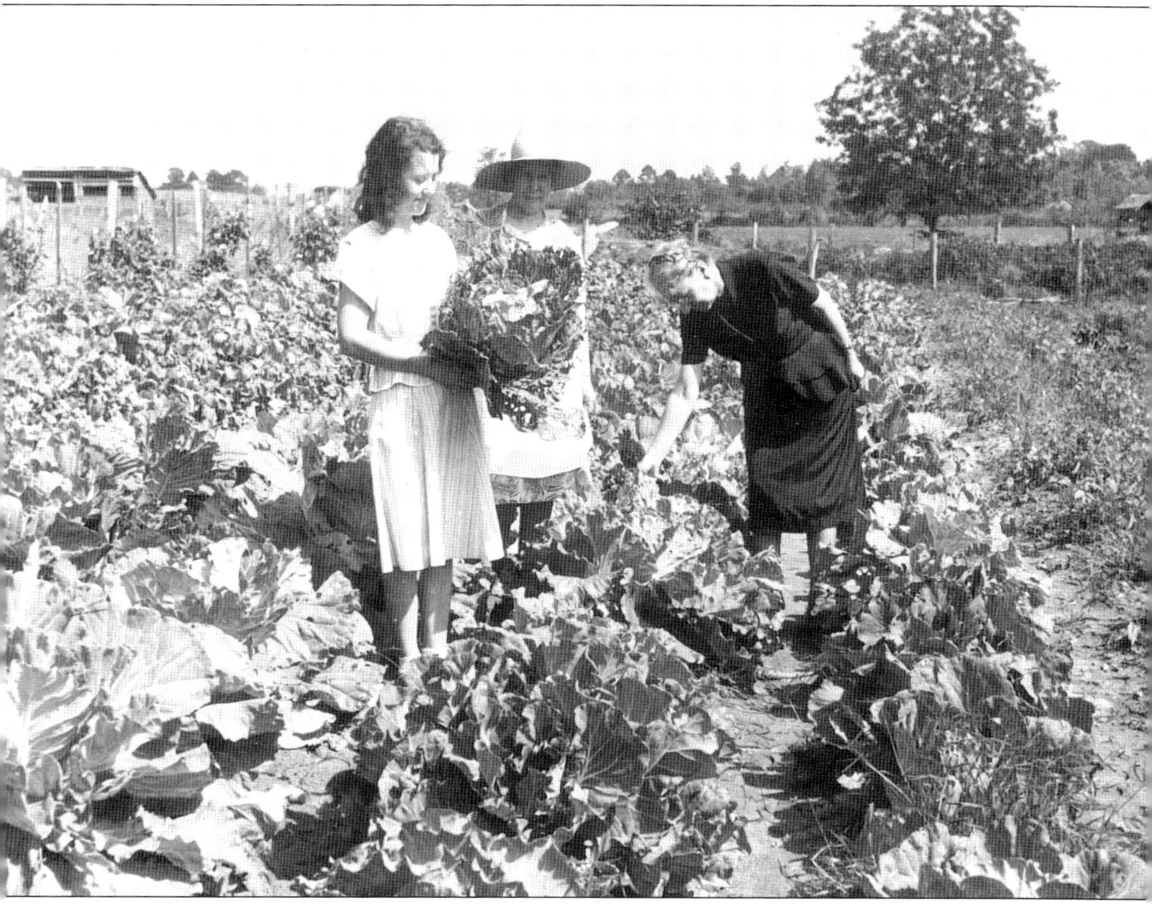

FALL GARDEN, 1948, NEWBERRY. Women took great pride in their gardens. Their efforts yielded extra food for their families and, if they sold their produce, extra dollars.

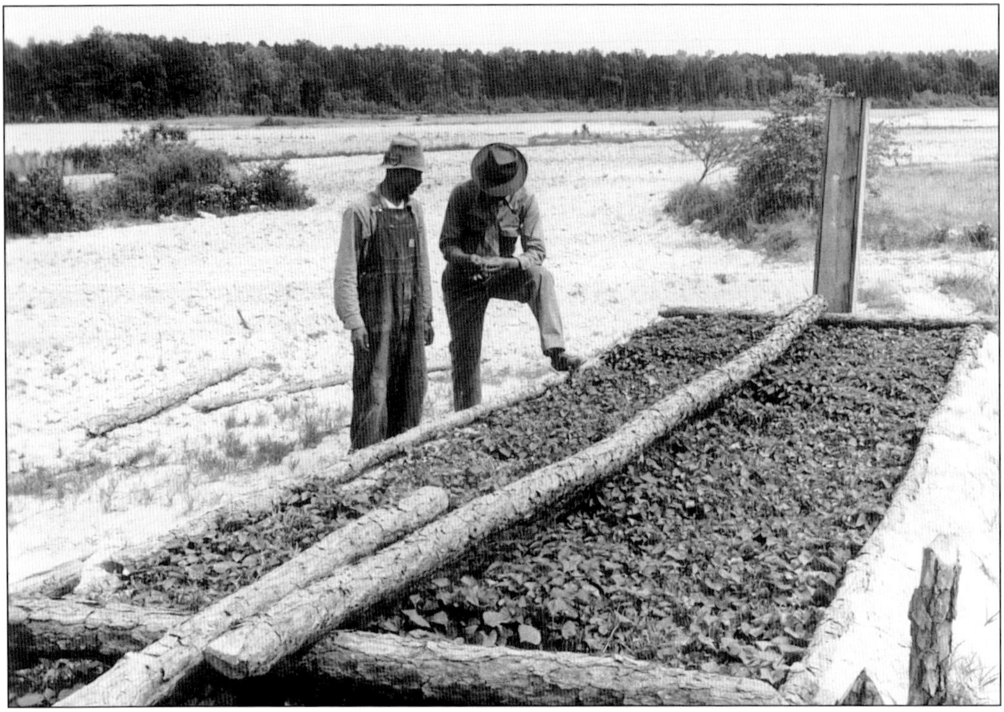

HOTBED FOR SWEET POTATO PLANTS, 1941, UNION.

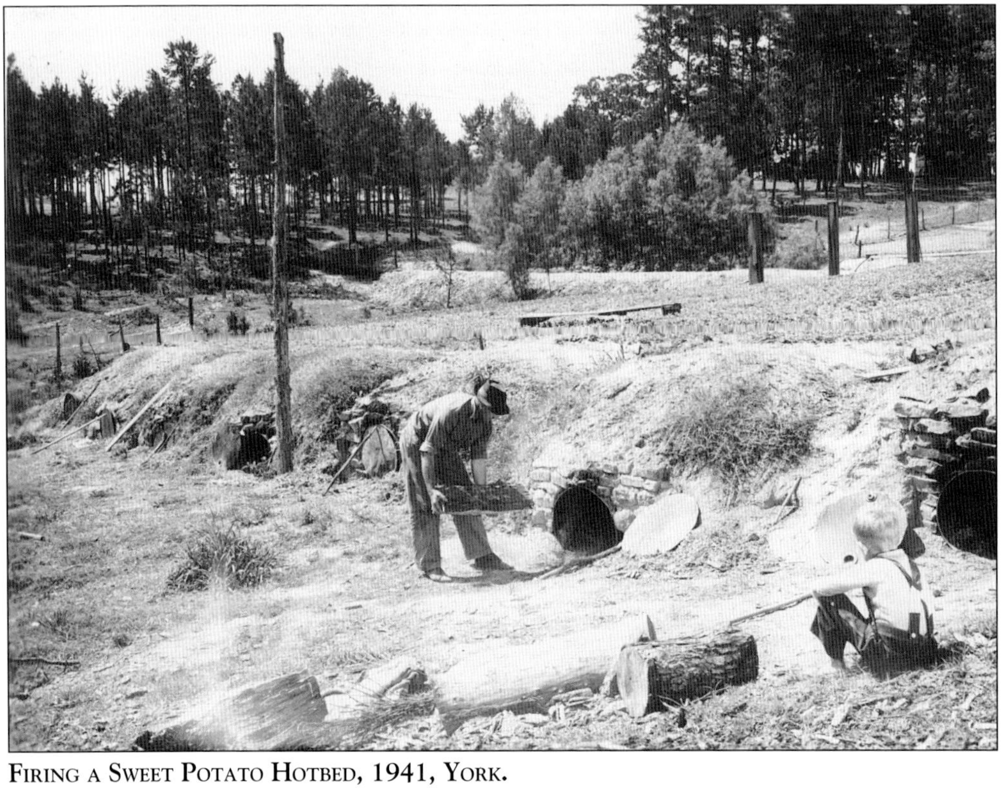

FIRING A SWEET POTATO HOTBED, 1941, YORK.

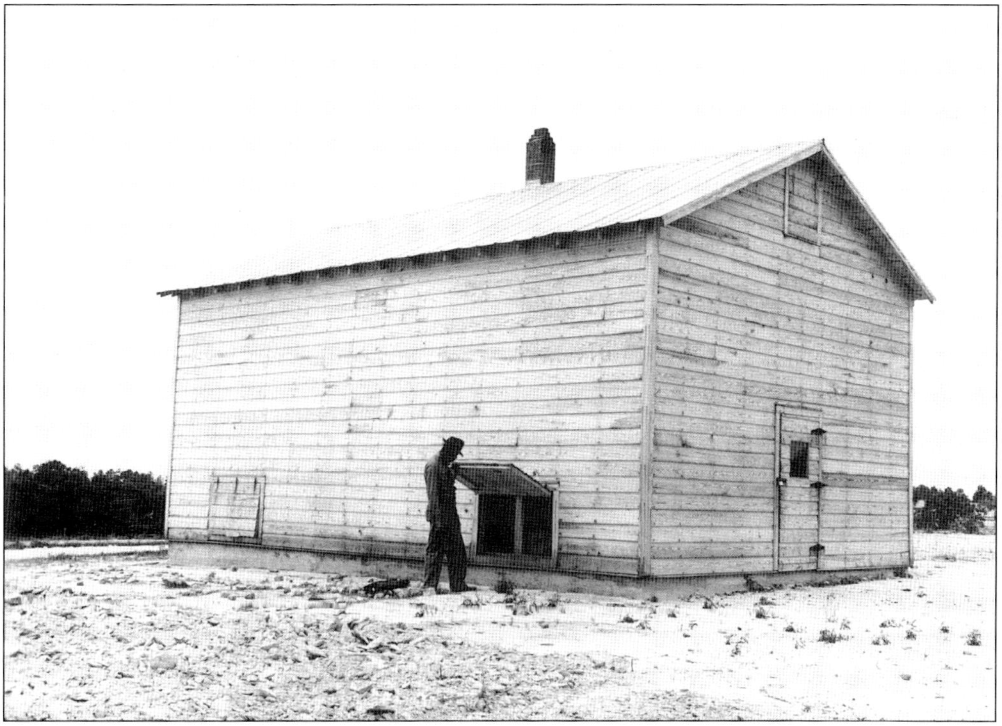

Storage House for Curing Sweet Potatoes, 1941, Union.

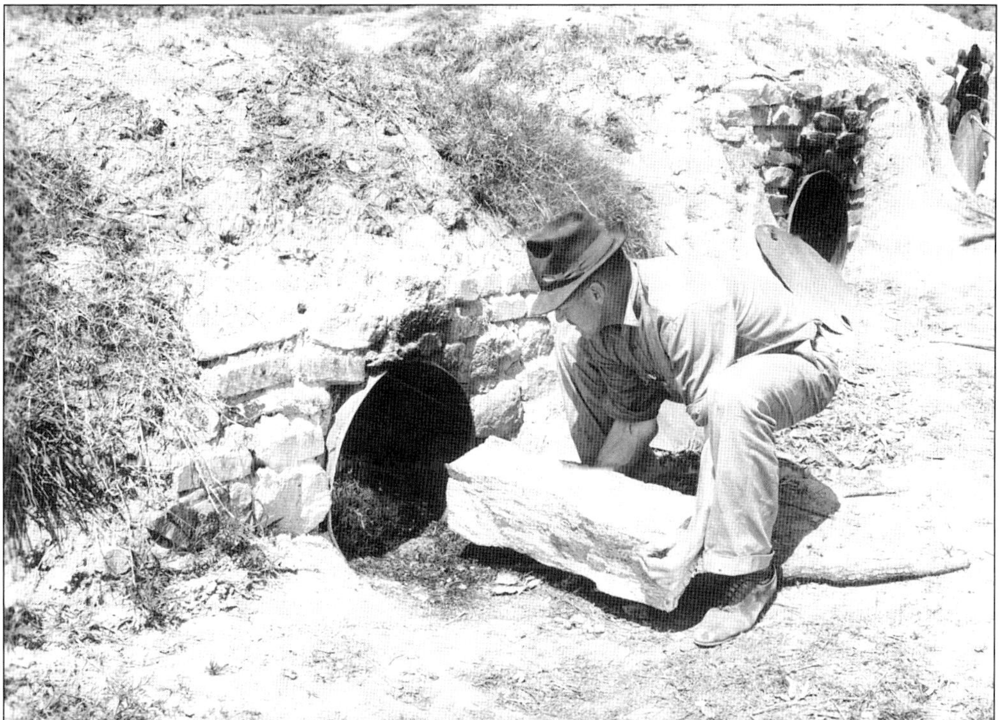

Firing a Sweet Potato Hotbed, 1941, York.

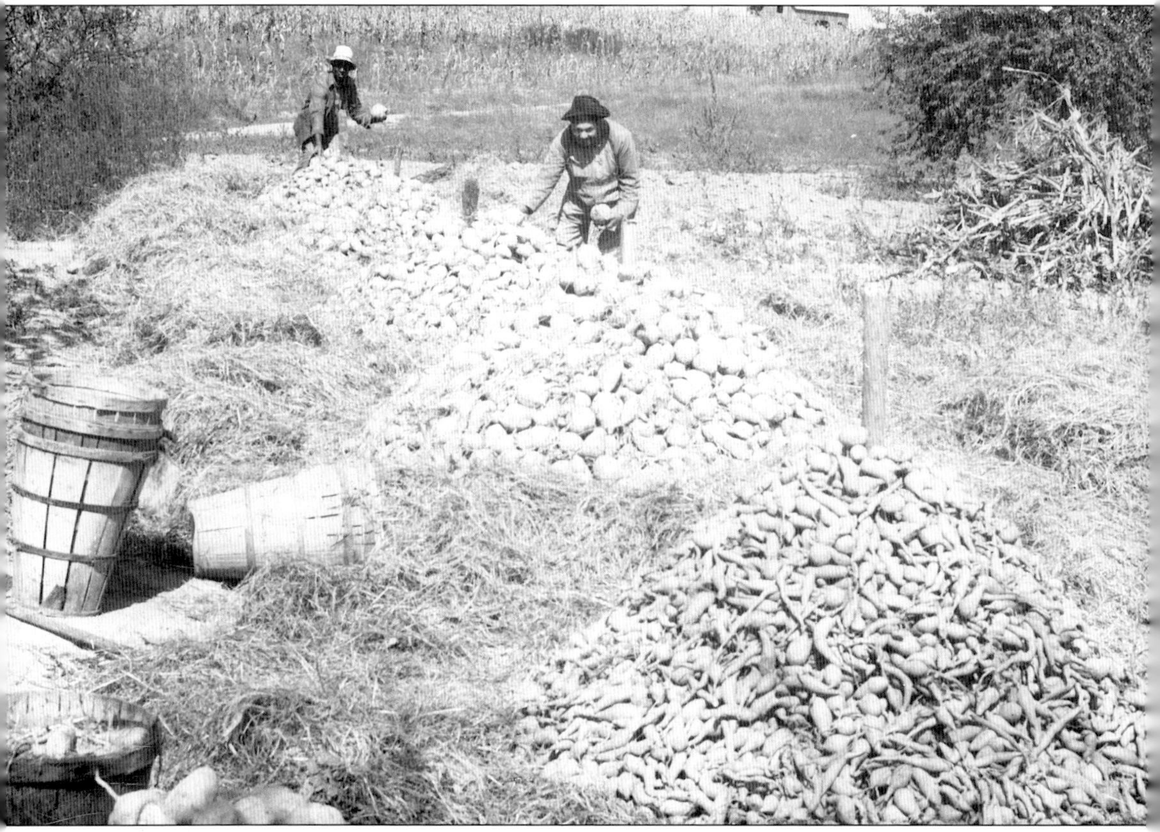

SWEET POTATO HARVEST, 1938, GREENVILLE. Sweet potatoes served as an excellent source of nutrition for many in the Piedmont. Cooks served sweet potatoes in a variety of ways, such as candied, baked, boiled, and mashed. No potato was complete without a pat of butter. The best-known use for sweet potatoes, however, was the Southern specialty, sweet potato pie. The Extension Service even issued a bulletin devoted to recipes using these savory vegetables.

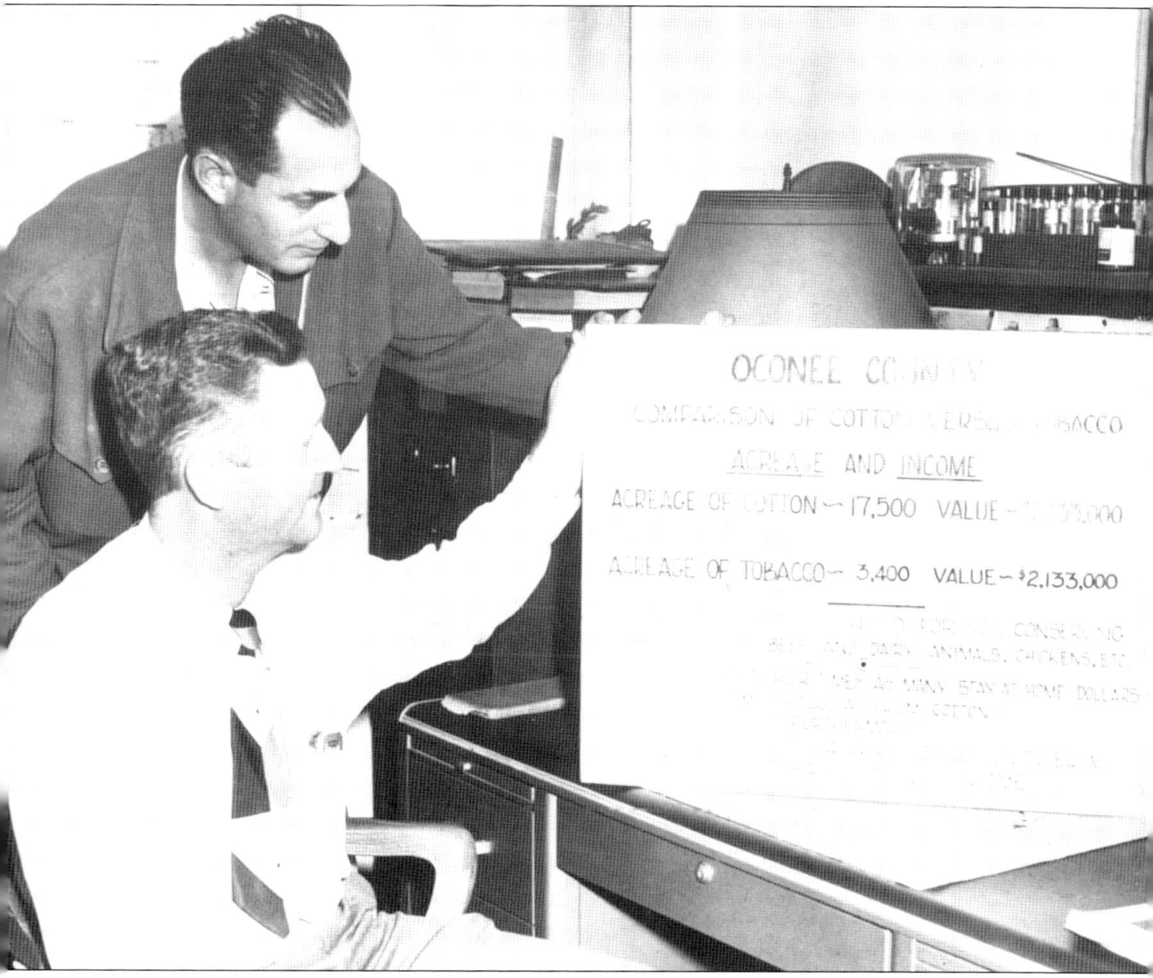

CLEMSON EXTENSION AGENTS BOB MATTISON AND RED MARTIN SHOWING STATISTICS ON TOBACCO AND COTTON, 1946.

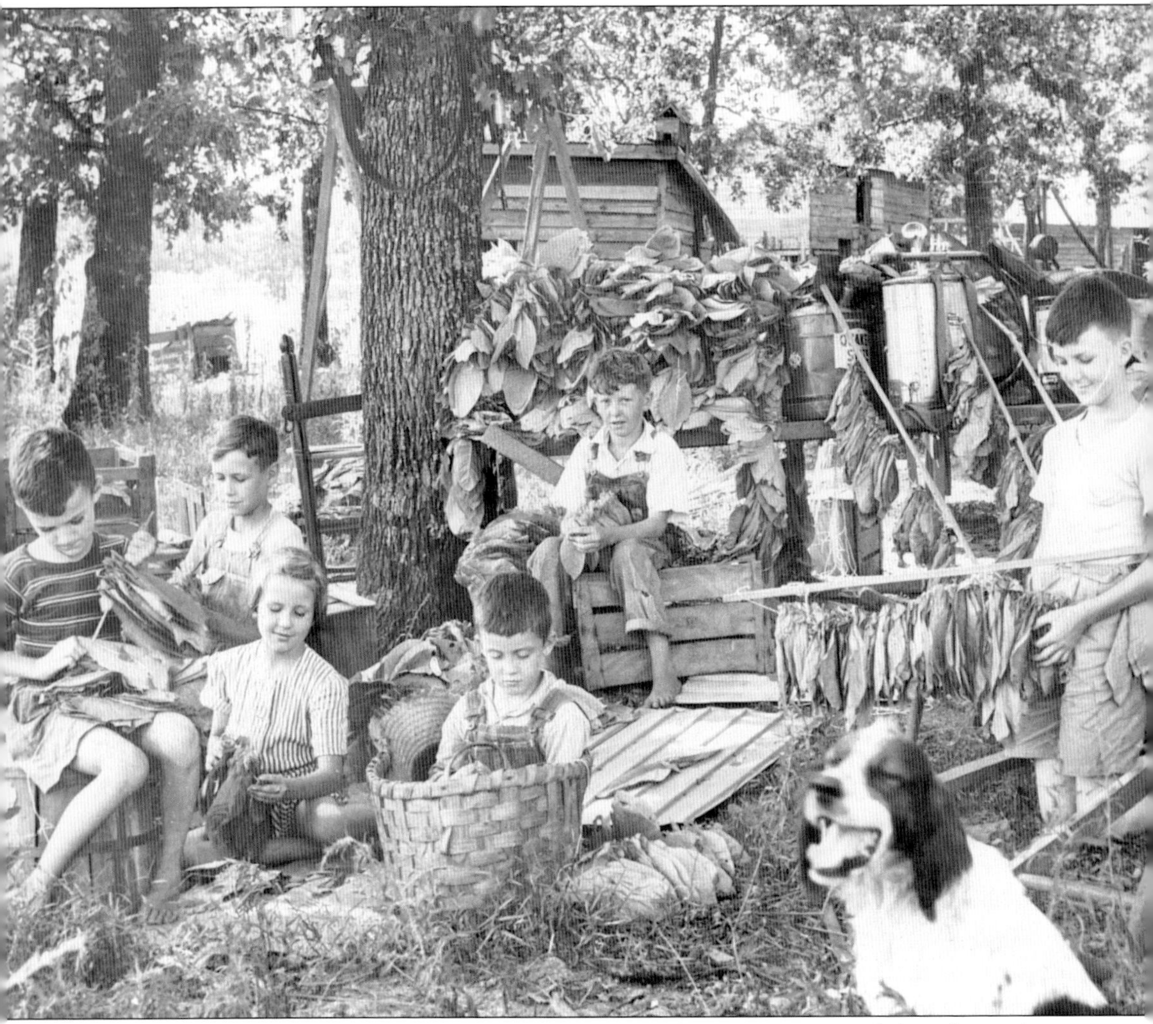

FAMILY STRINGING TOBACCO, 1946, OCONEE COUNTY. Stringing permitted the tobacco leaves to cure properly.

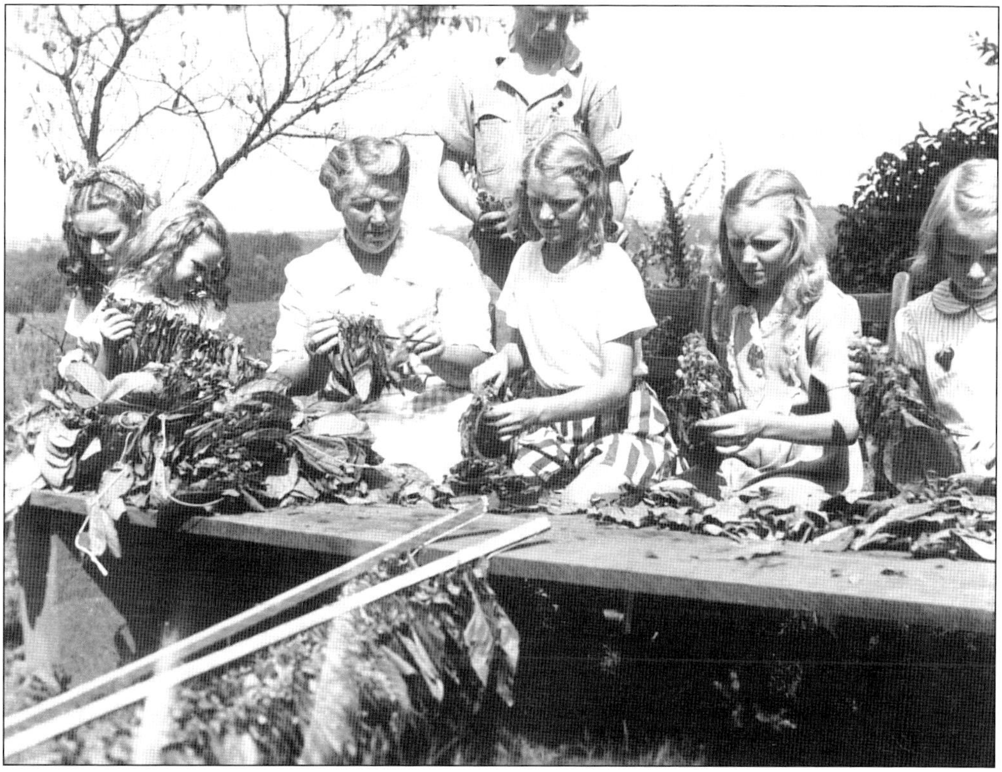

STRINGING TOBACCO FOR CURING, 1946, OCONEE COUNTY. The Turkish tobacco program was sponsored by Duke University and Clemson Cooperative Extension Service.

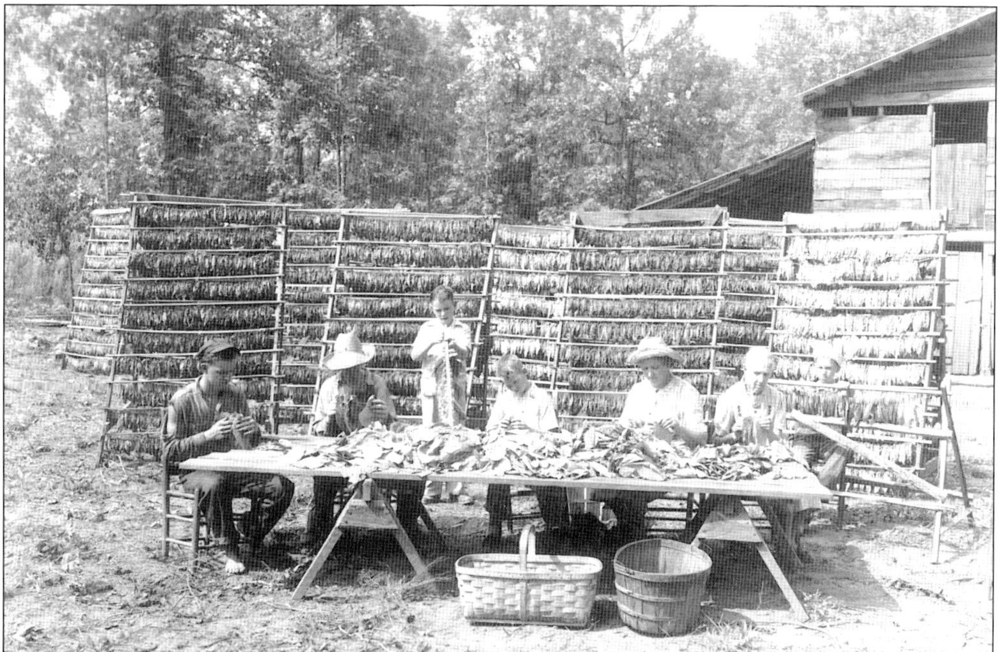

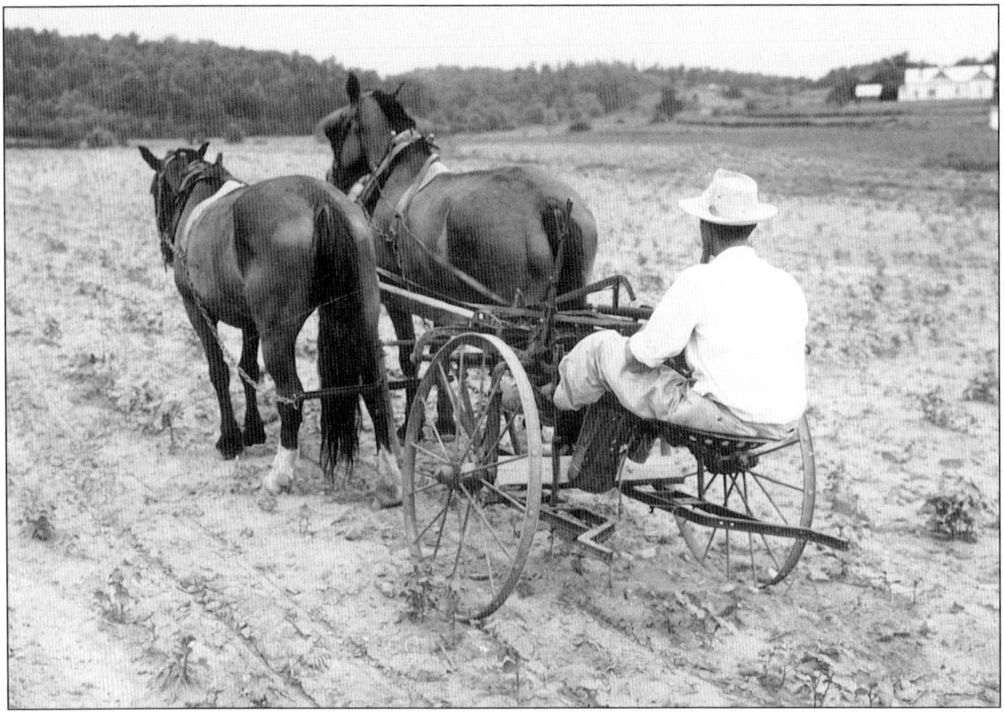

SPRAYING COTTON PLANTS, 1950, PICKENS COUNTY. This farmer uses a sprayer he made himself.

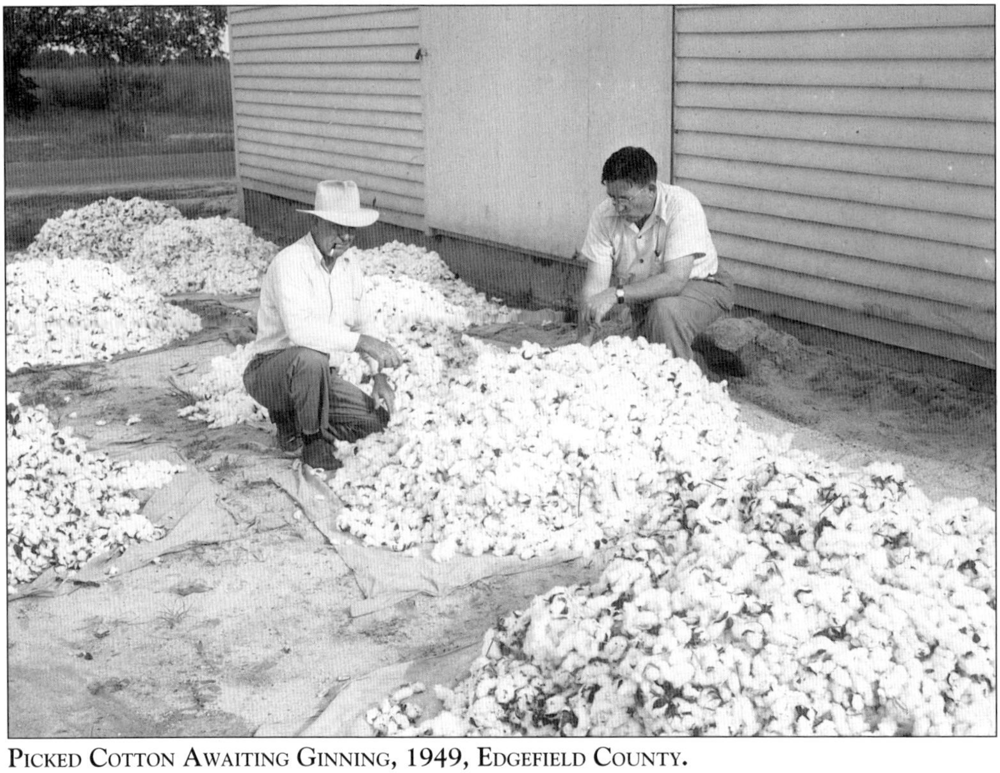

PICKED COTTON AWAITING GINNING, 1949, EDGEFIELD COUNTY.

COTTON PICKER, 1949, PICKENS COUNTY.

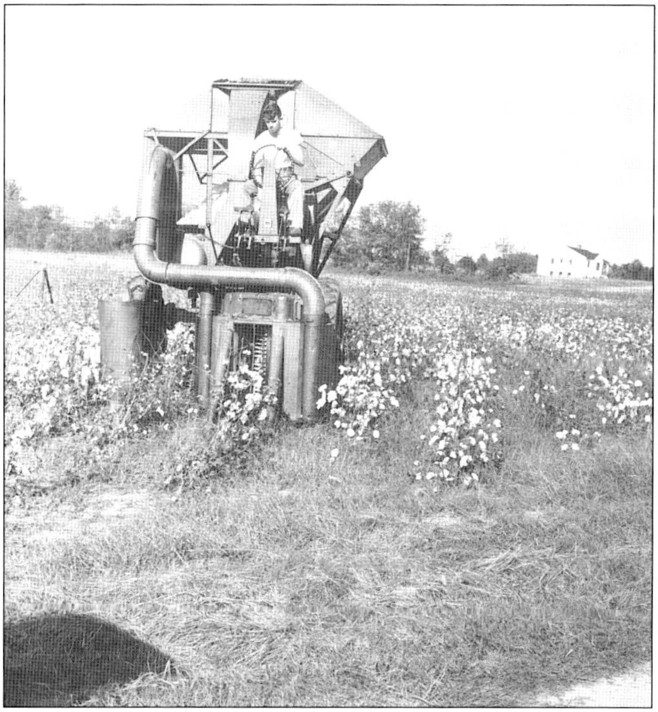

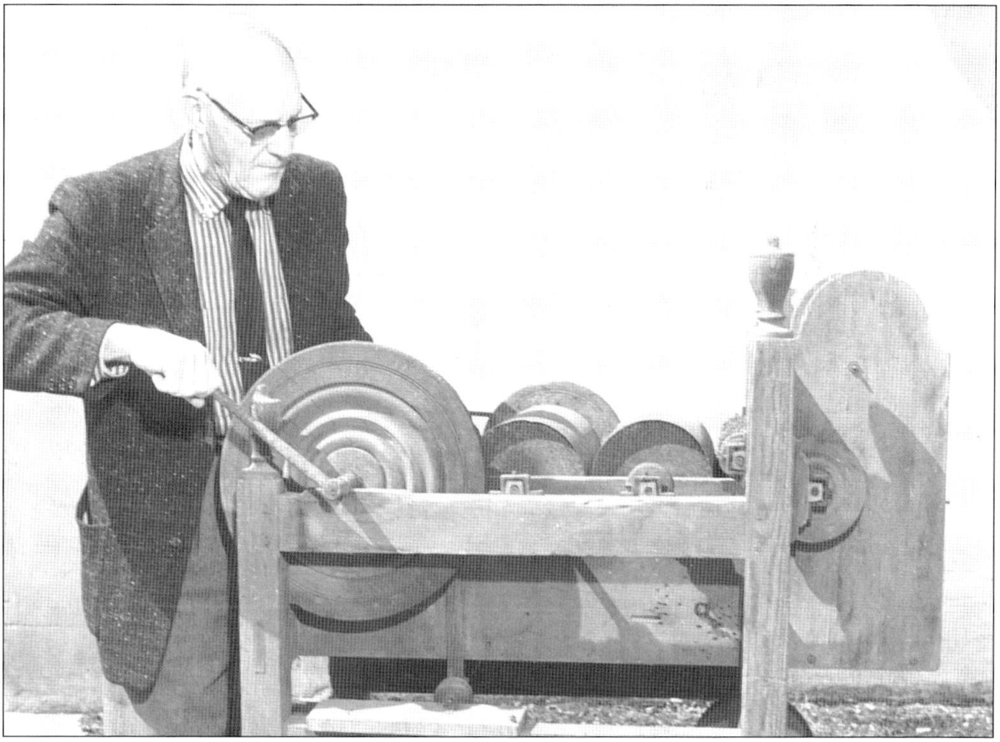

SAM WILLIAMS, COTTON-GINNING SPECIALIST OF EDGEFIELD COUNTY, DEMONSTRATING HOLMES GIN, 1964. Hodgen Holmes was granted a patent in 1796 for this gin, which used iron disks with teeth rather than a spiked cylinder used on the gin invented by Eli Whitney.

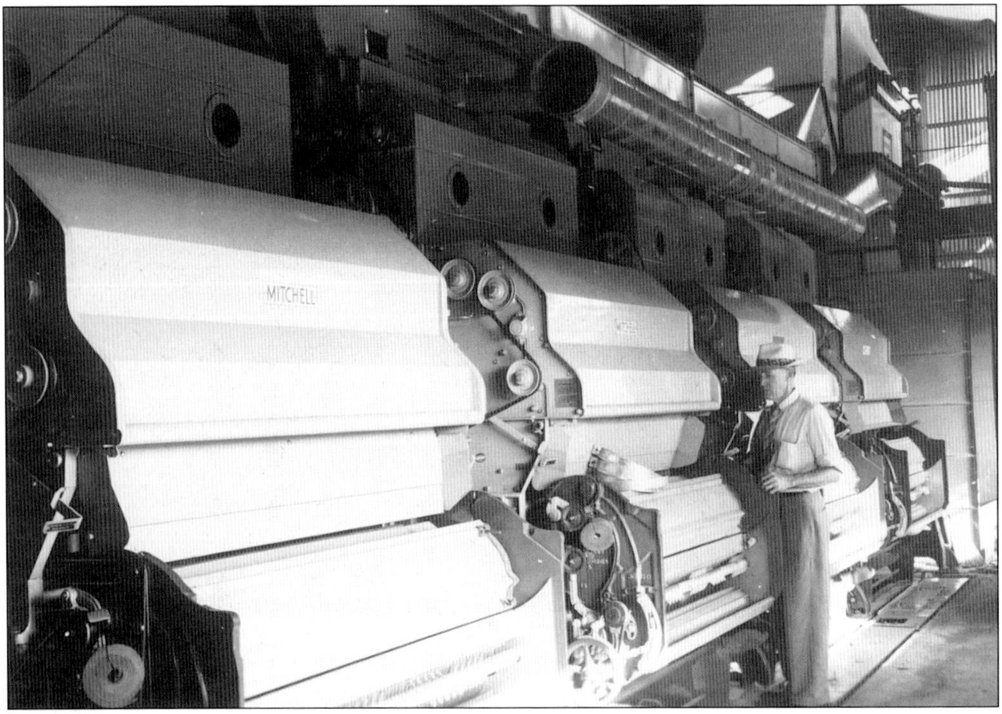

COTTON GIN, 1948, HONEA PATH. The textile industry afforded work for thousands of South Carolinians.

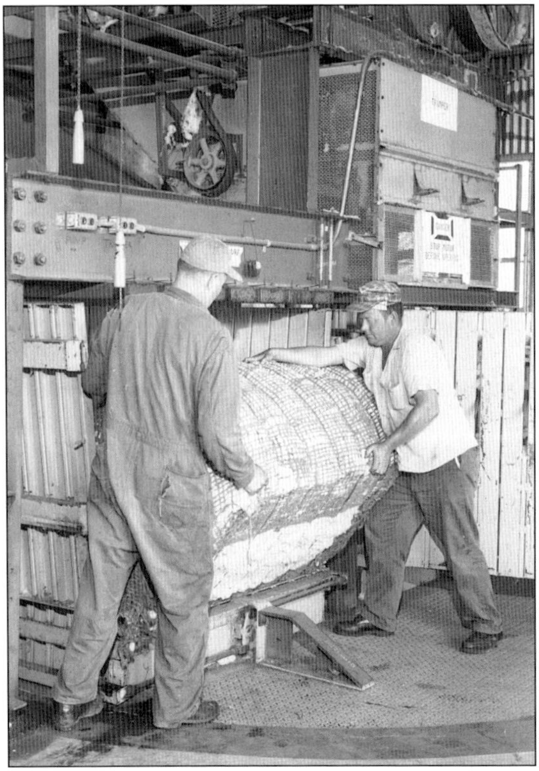

COTTON GIN, C. 1965, LOCATION UNKNOWN.

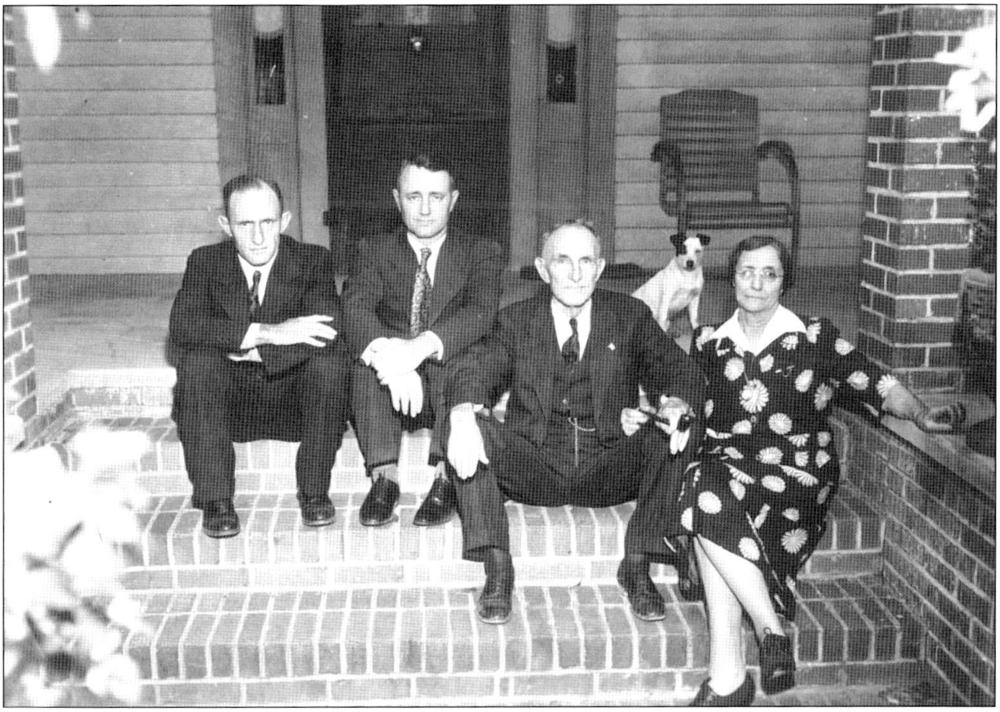

BOB SMITH FAMILY OF EDGEFIELD, RECIPIENTS OF NUMEROUS COTTON-GROWING AWARDS, 1944.

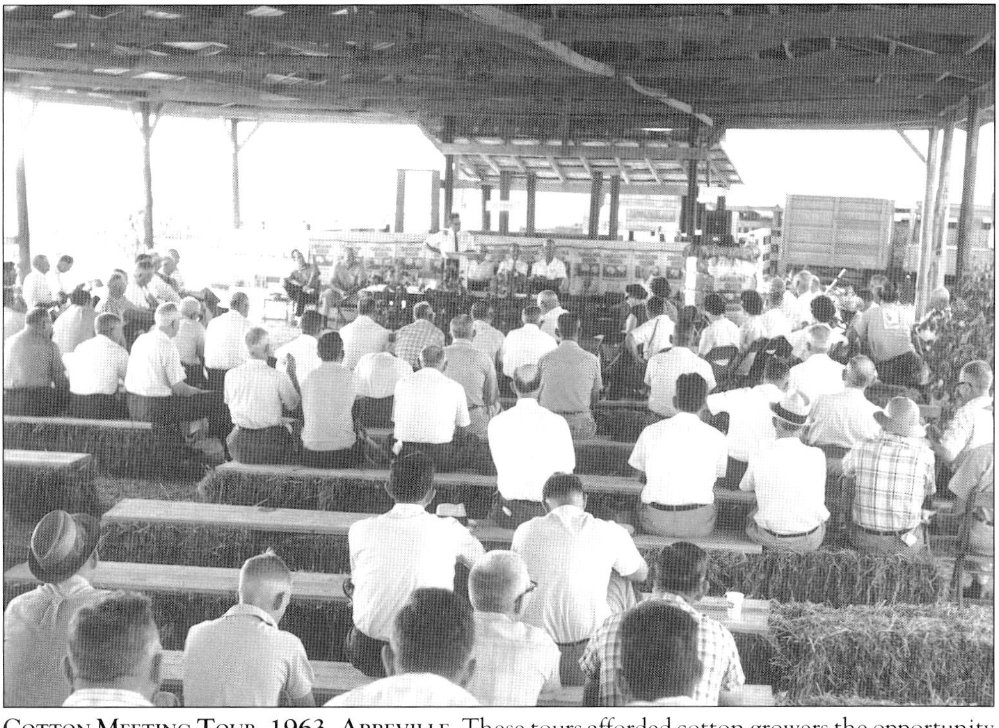

COTTON MEETING TOUR, 1963, ABBEVILLE. These tours afforded cotton growers the opportunity to meet and discuss issues affecting cotton growing.

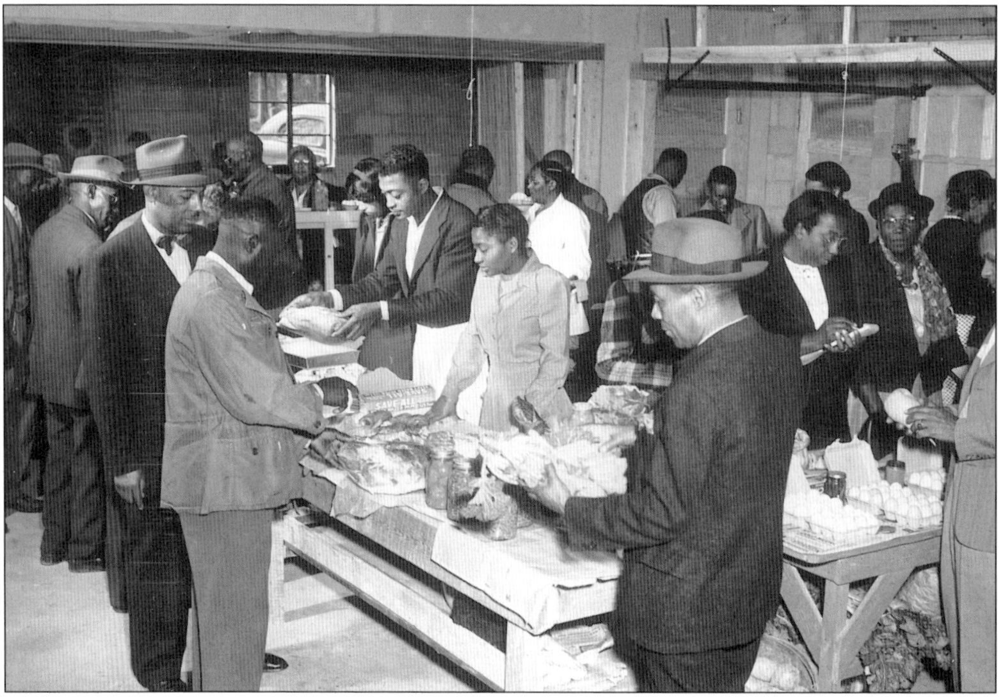

CO-OP MARKET FOR AFRICAN AMERICANS, 1950, CHESTER COUNTY. This co-op market allowed members to buy fresh meats and produce at affordable prices.

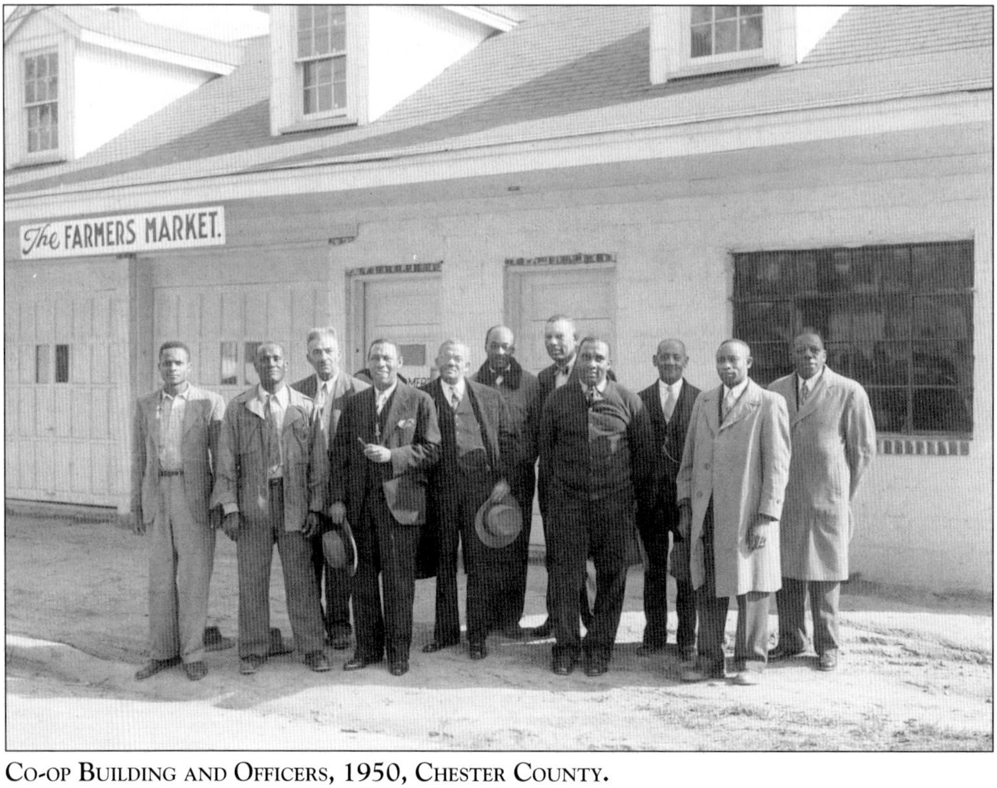

CO-OP BUILDING AND OFFICERS, 1950, CHESTER COUNTY.

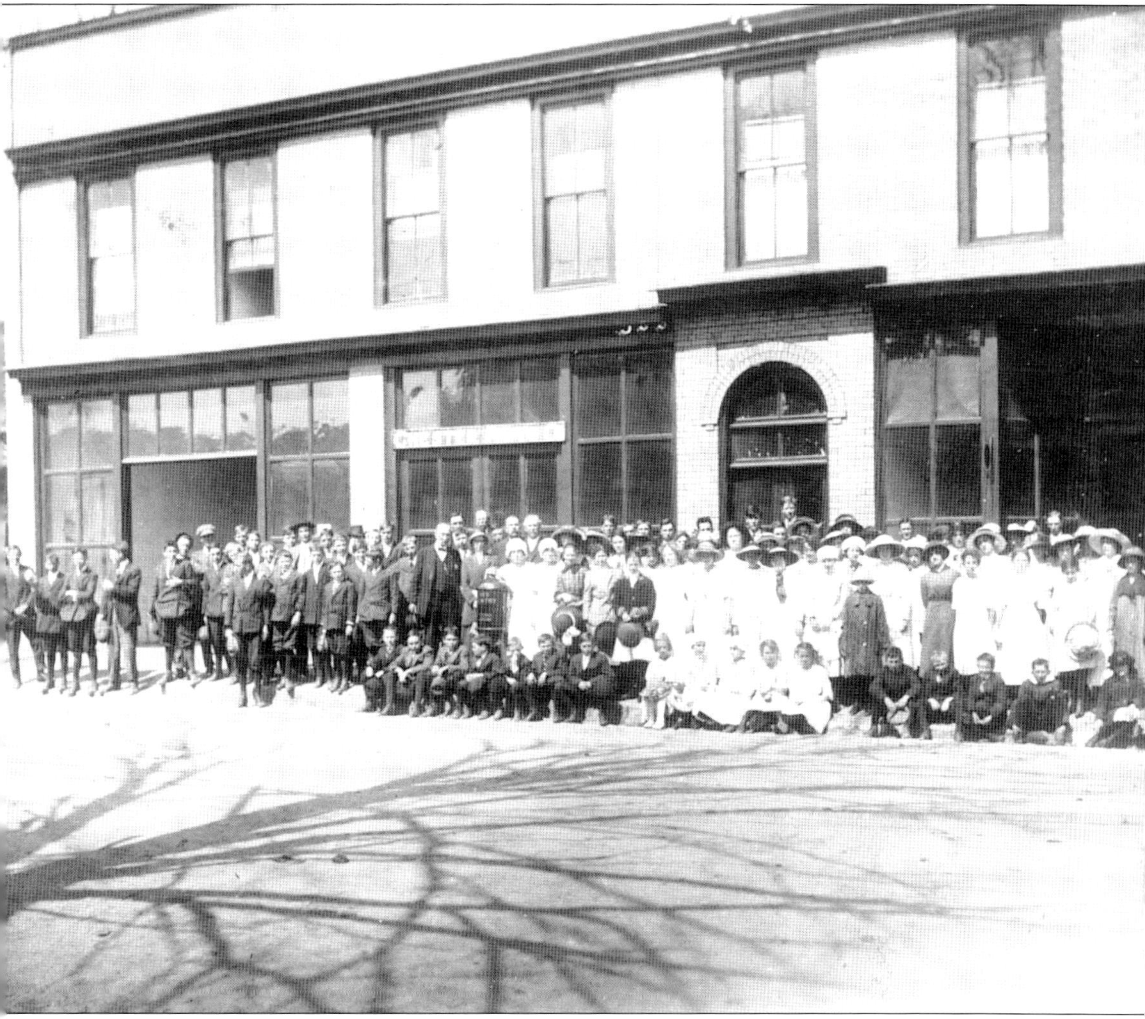

FARMERS COOPERATIVE, C. 1939, CHESTER.

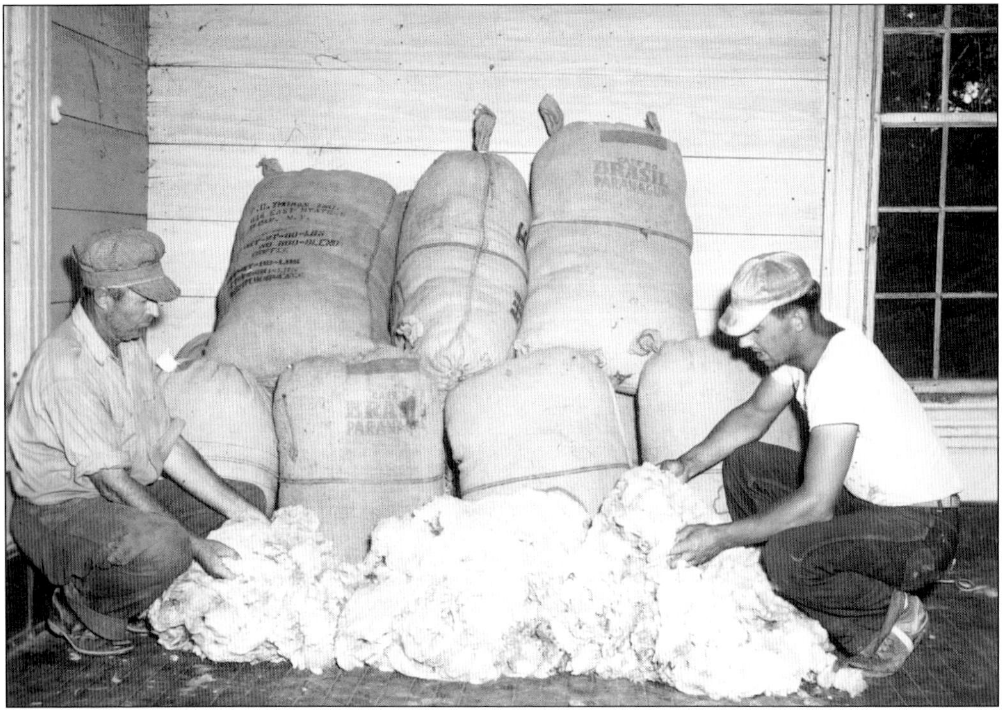

BAGS OF FLEECE, 1952, DICKSON FARM, LAURENS.

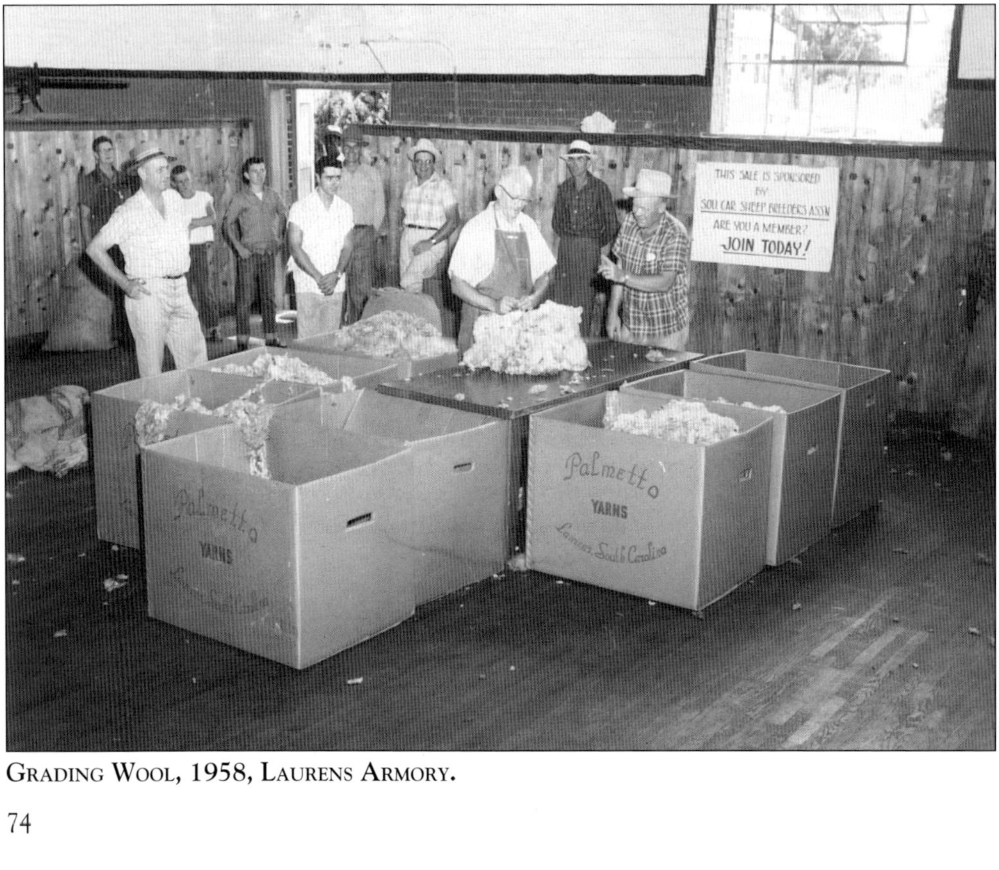

GRADING WOOL, 1958, LAURENS ARMORY.

Four

LIVESTOCK

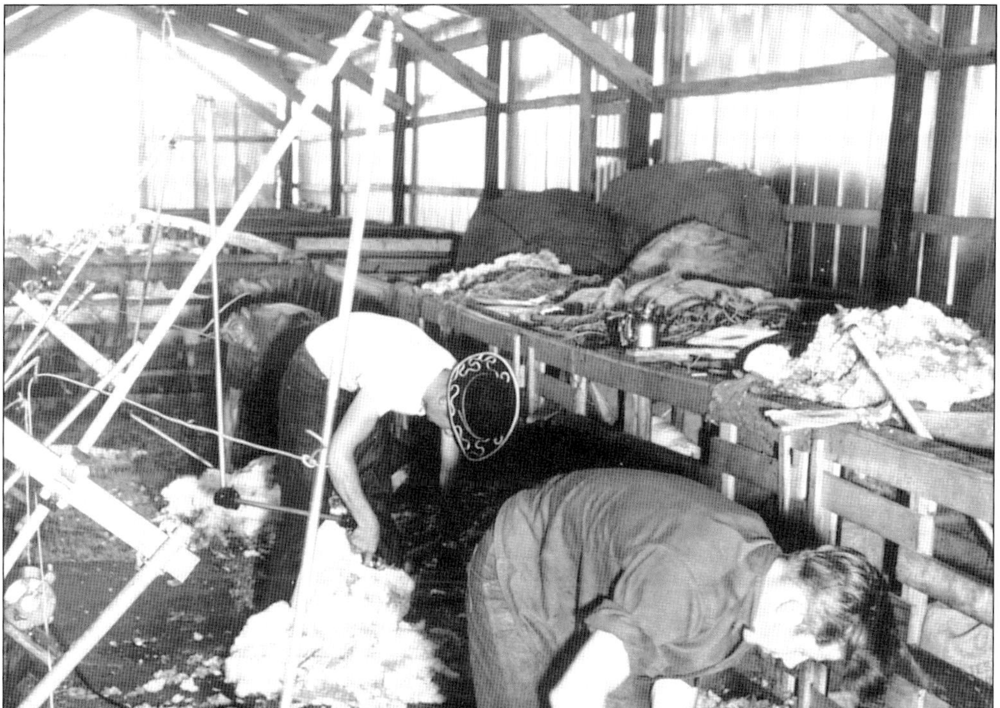

SHEARING SHEEP, C. 1950, LOCATION UNKNOWN. Most sheep were shorn once a year. A skilled shearer could clip 100 to 300 sheep in a day.

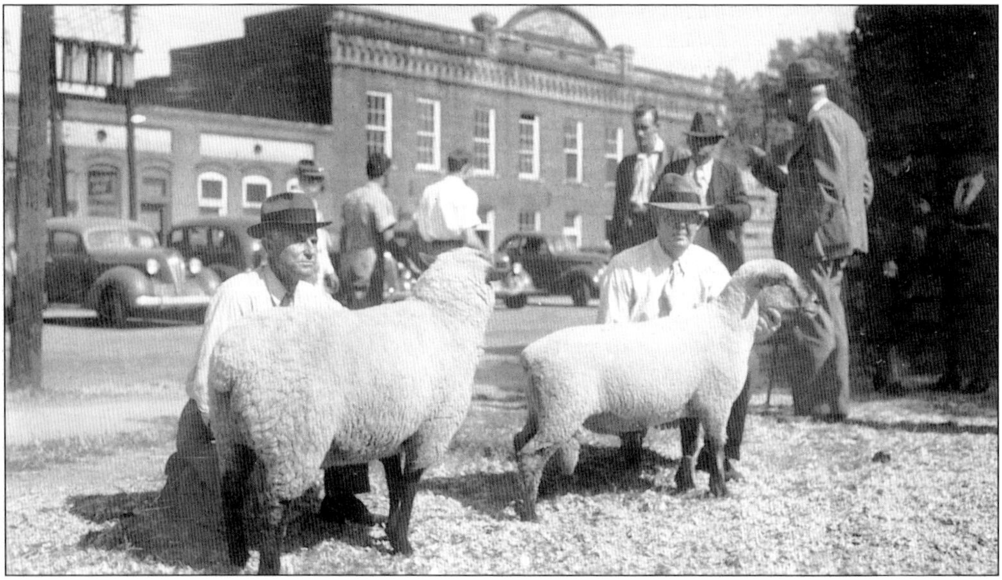

Sheep at Fair, 1938, Winnsboro.

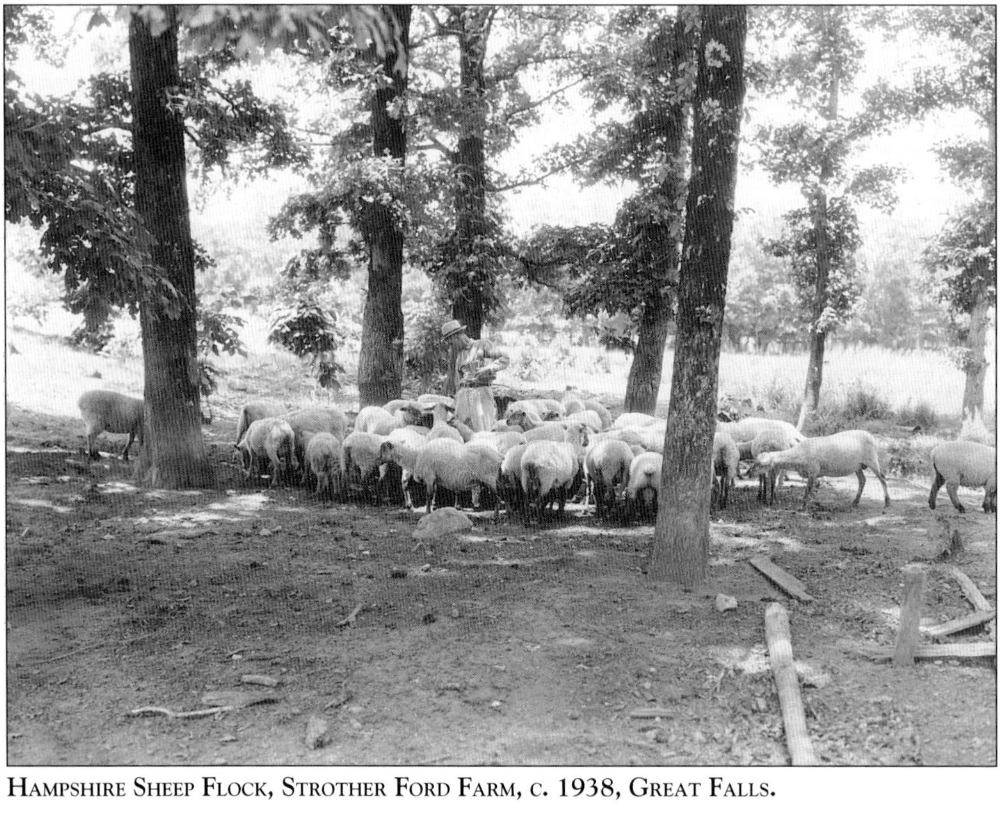

Hampshire Sheep Flock, Strother Ford Farm, c. 1938, Great Falls.

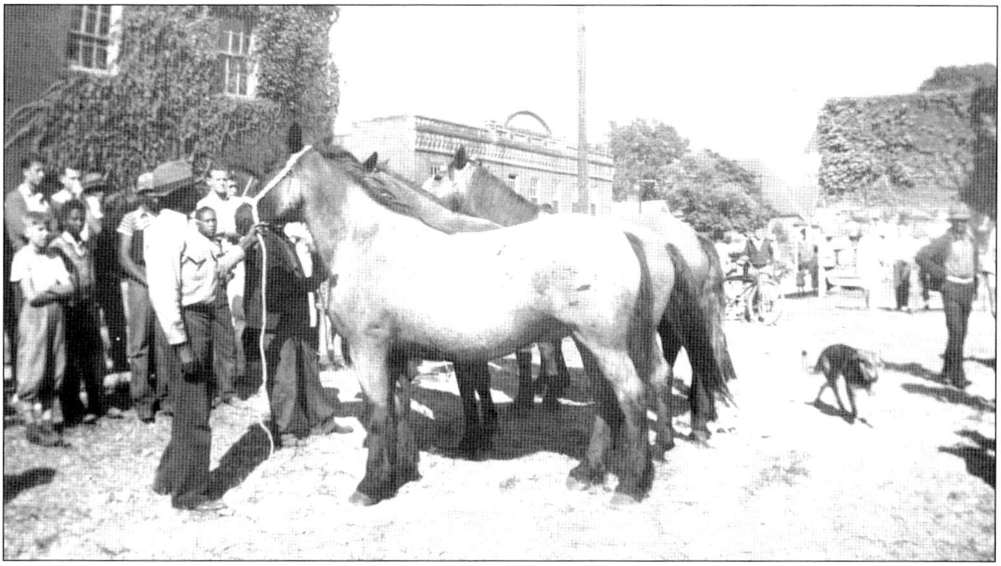

HORSE SHOW AT COUNTY FAIR, 1938, WINNSBORO.

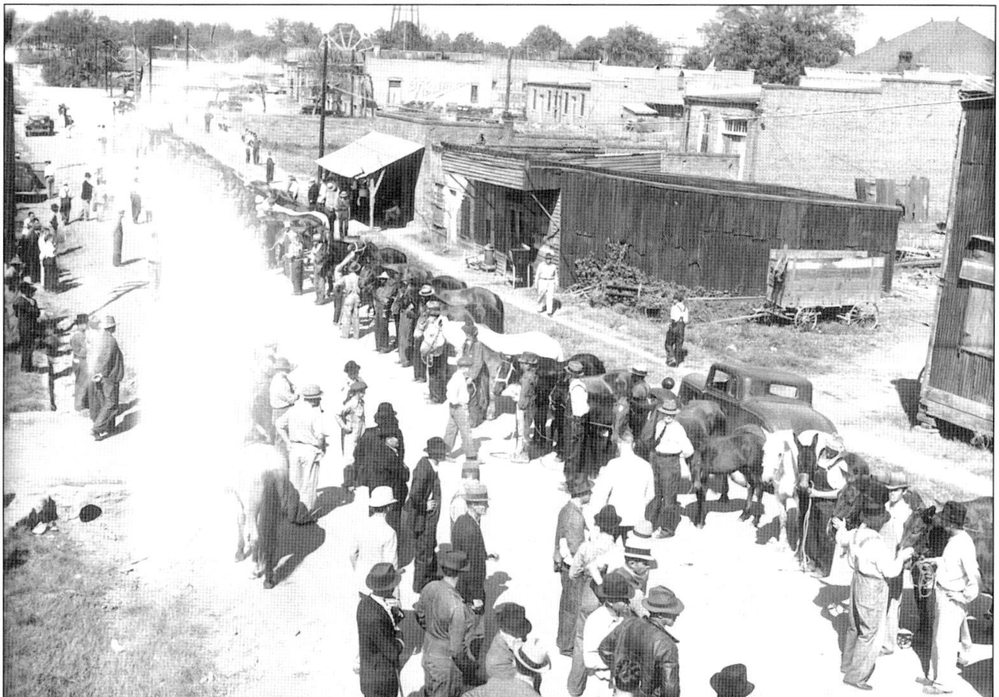

BROOD MARES LINED UP FOR JUDGING, 1938, WESTMINSTER. Brood mares were mares kept exclusively for breeding.

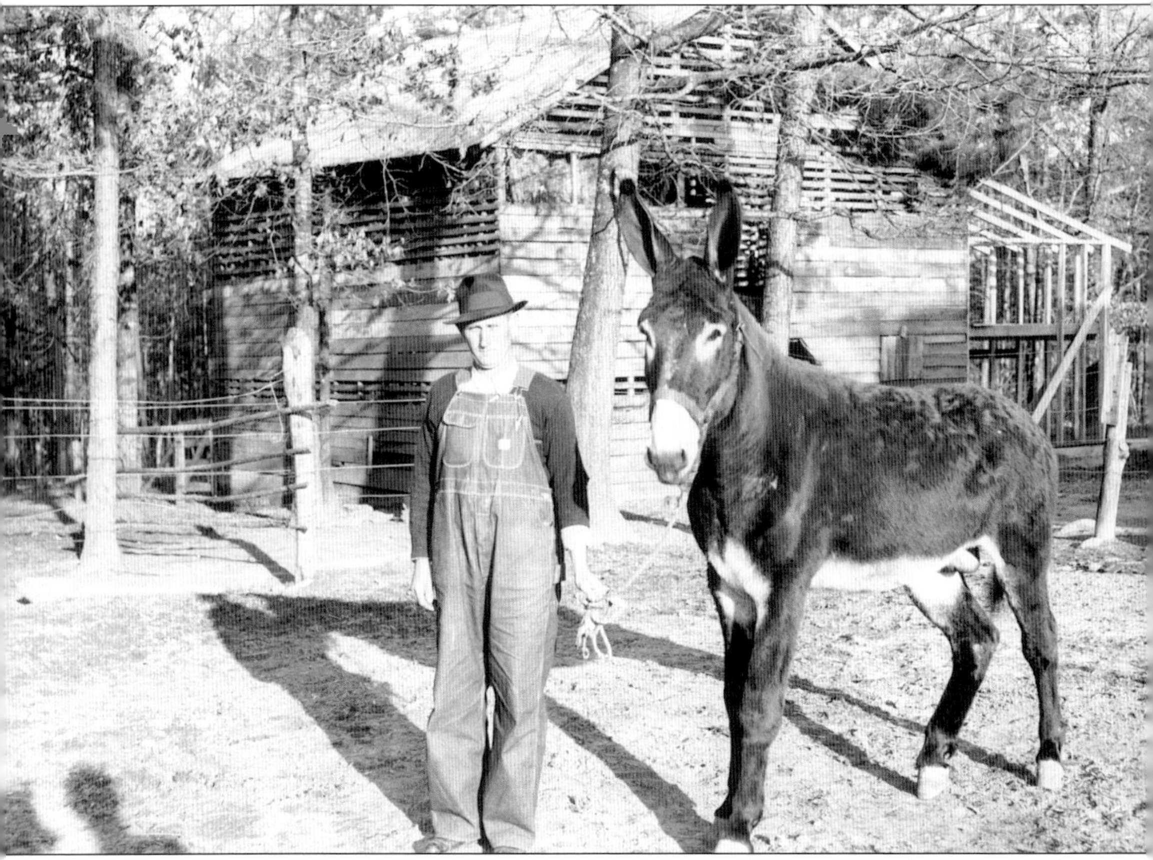

FARMER AND HIS MULE, C. 1945, FAIRFIELD. A mule, the offspring of a male donkey and a mare, while popularized as stubborn and obstinate, was actually a highly respected and essential farm animal.

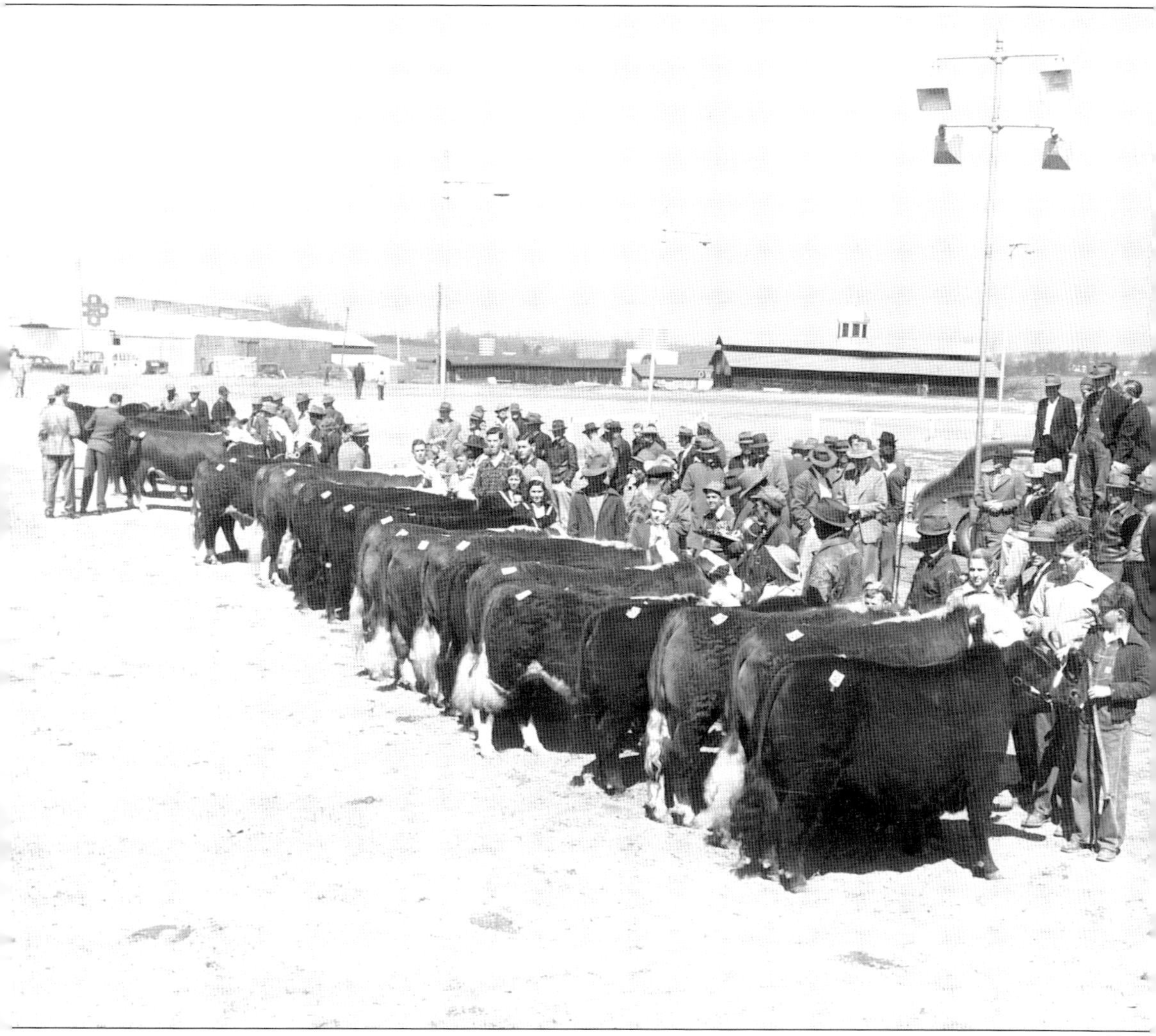

Blue Ribbon Steers, 1949, Anderson. Steers were judged on overall categories of finish, form, and quality. These categories were further divided into such characteristics as body symmetry, glossiness of coat, and smoothness of body. It is worthy to note that girls, as frequently as boys, raised prize-winning steers.

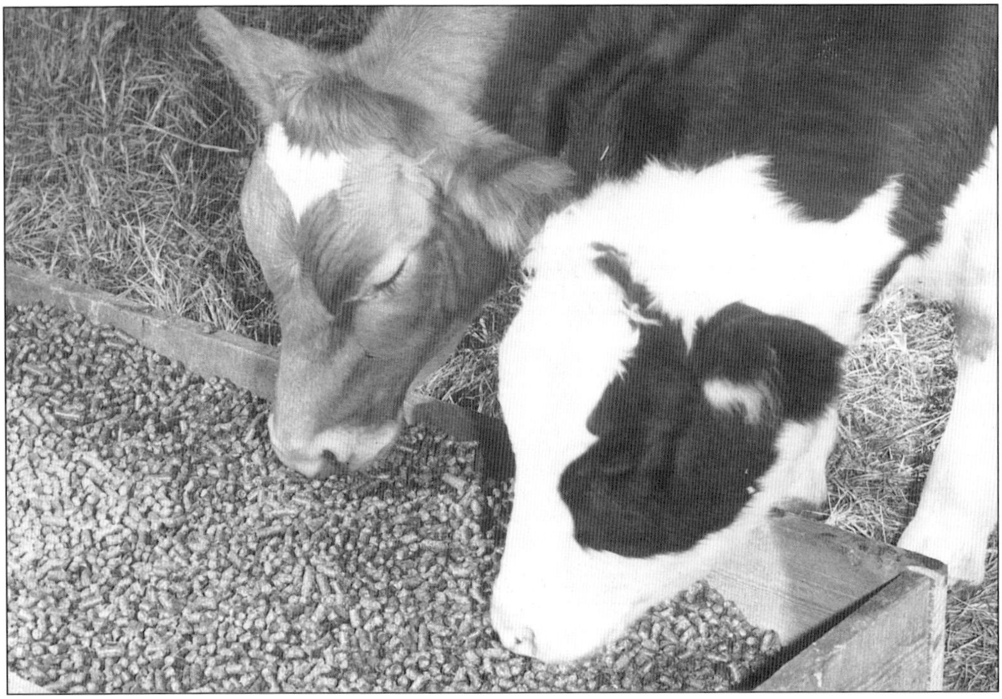

Pelletized Feed, 1950s. Pelleted feed improved palatability and was easier to handle and store than regular feed. Animals also consumed it in greater quantities.

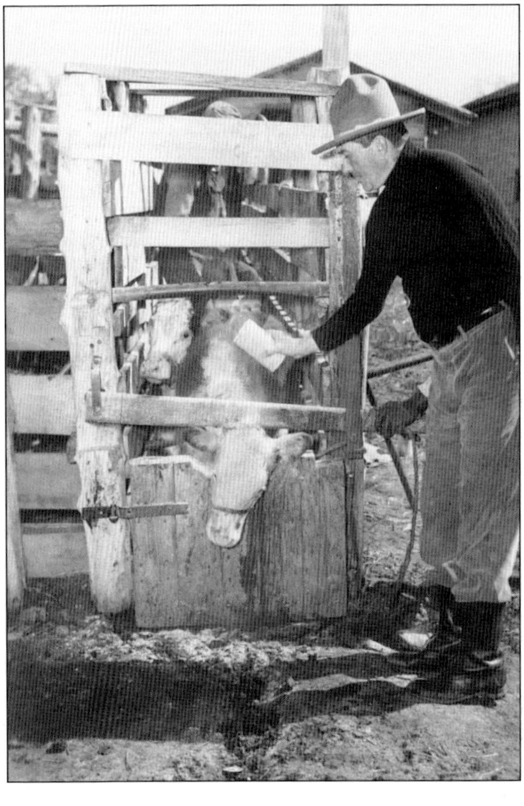

Dehorning a Steer, Dows farms, 1944, Greenwood. Cattle were dehorned to prevent injury to people and other animals and to make feeding easier.

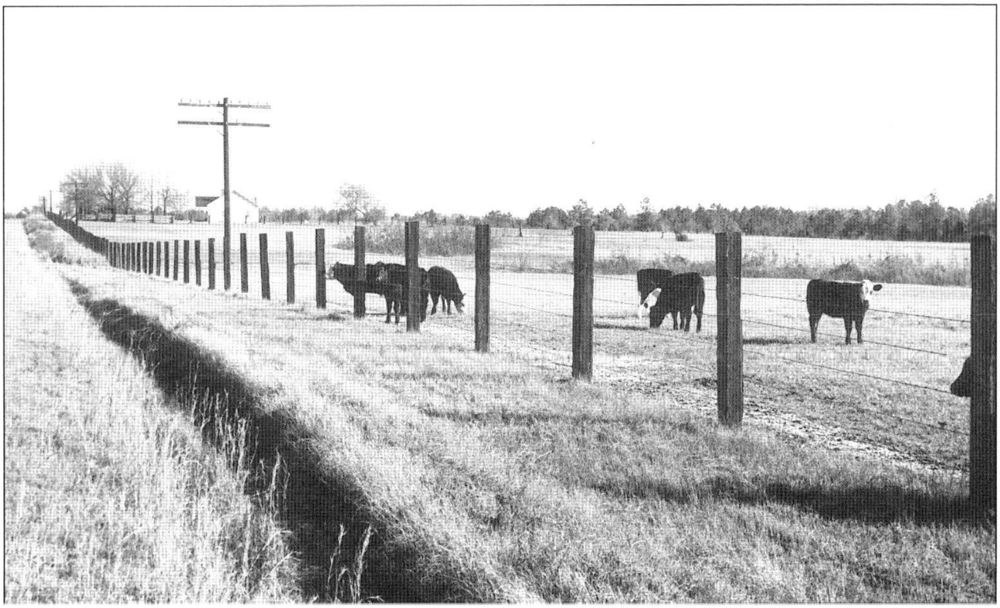

Fence Made from Railroad Ties, 1953, Greenwood.

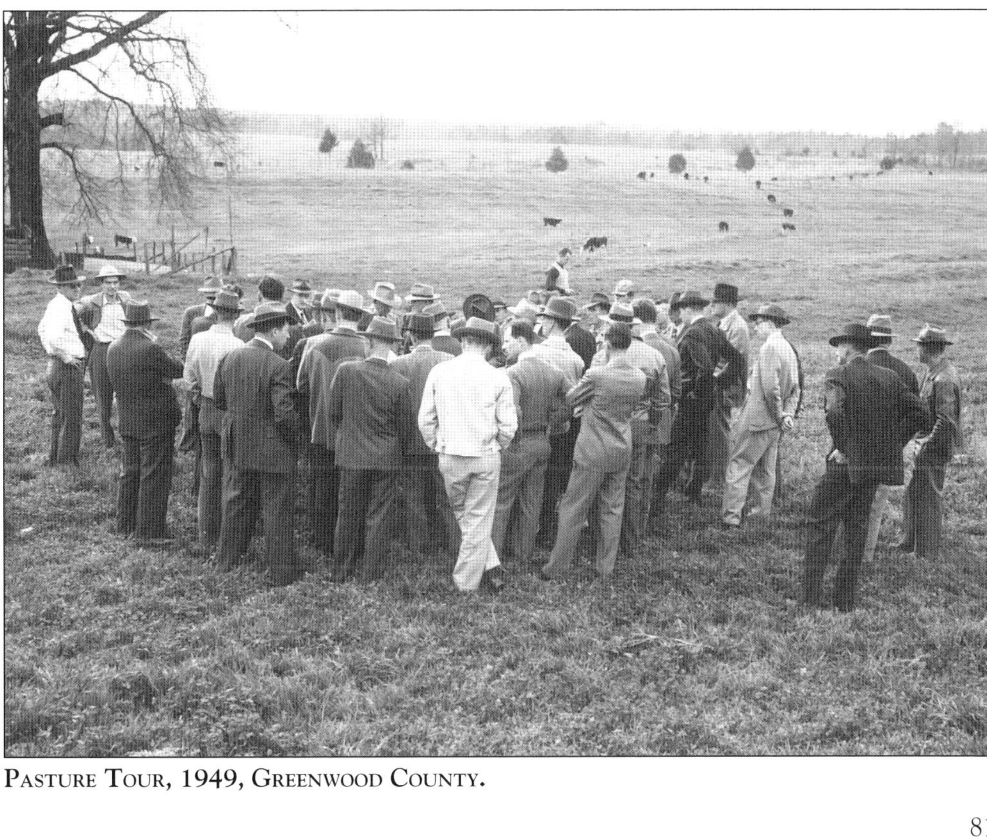

Pasture Tour, 1949, Greenwood County.

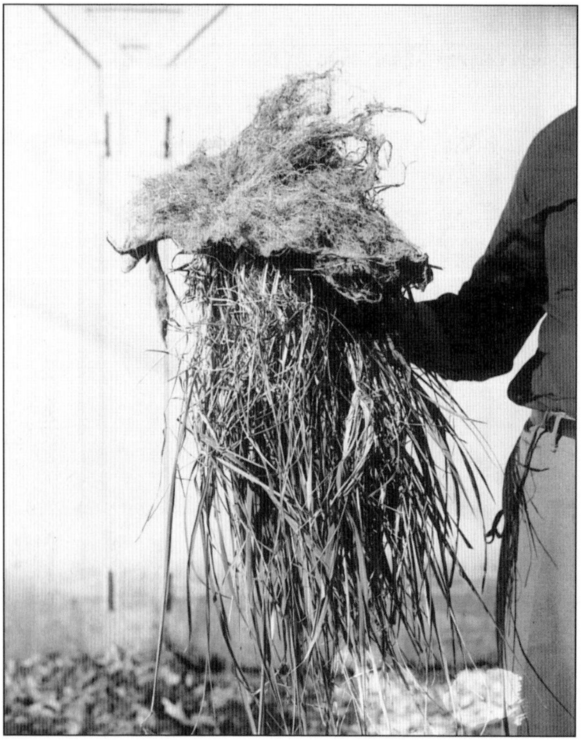

Fescue Plant, 1949, Pickens County. Kentucky fescue was commonly used for pasture planting. Its extensive root system allowed repeated mowings and quick growth.

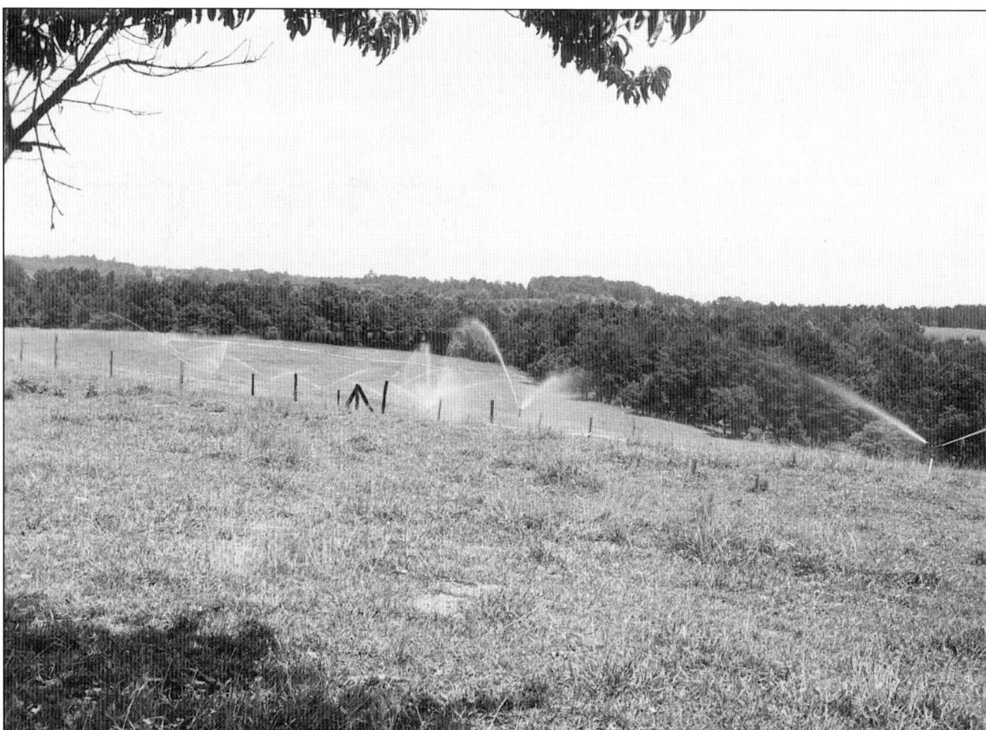

Irrigating Pasture Land, c. 1949, Powdersville.

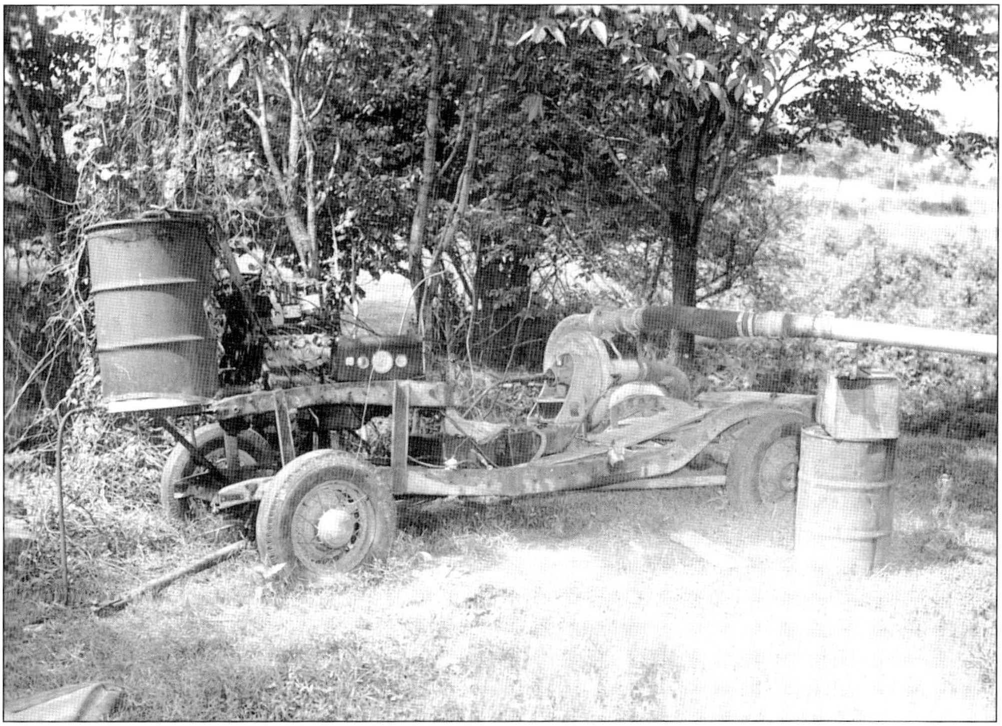

IRRIGATION PUMP, 1953, ANDERSON. An automobile engine was used to make the pump.

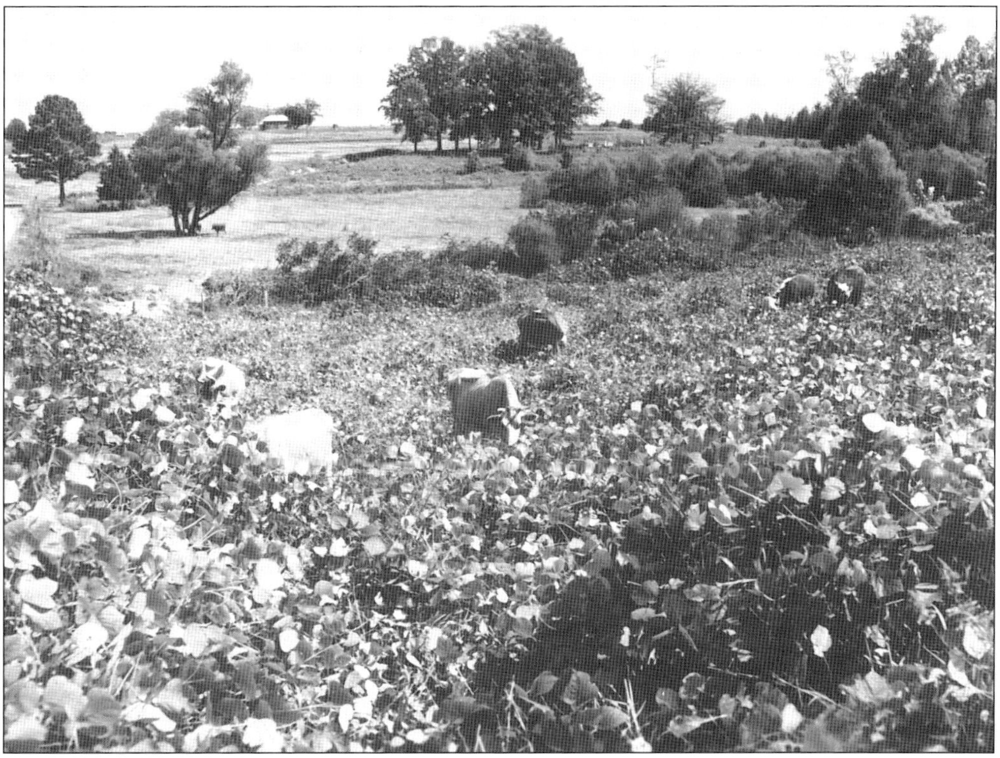

COWS GRAZING ON KUDZU, DATE AND LOCATION UNKNOWN.

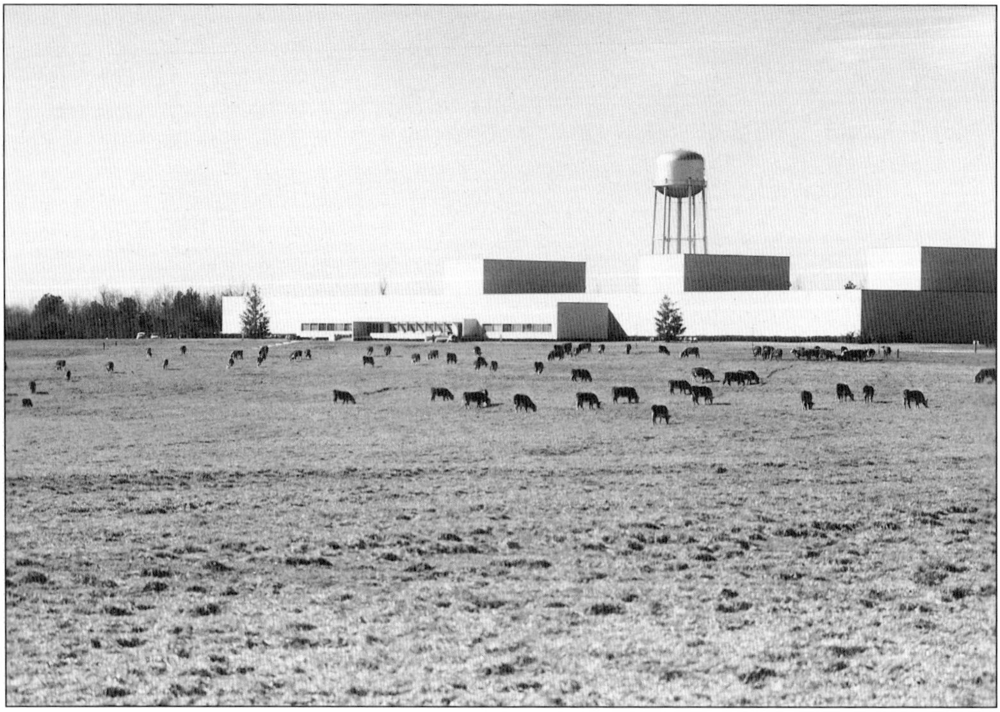

DEERING-MILLIKEN PLANT, 1952, PENDLETON.

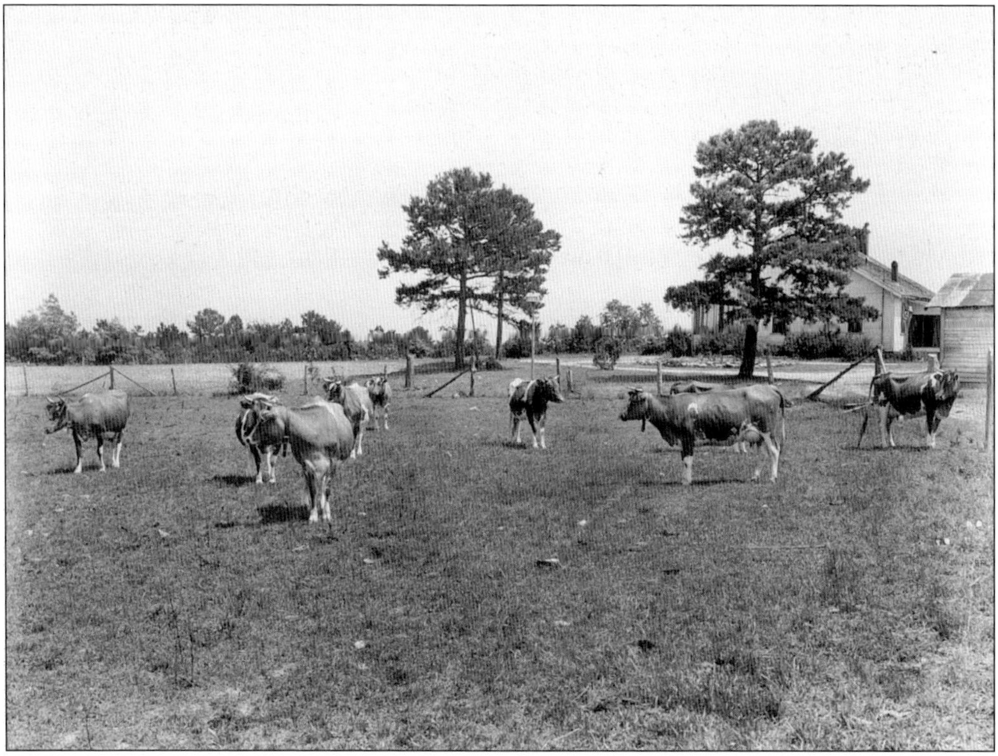

HERD OF PUREBRED GUERNSEY COWS, L.E. STROUD FARM, 1936, GREAT FALLS.

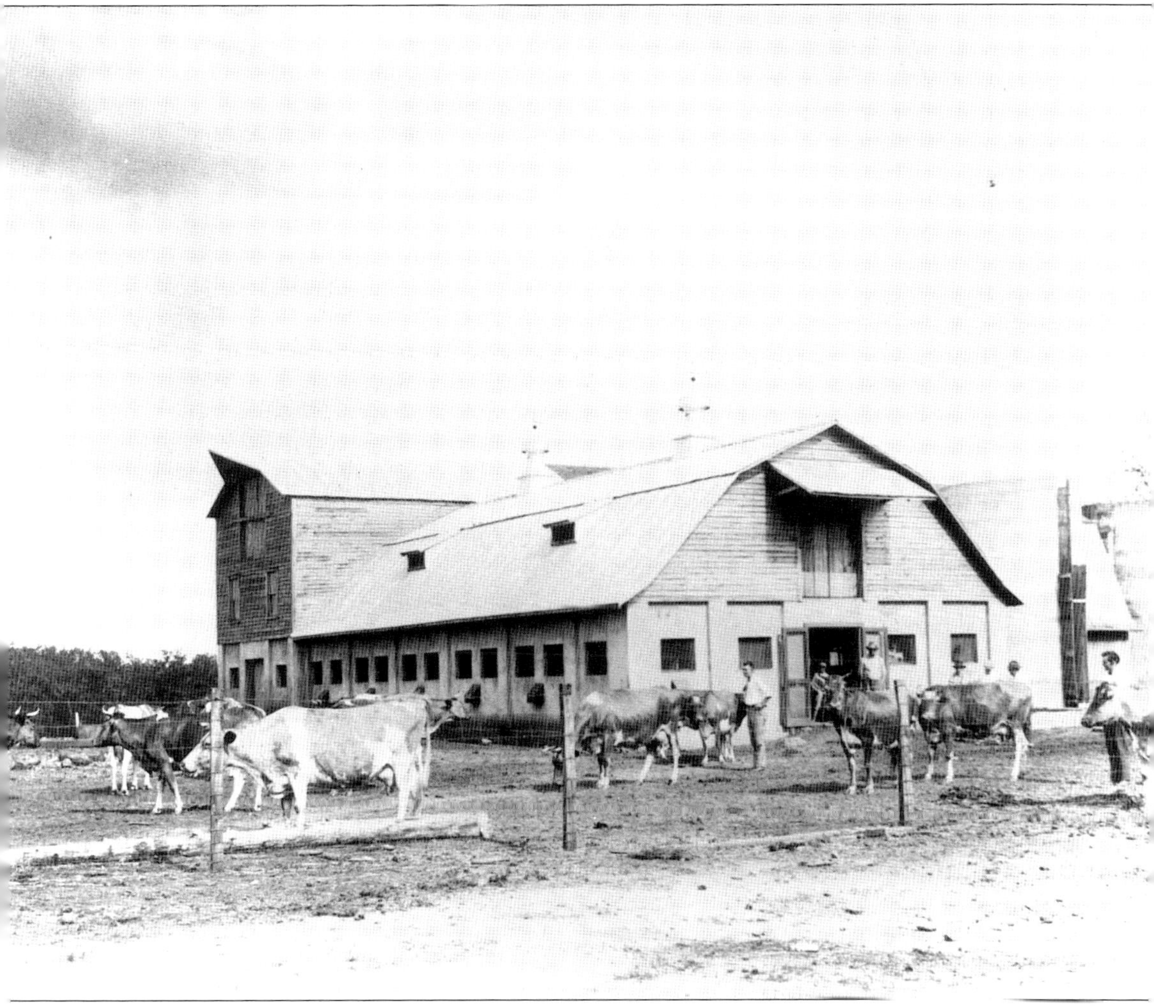

Dairy Barn and Herd, R.C. Guy Farm, 1924, Chester. Three milk cow varieties include jersey, guernsey, and holstein. Jersey cows, which are yellow, brown, or fawn colored, produce very rich milk with heavy cream. Guernsey cows, fawn and white in color, are larger than jerseys but also produce very rich milk. Holsteins on the other hand are black and white and produce large amounts of milk comparitively low in fat.

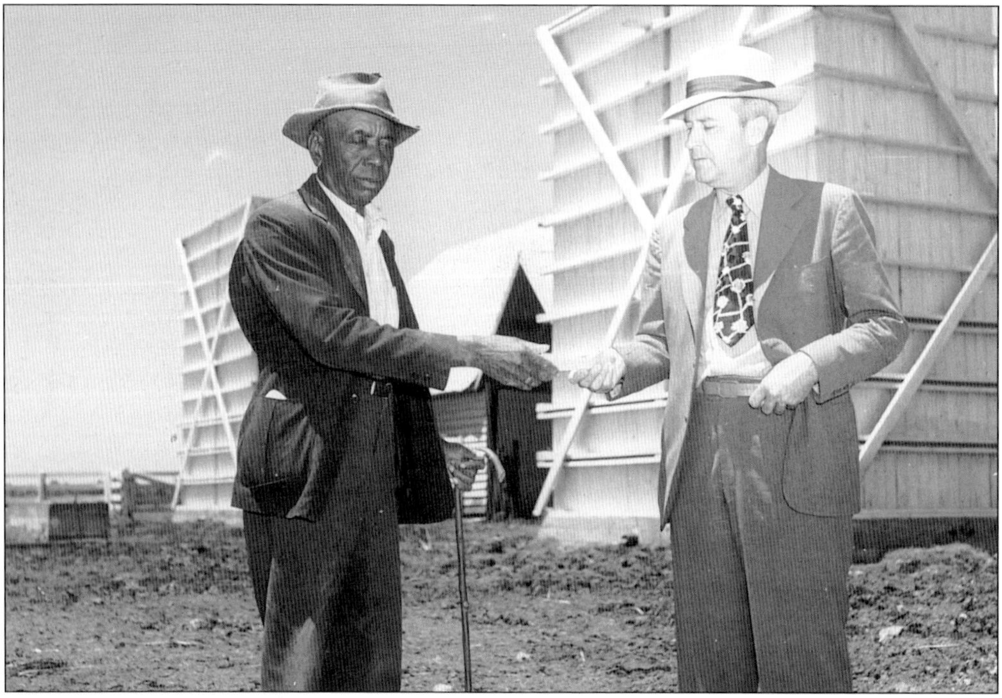

Alec Oliphant (right) Presenting Sharecropper (unidentified) with Check for Milk Produced, 1946, Chester County.

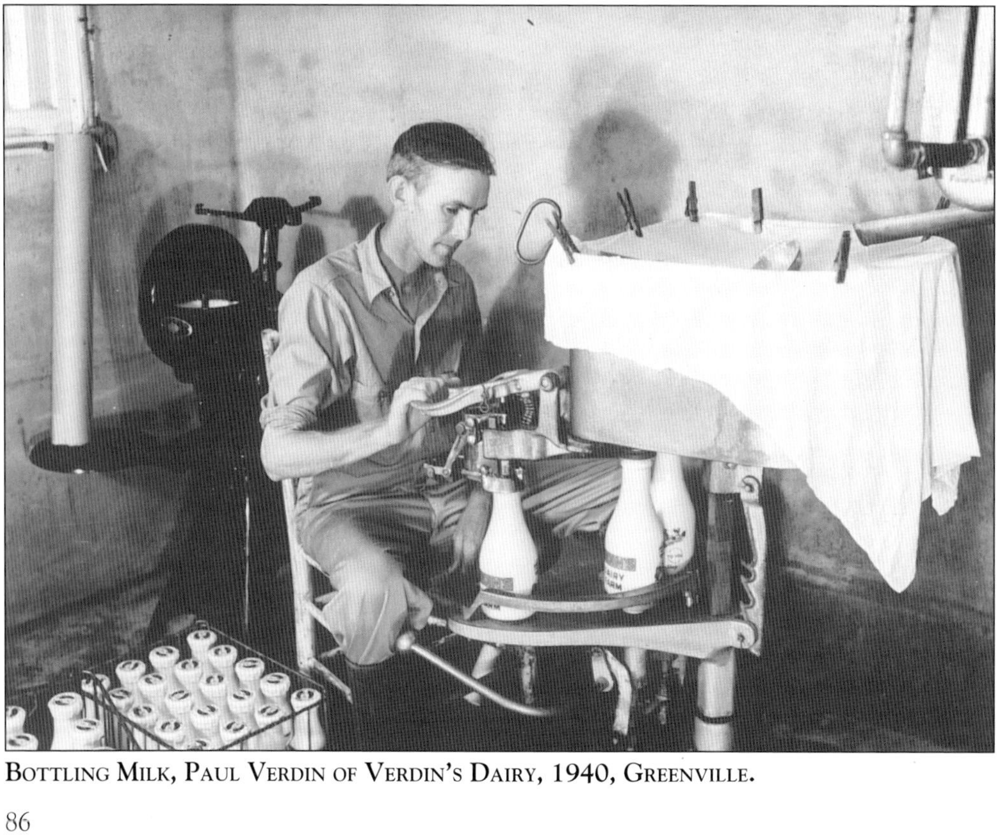

Bottling Milk, Paul Verdin of Verdin's Dairy, 1940, Greenville.

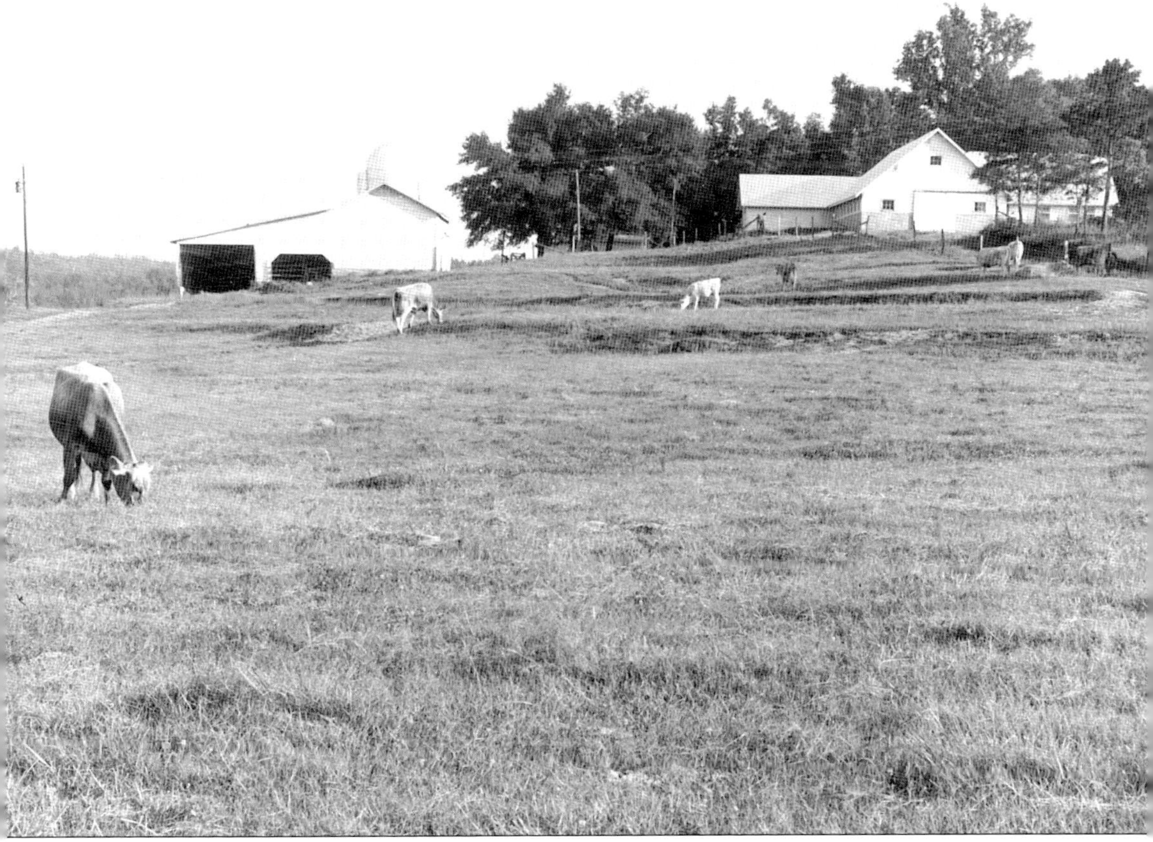

Brown Swiss Herd of W.T. McClure, 1948, Oconee County. The building on the right was constructed using Extension Service plans.

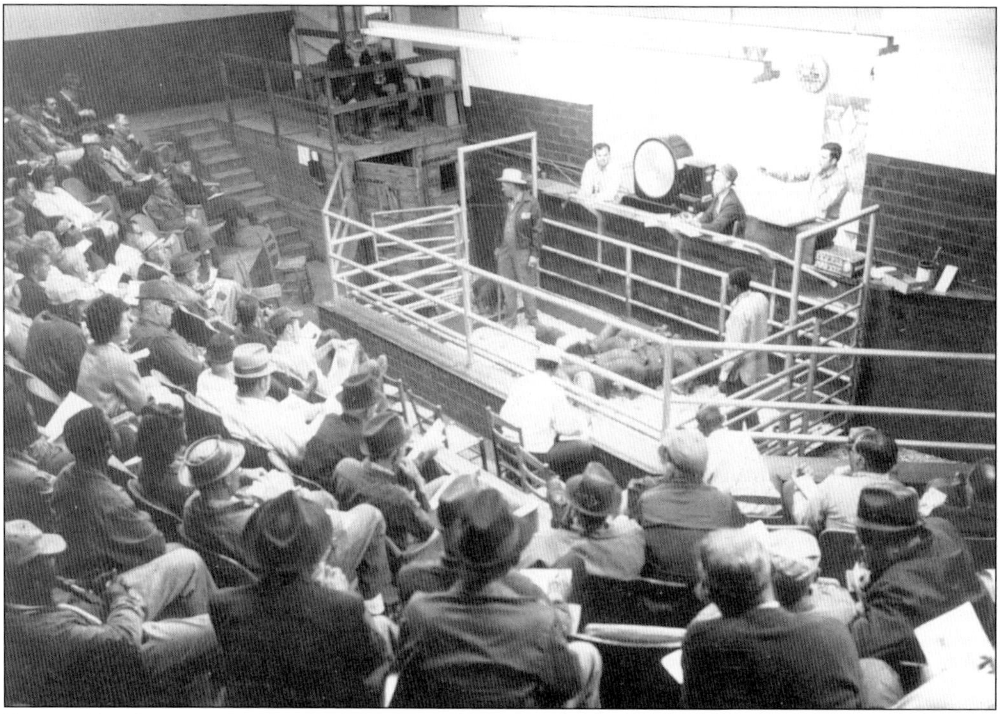

FEEDER PIG SALE, 1970, SALUDA.

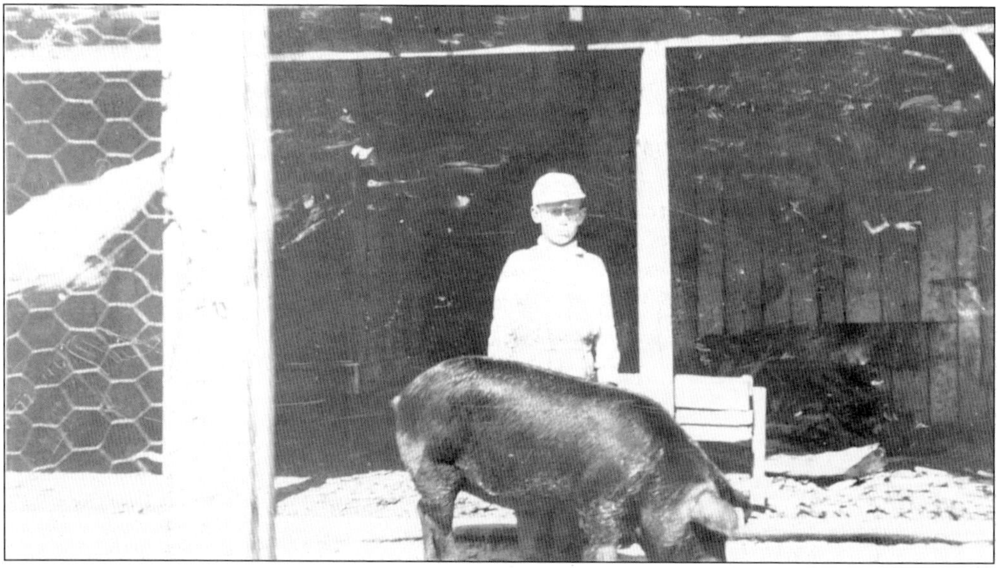

FRANCIS PARHAM WITH "MISS BOBBIE." Miss Bobbie was a pig Parham raised in the 1920s in Union. She sold for $150.

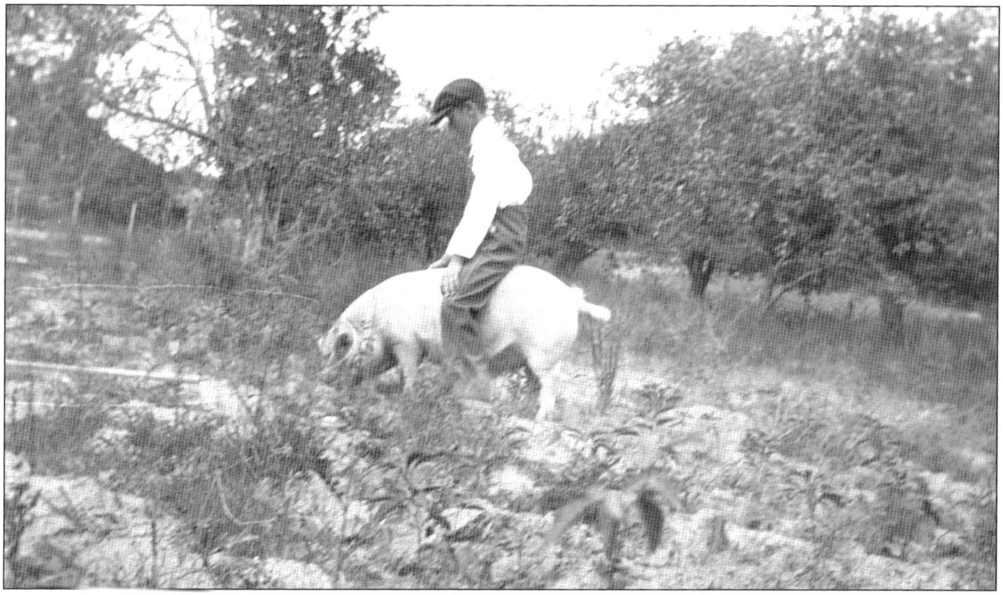

RYAN ROPER OF LAURENS RIDING HIS PIG, 1920. A note on the back reads, "on his way to college."

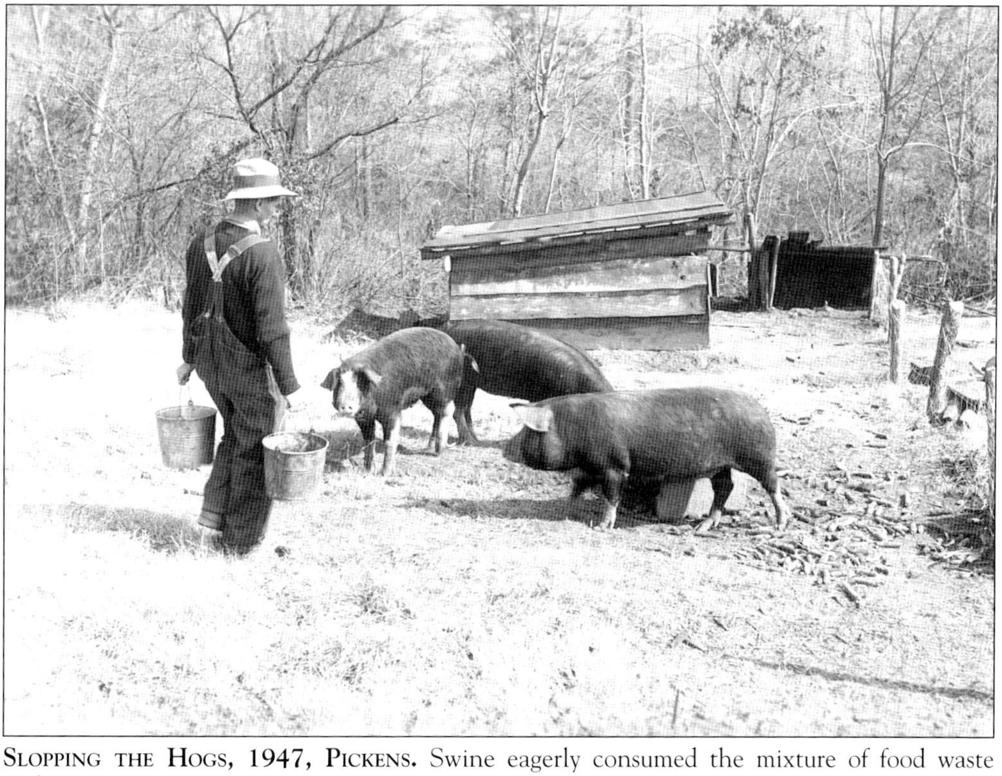

SLOPPING THE HOGS, 1947, PICKENS. Swine eagerly consumed the mixture of food waste and water.

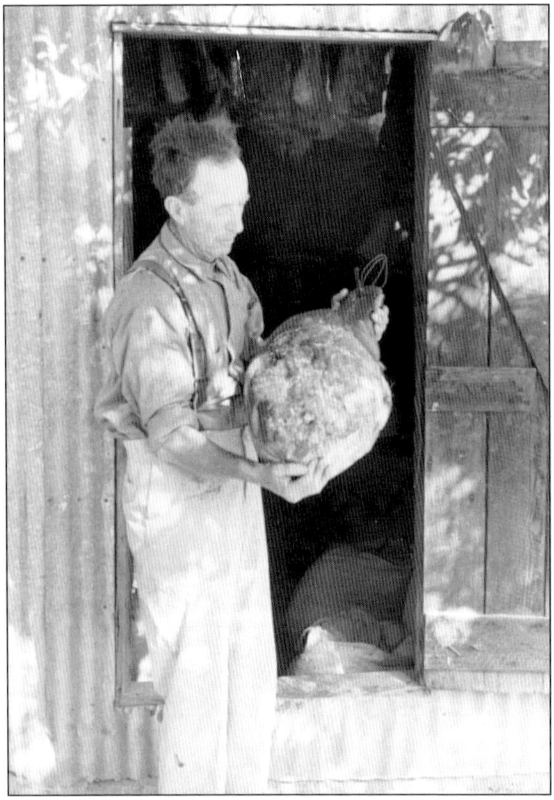

HOME-CURED HAM, 1947, FAIRFIELD. Hams could be salt cured, sugar cured, or smoked, depending on personal taste.

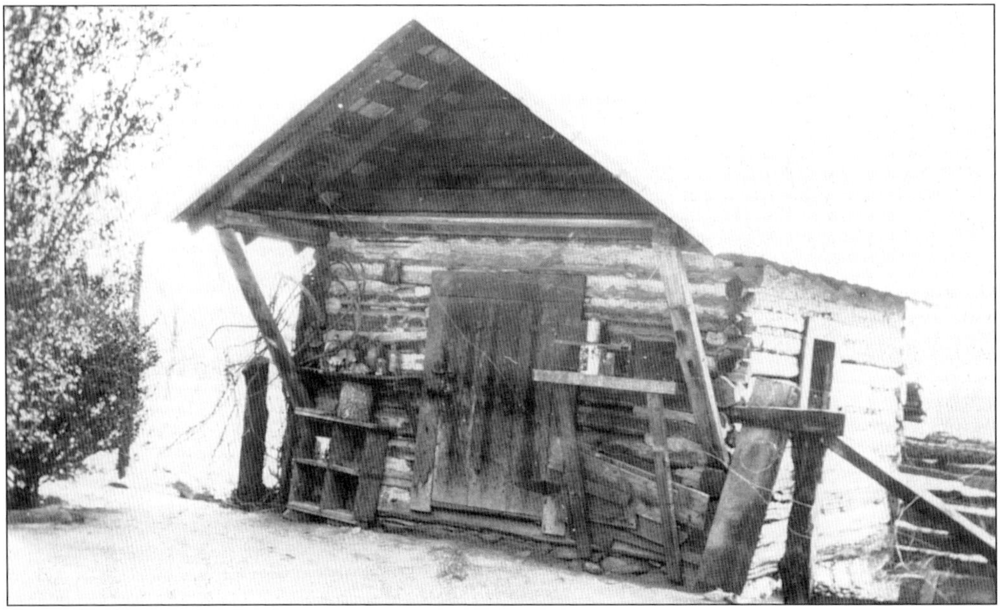

SMOKEHOUSE FOR MEAT CURING, C. 1920, SPARTANBURG.

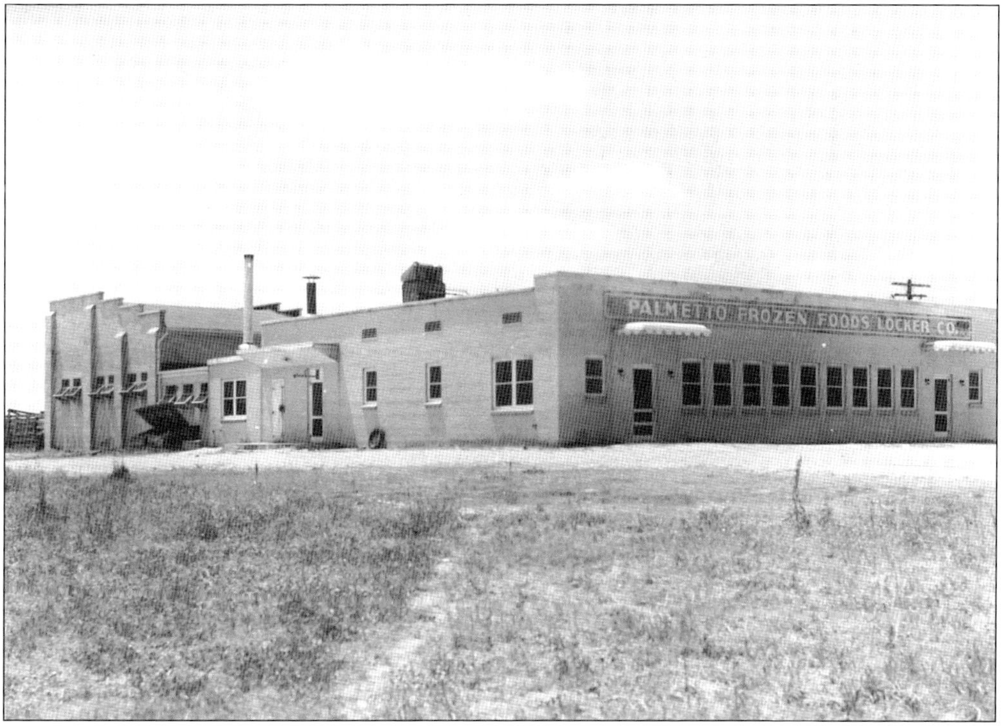

FROZEN LOCKER PLANT, 1947, FAIRFIELD.

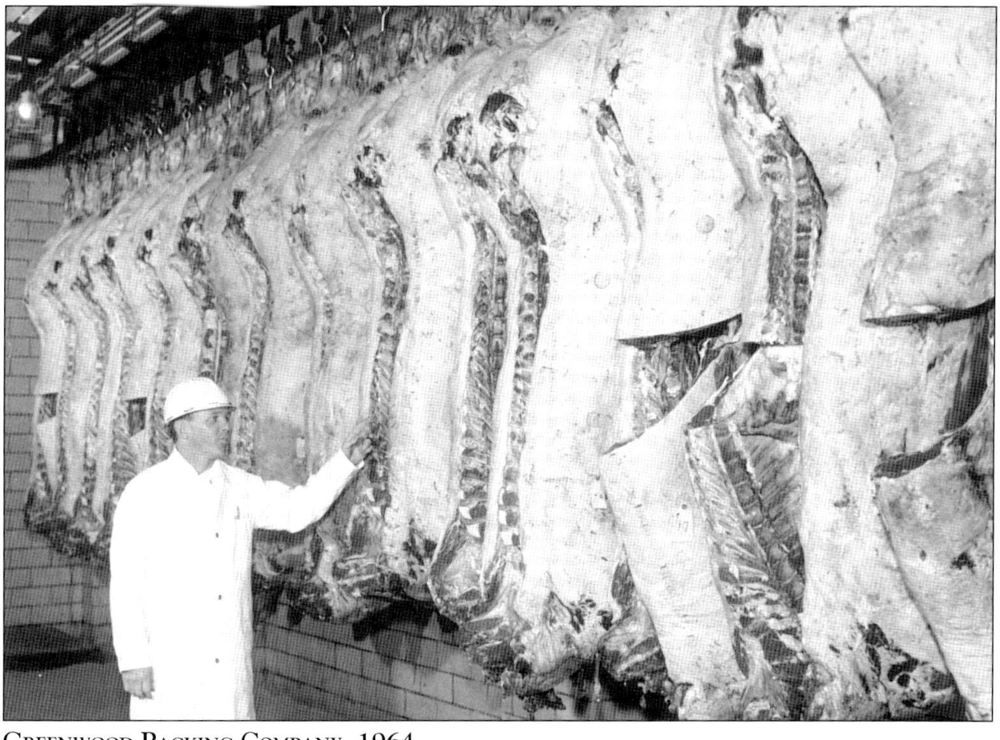

GREENWOOD PACKING COMPANY, 1964.

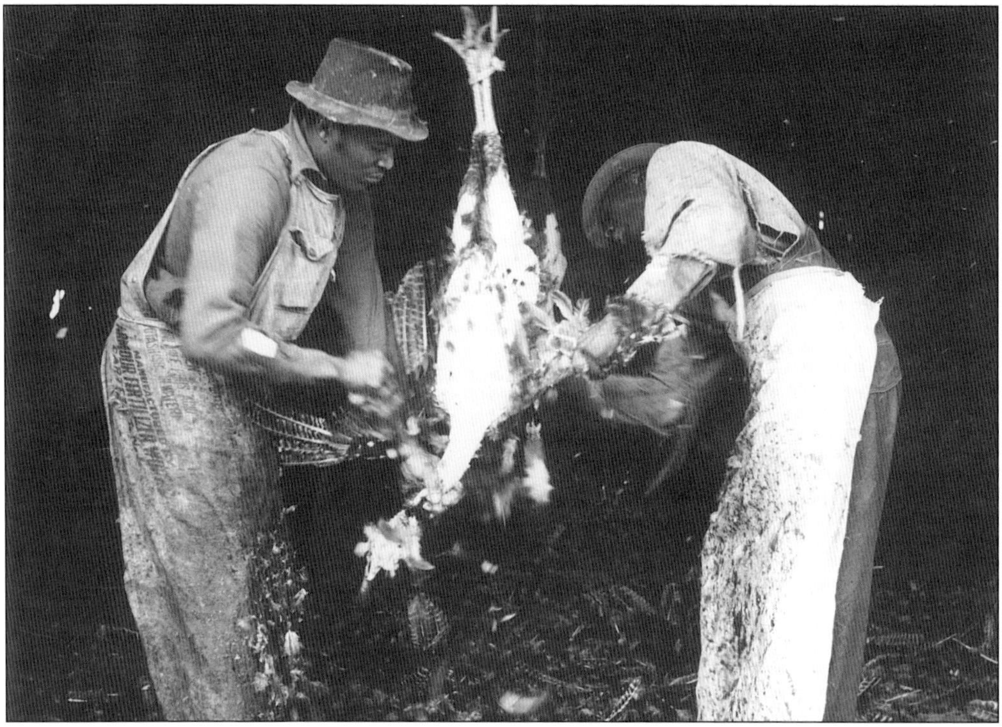

Picking Turkey Using Dry Method, 1941, York.

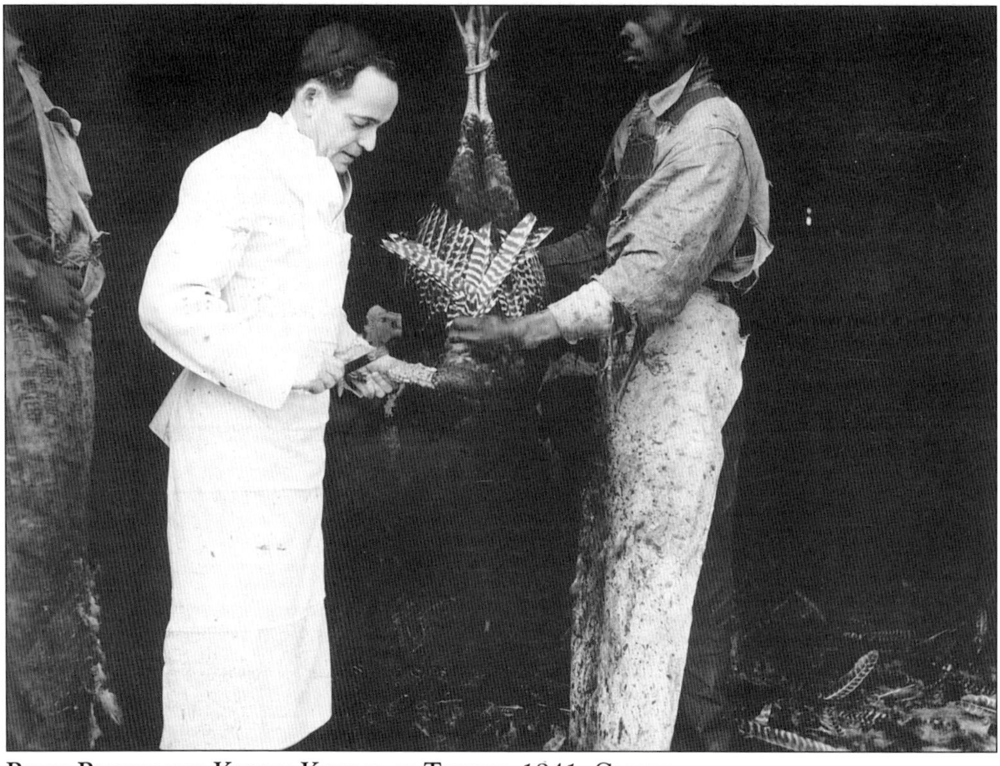

Rabbi Performing Kosher Killing of Turkey, 1941, Clover.

Five

POULTRY

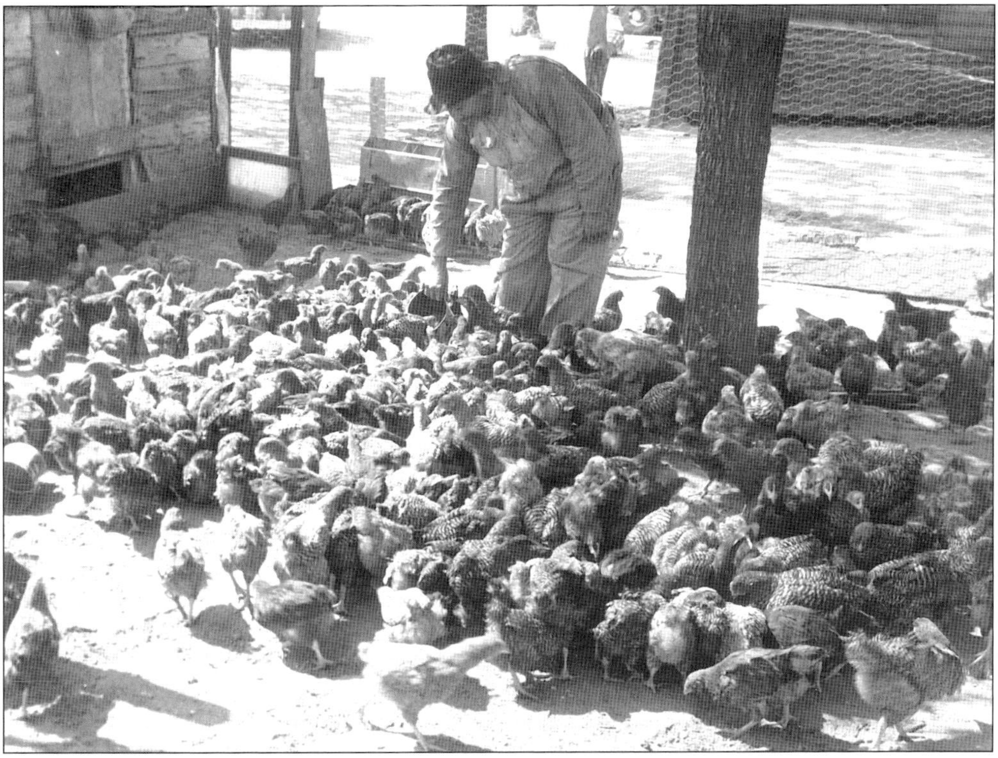

FARMER AND CHICKENS, 1938, GREENVILLE. Only five chickens were lost out of 400.

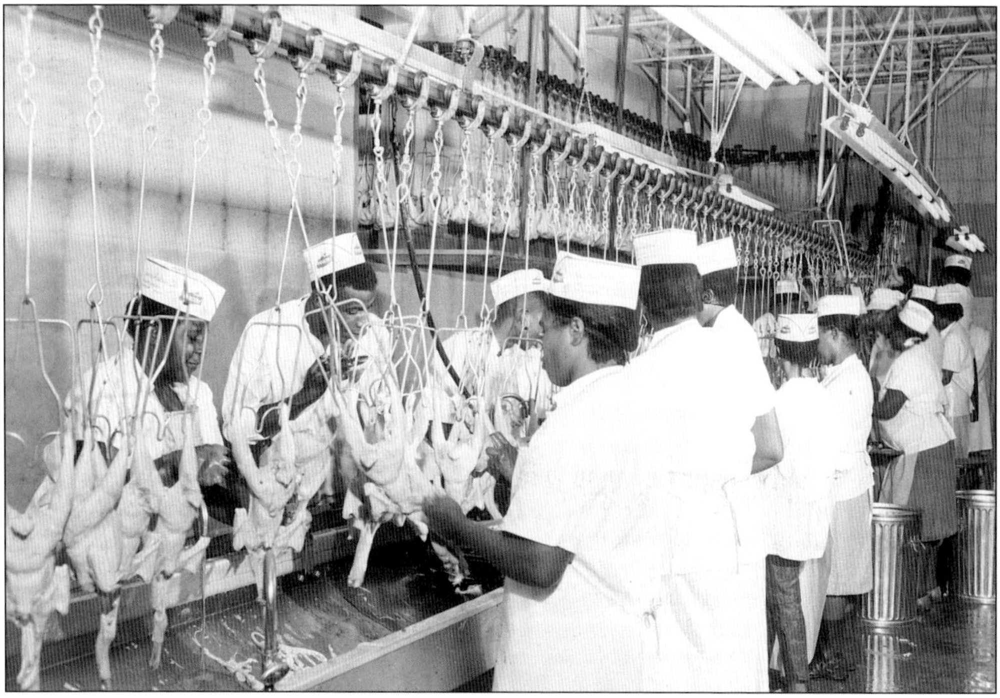

MARSHALL FARMS PROCESSING PLANT, 1962, GREENVILLE.

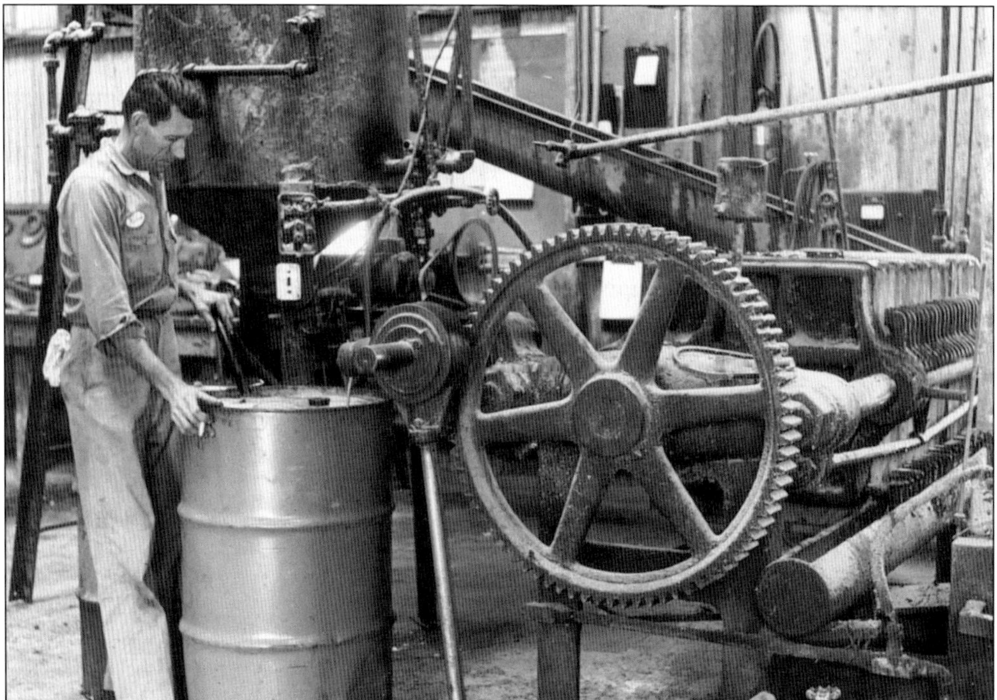

PROCESSING CHICKEN FAT, FORT MILL INDUSTRIES, 1964. Modern processing methods were so efficient that they used, according to some growers, "every part of the chicken except the cackle."

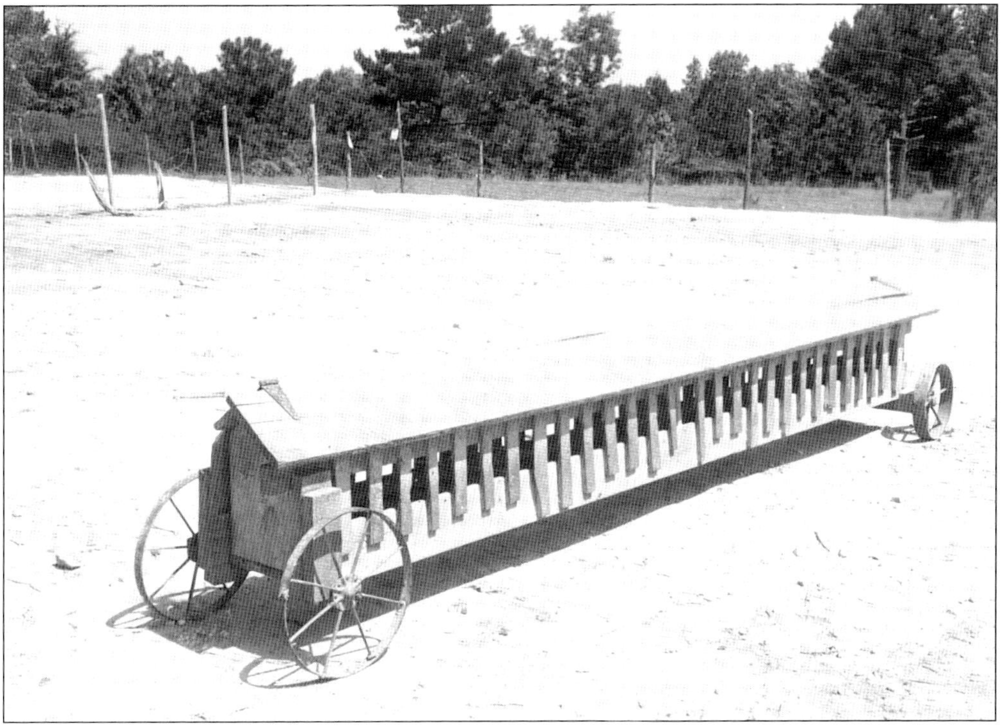

TURKEY RANGE FEEDER, HAROLD BISHOP FARM, 1946, CLINTON.

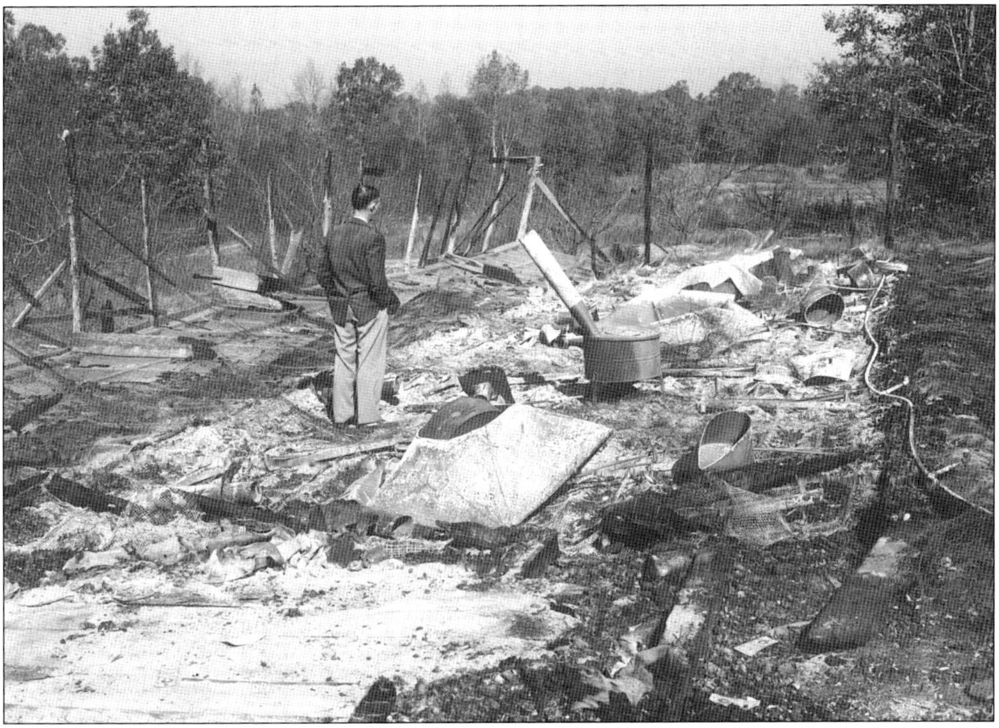

TURKEY HOUSE DESTROYED BY FIRE, 1950, YORK. The plight of many growers was worsened by being uninsured.

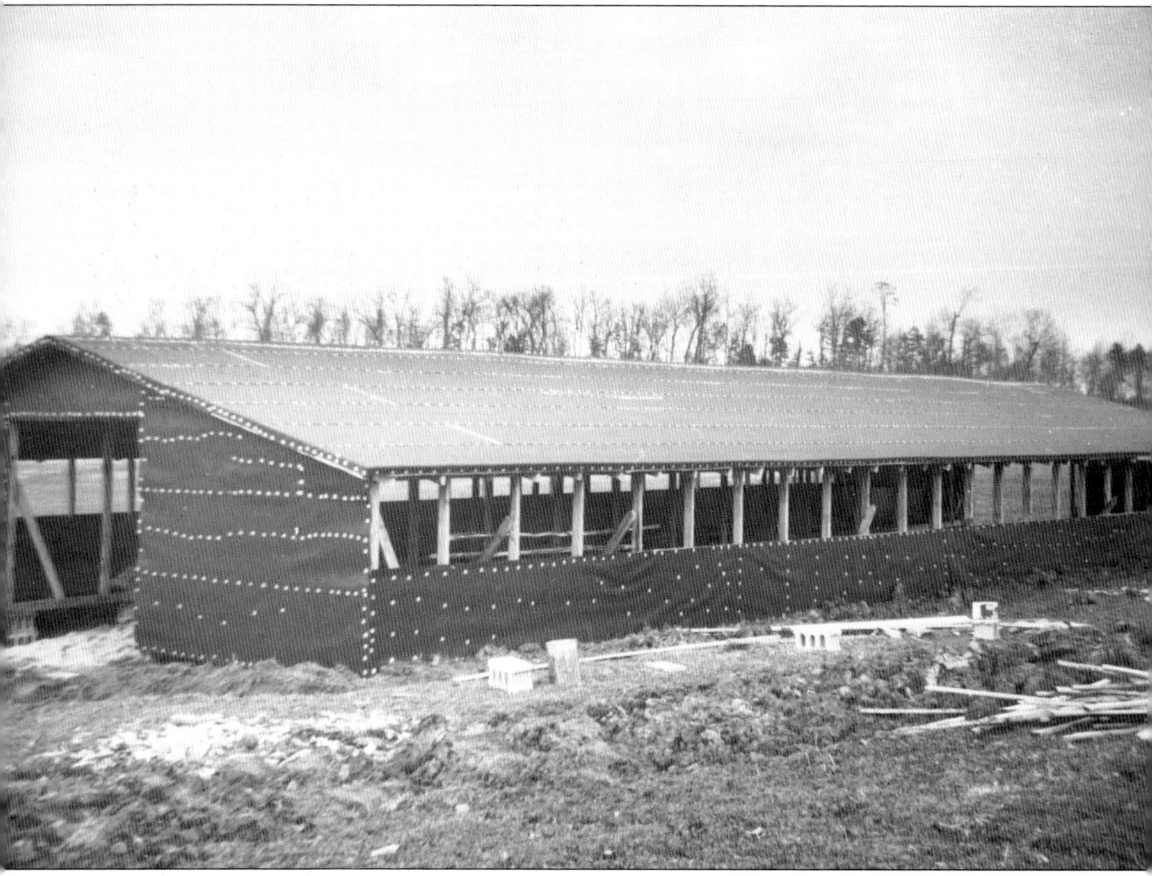

Poultry House under Construction, Duncan Brothers Farm, 1949, York. Poultry houses during this time were ventilated by windows. Later construction provided for mechanical ventilation.

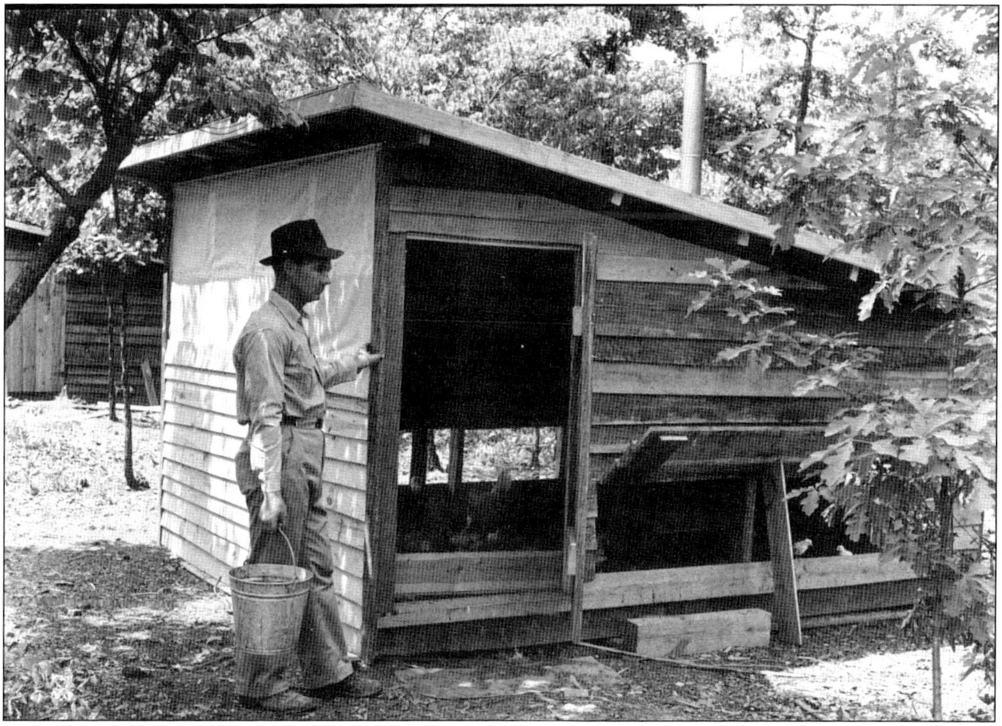

BROODER HOUSE OF FRED WEBB, 1941, SALUDA.

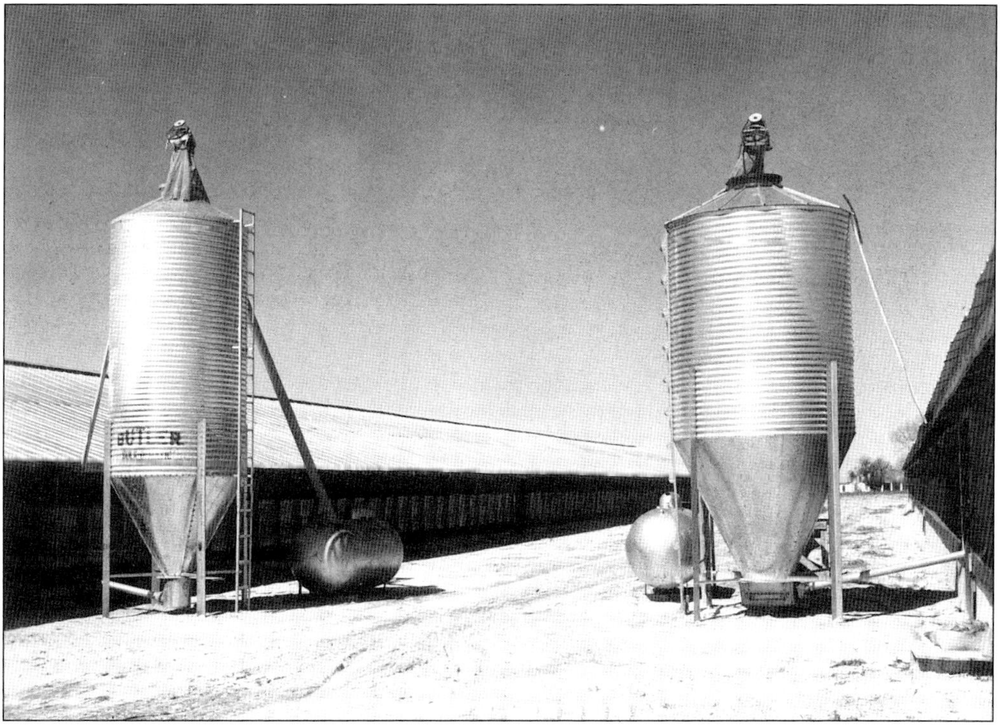

MODERN POULTRY HOUSE, 1958, LOCATION UNKNOWN. With automated equipment, chickens could be fed special feed mixtures at precise intervals.

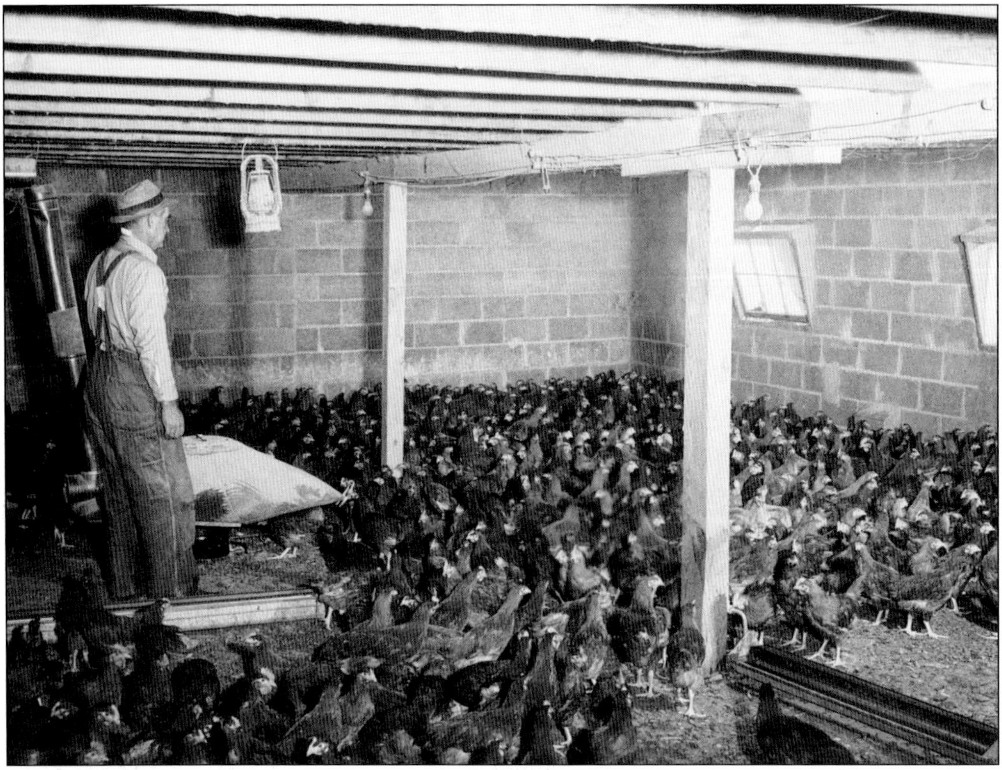

Broilers, 1950, Spartanburg. Broilers were young chickens of up to 2.5 pounds dressed weight.

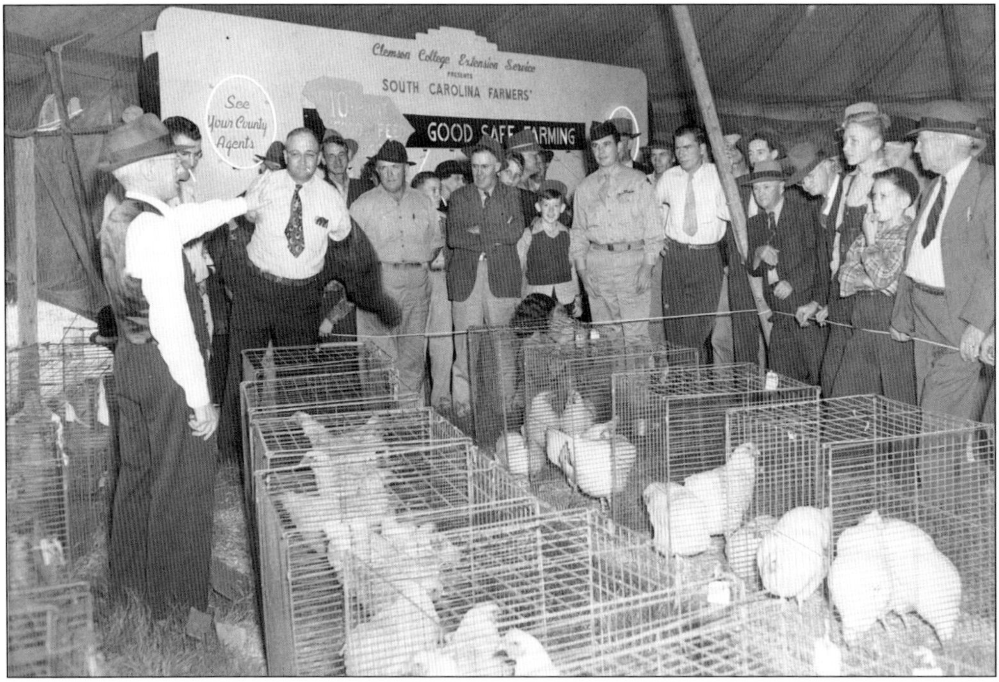

Poultry Exhibit at Union County Fair, 1945.

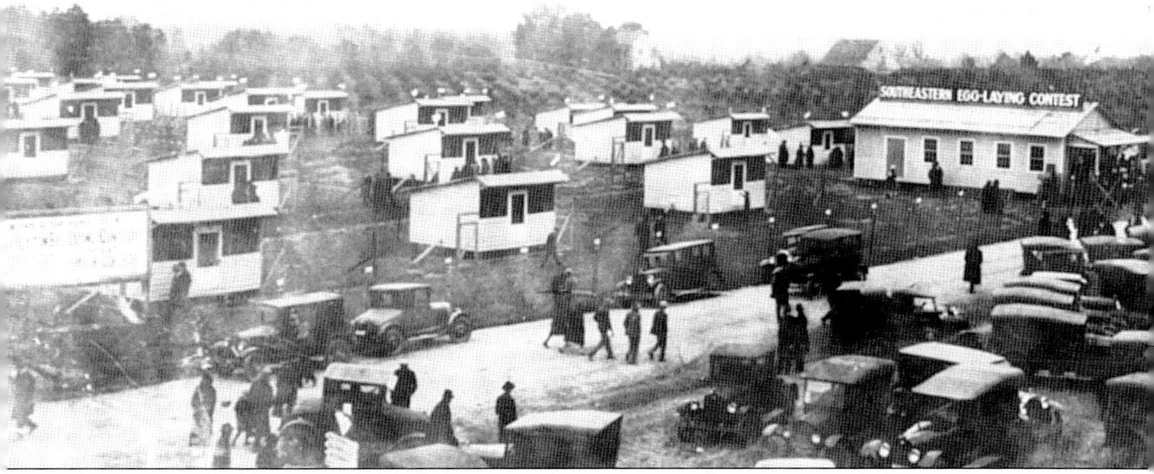

EGG CONTEST, 1925–1926, MCCORMICK. Tom Morgan of the Extension Service organized the contest.

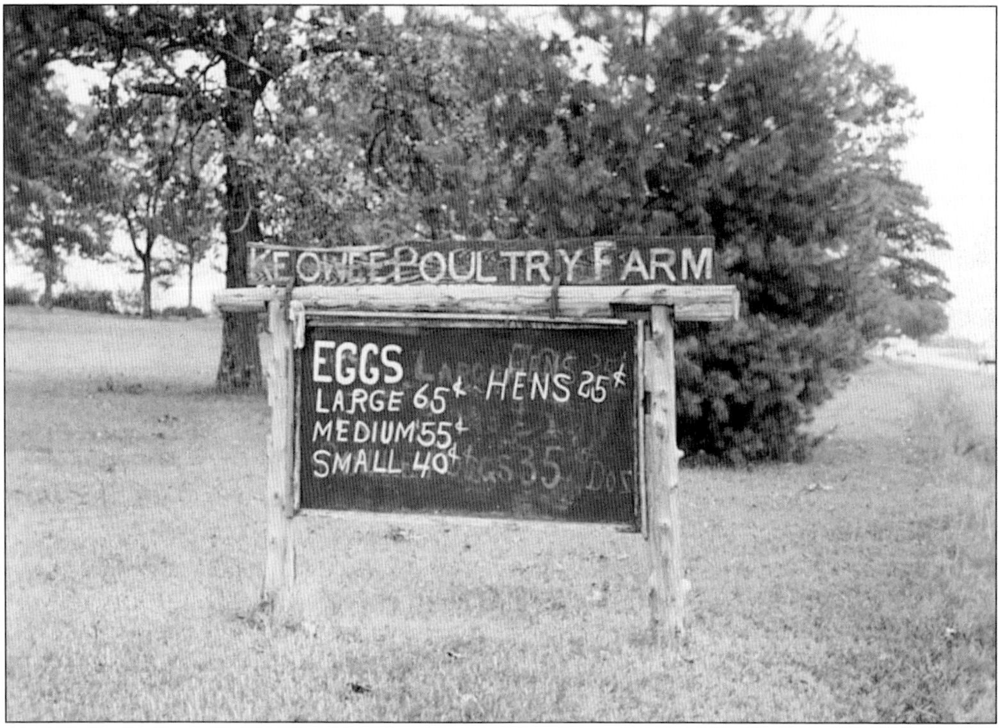

SIGN FOR KEOWEE POULTRY FARM, C. 1948, OCONEE COUNTY.

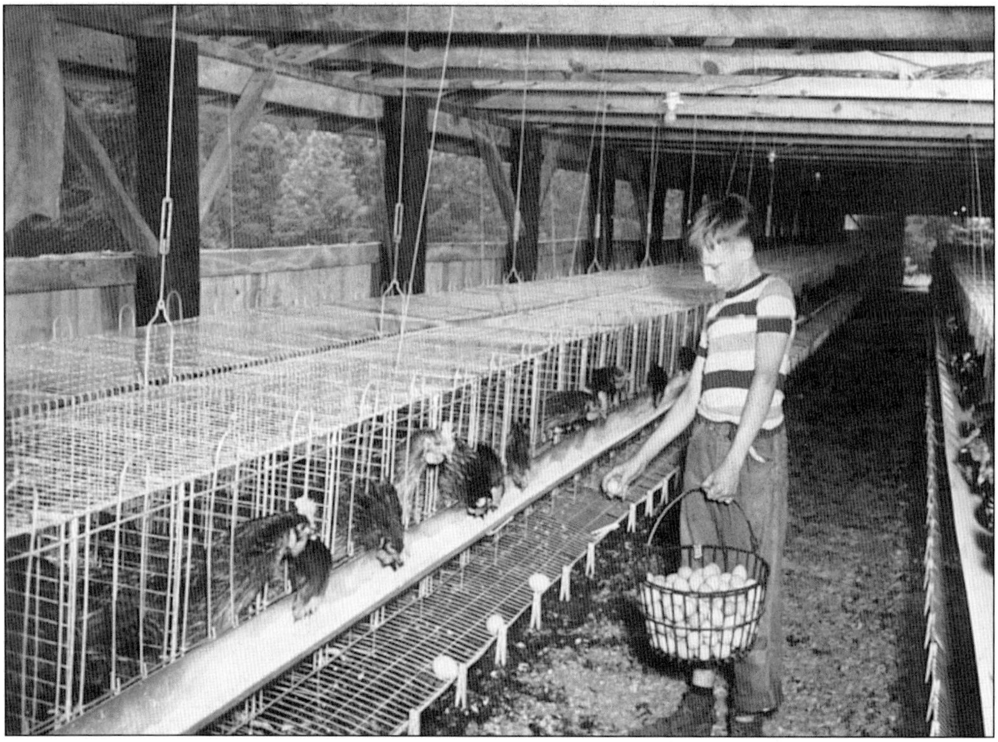

GATHERING EGGS, 1954, YORK COUNTY.

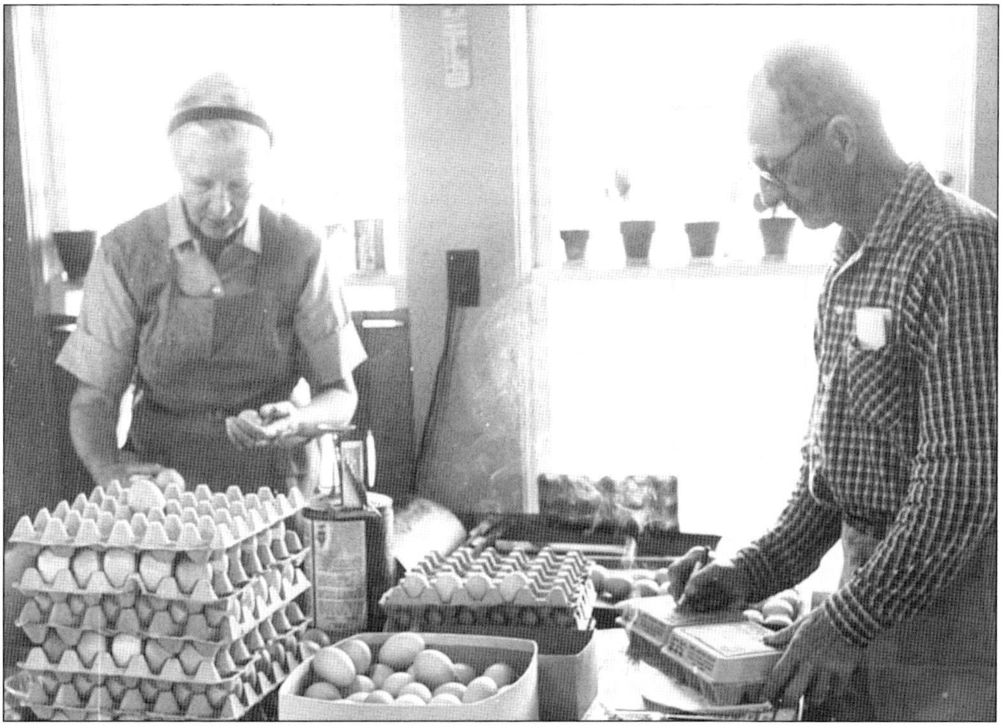

GRADING EGGS, C. 1960, LAURENS.

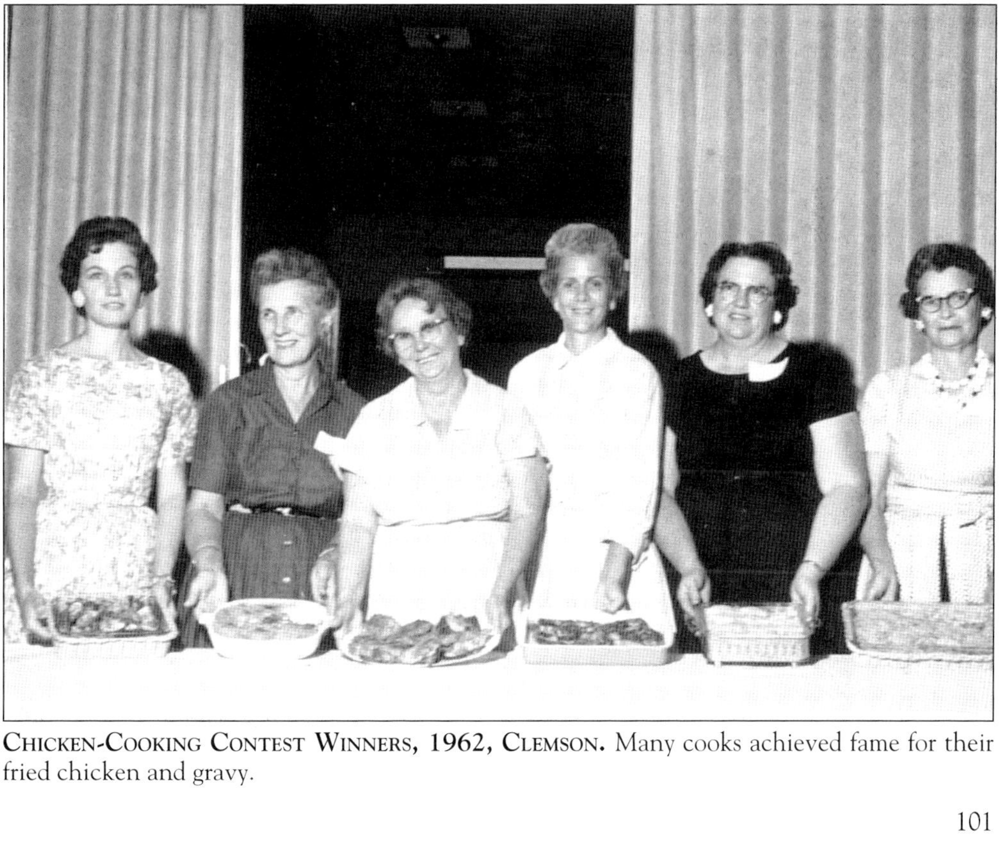

CHICKEN-COOKING CONTEST WINNERS, 1962, CLEMSON. Many cooks achieved fame for their fried chicken and gravy.

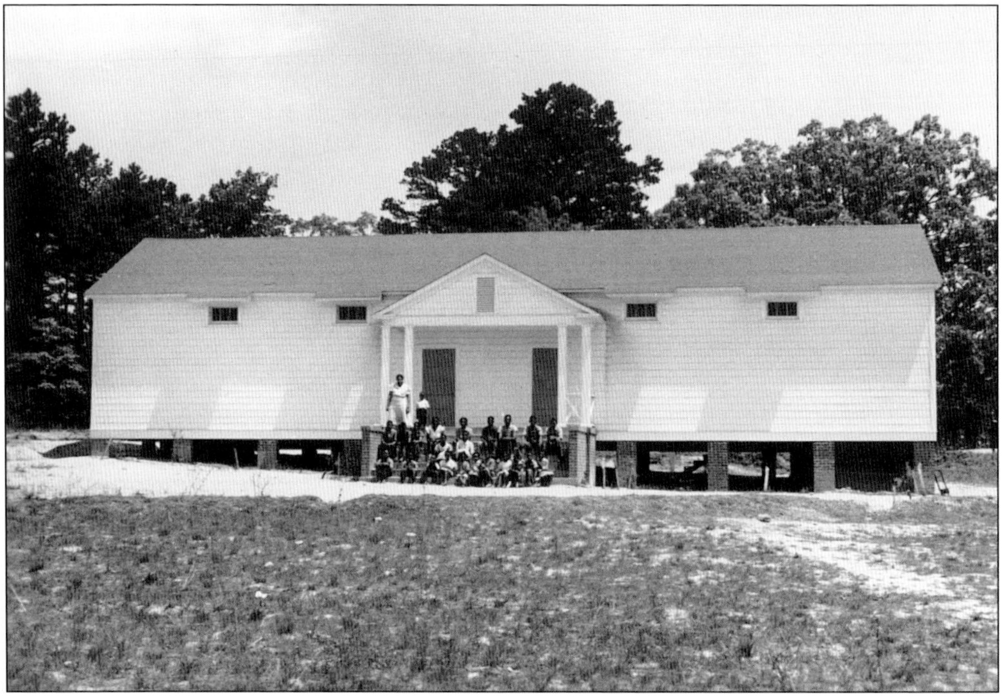

Shiloh School, 1947, Anderson County.

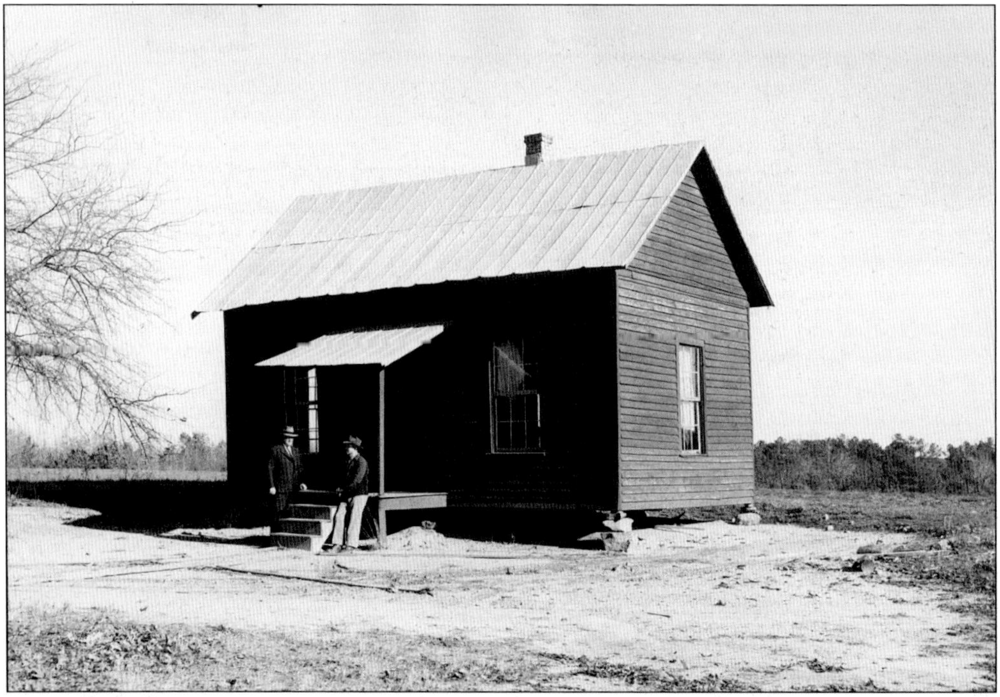

One-Room School, C.T. Smith Farm, 1953, Newberry. It was not uncommon for students of every age group to learn together. Teachers advised their pupils: "Older ones lead, younger ones follow."

Six

EDUCATION AND LEISURE

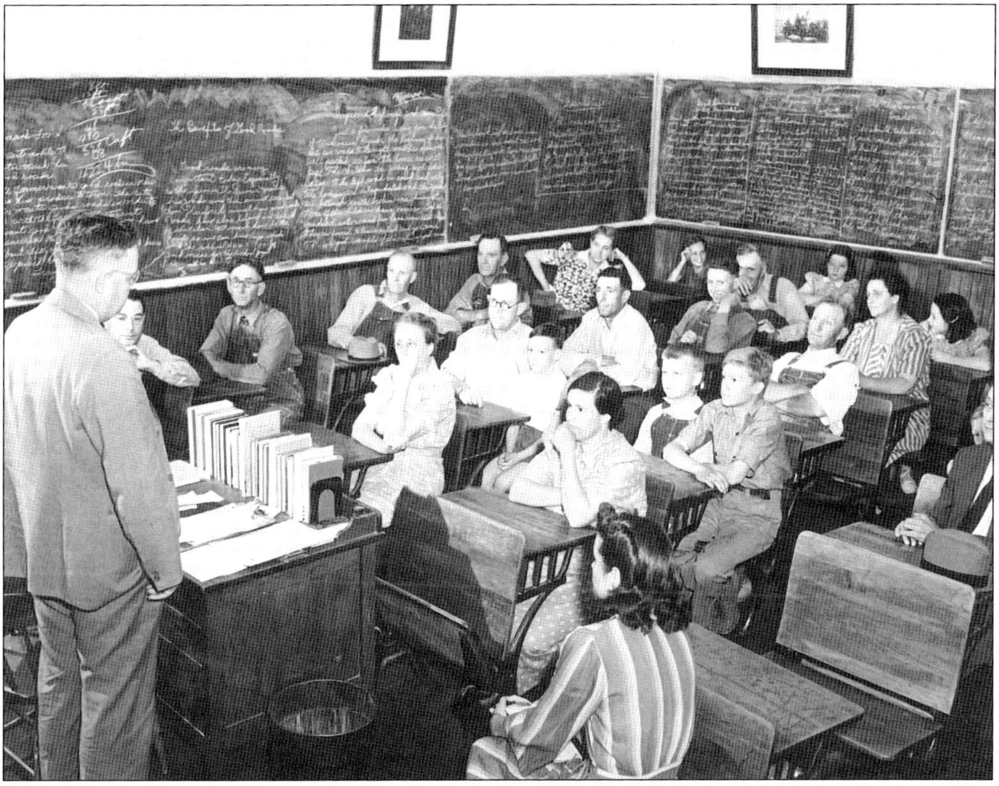

COUNTY AGENT PAUL EZELL MEETING WITH FARM FAMILIES, C. 1935, NEWBERRY.

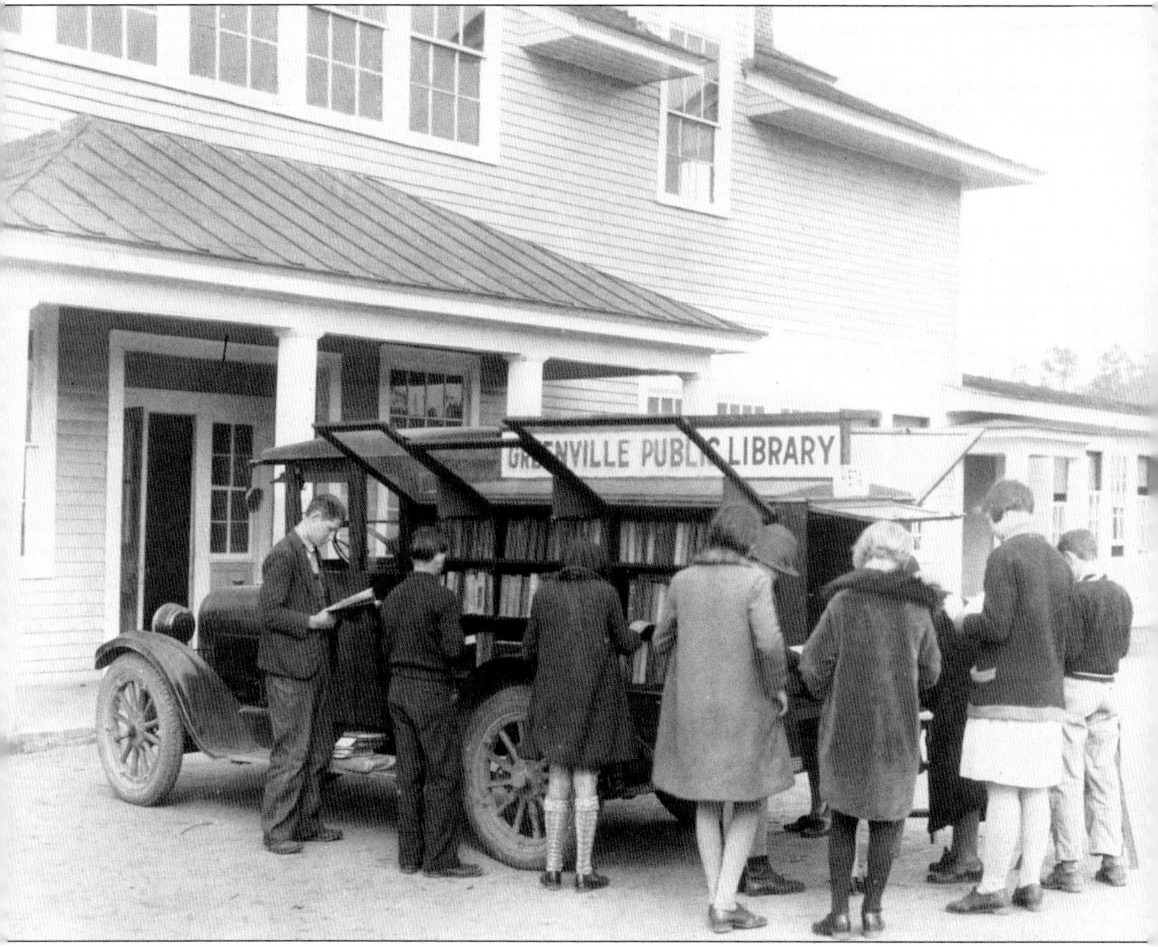

BOOKMOBILE, C. 1940, GREENVILLE. Greenville County first used a small truck to transport books to mill villages in October 1923. Greenville also took the lead in support for public libraries by legislating tax money for their development. Summer reading programs for children, as well as other outreach activities, supplemented education provided by the schools and at home.

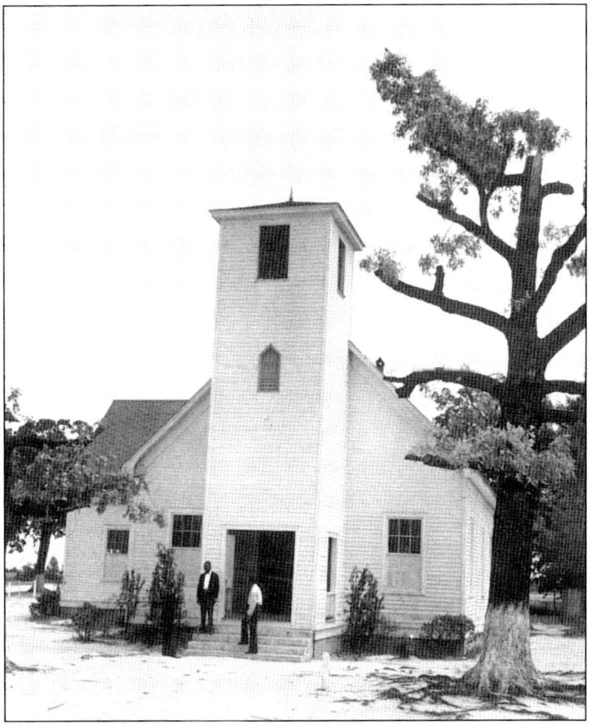

MOUNT MORIAH BAPTIST CHURCH, 1941, ANDERSON COUNTY. Mount Moriah was founded in 1878.

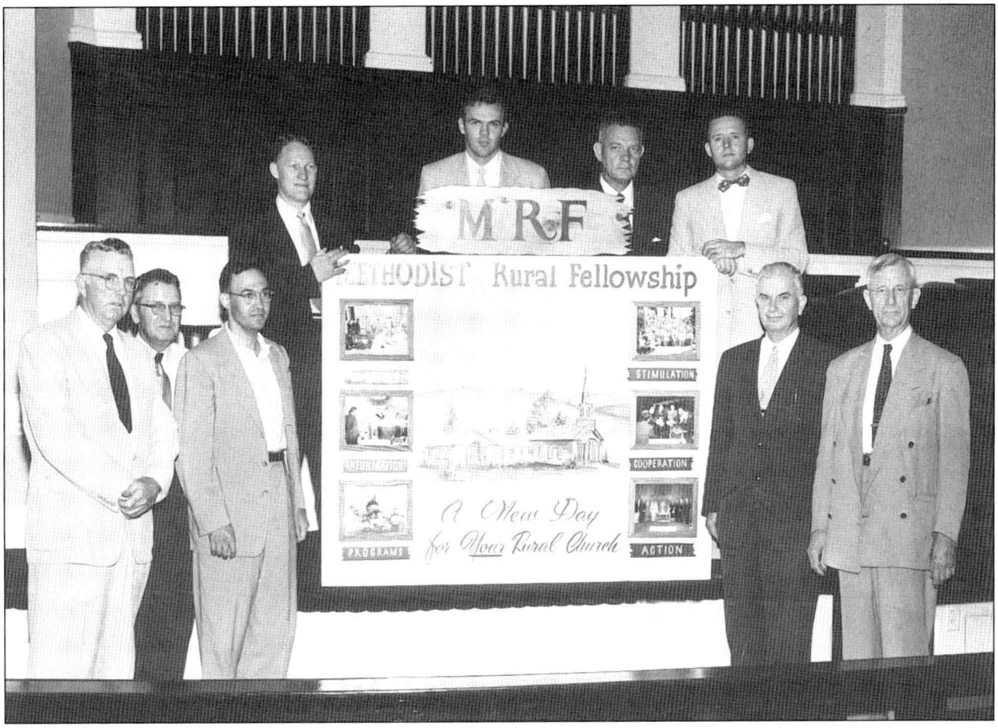

METHODIST RURAL FELLOWSHIP, DATE AND LOCATION UNKNOWN. One of several religious groups in the overwhelmingly Protestant Piedmont, Methodism afforded opportunities for worship, fellowship, and service.

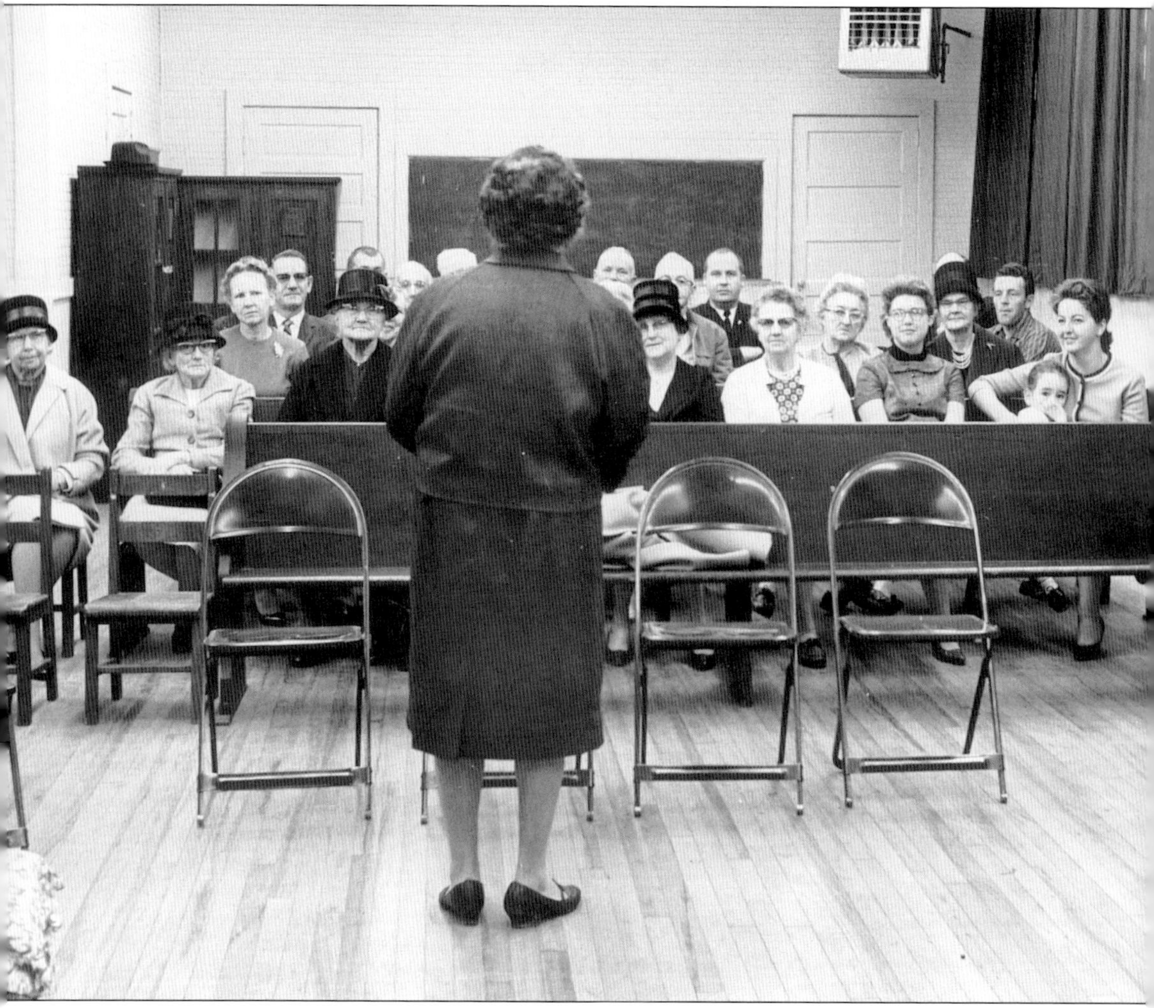

HOME DEMONSTRATION AGENT, C. 1960, RICH HILL. Home demonstration agents worked tirelessly to improve nutrition, clothing, and housing for all South Carolinians.

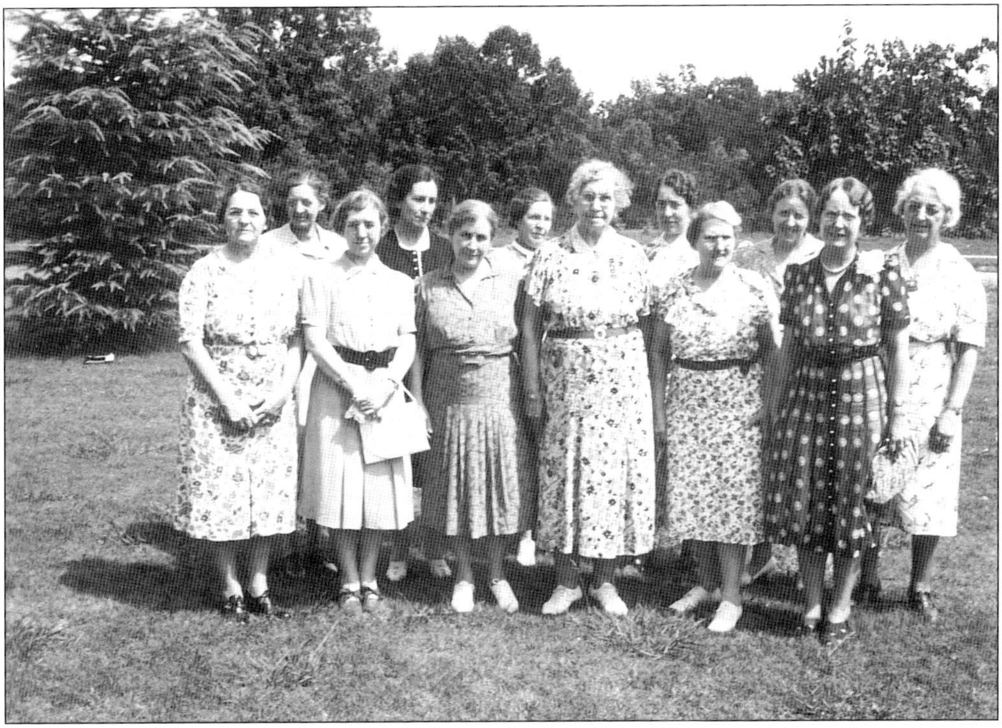

EXTENSION HOME DEMONSTRATION WORKERS, 1939.

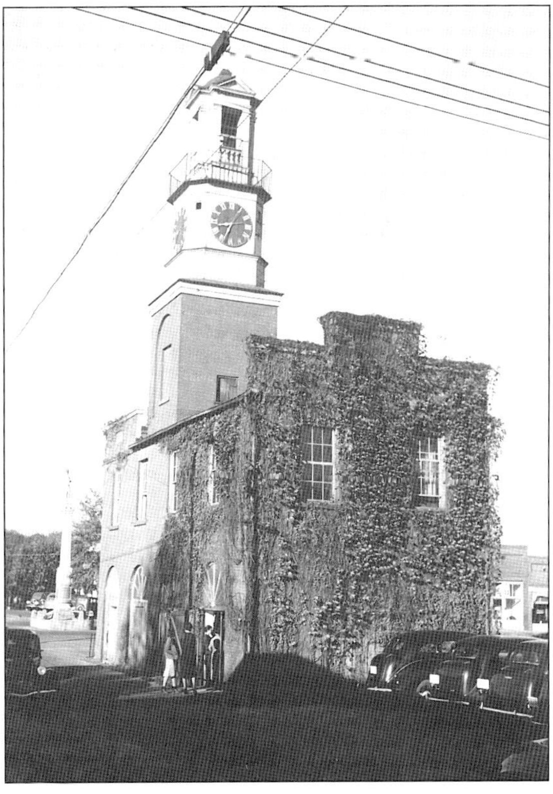

CLOCK TOWER, 1938, WINNSBORO. This was the site of the Home Demonstration market every Saturday morning.

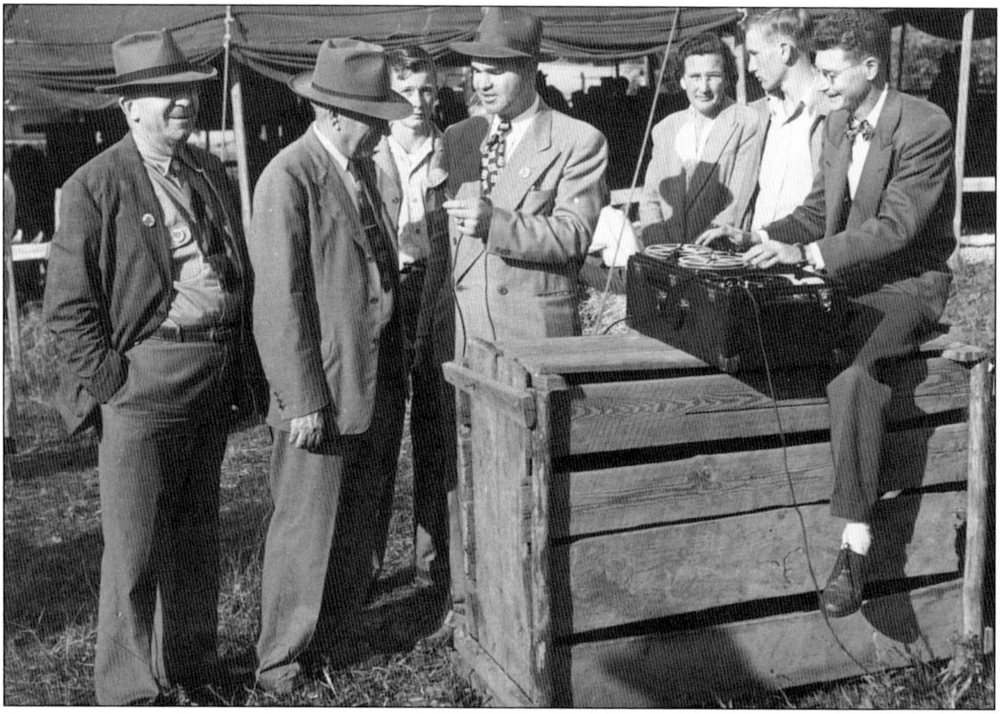

County Agent Griffin Recording a Radio Program for WFBC, 1947.

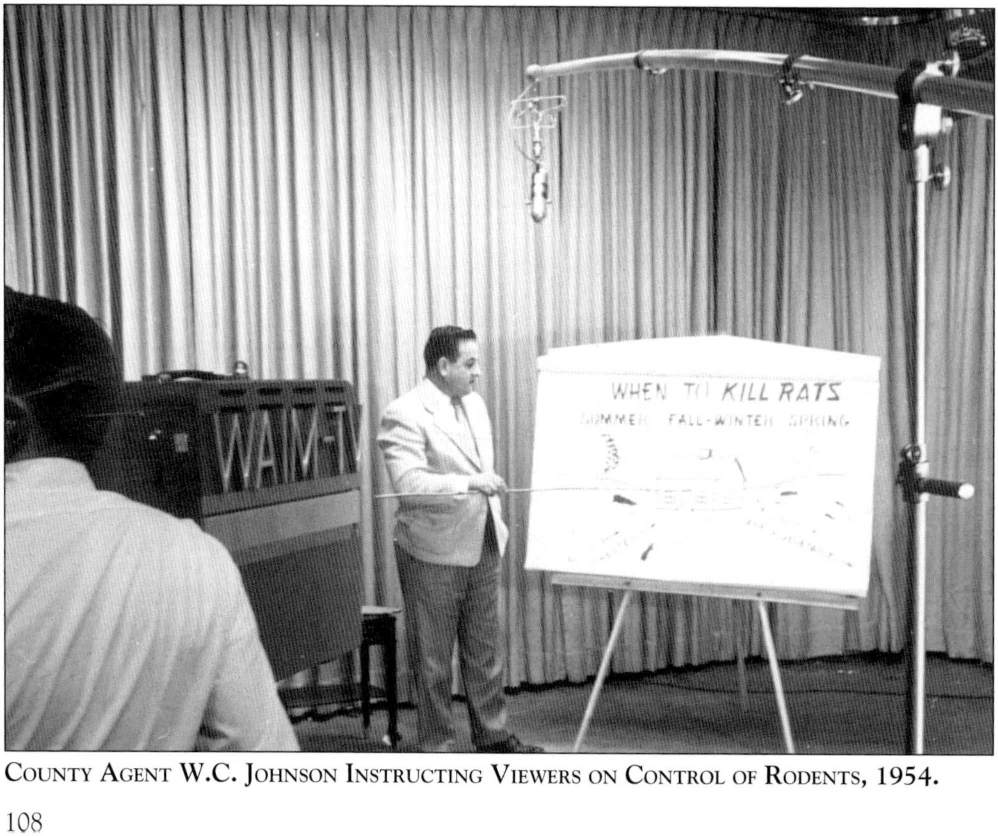

County Agent W.C. Johnson Instructing Viewers on Control of Rodents, 1954.

AGENT INSTRUCTING A WOMAN ON THE REPAIR OF HER COFFEE POT AT THE APPLIANCE REPAIR SCHOOL, C. 1940, GREENVILLE.

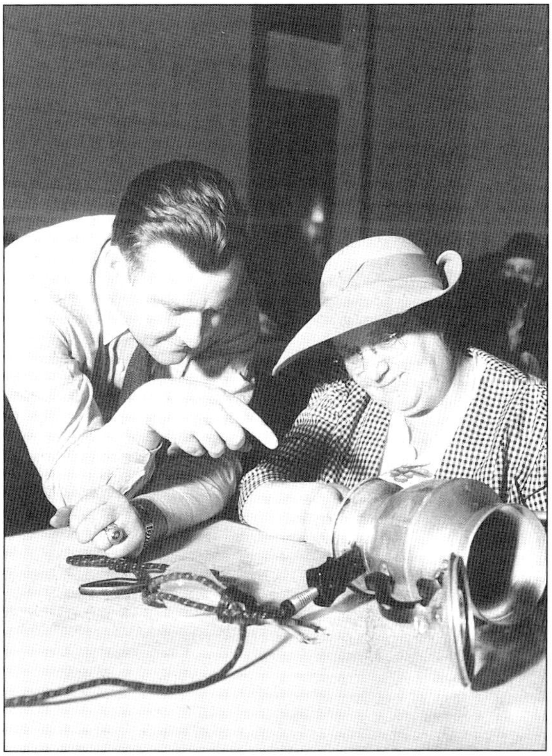

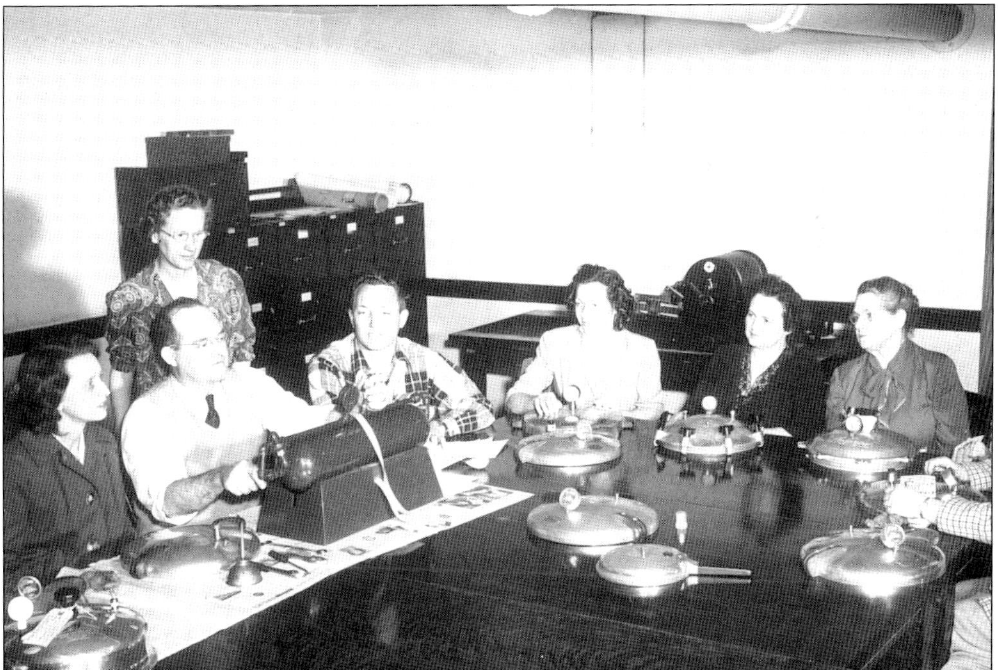

PRESSURE COOKER CLINIC, C. 1950, GREENVILLE. Many homemakers feared pressure cookers because they often exploded. Used correctly, however, pressure cookers greatly reduced cooking time and were essential for canning food at home.

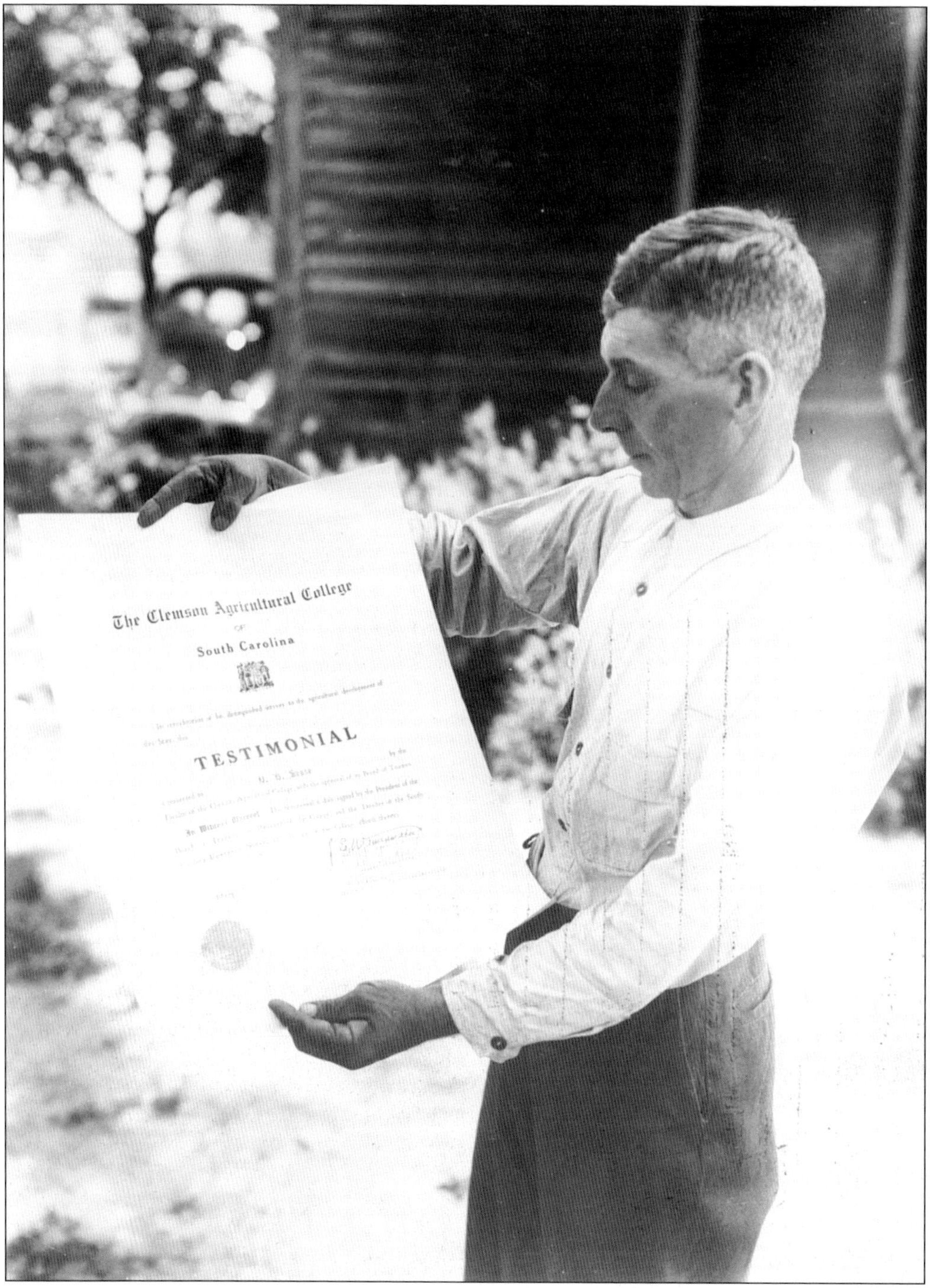

D.B. SEASE, NEWBERRY. He is holding a certificate recognizing service to agricultural development in South Carolina.

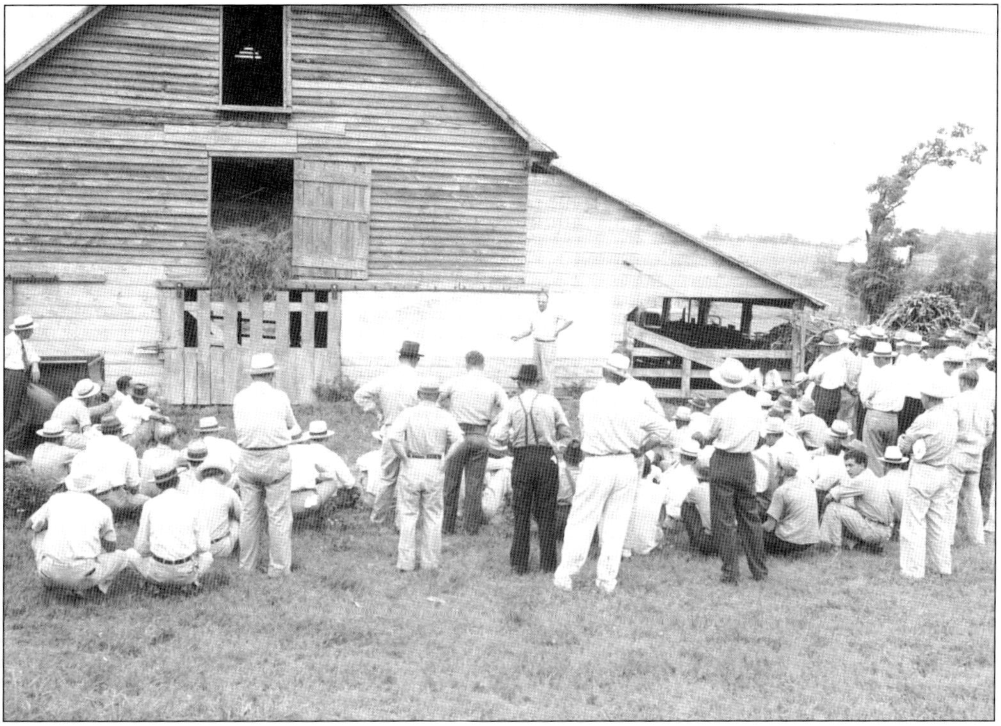

Farm Forage School, Dobbins Farm, 1946, Anderson County.

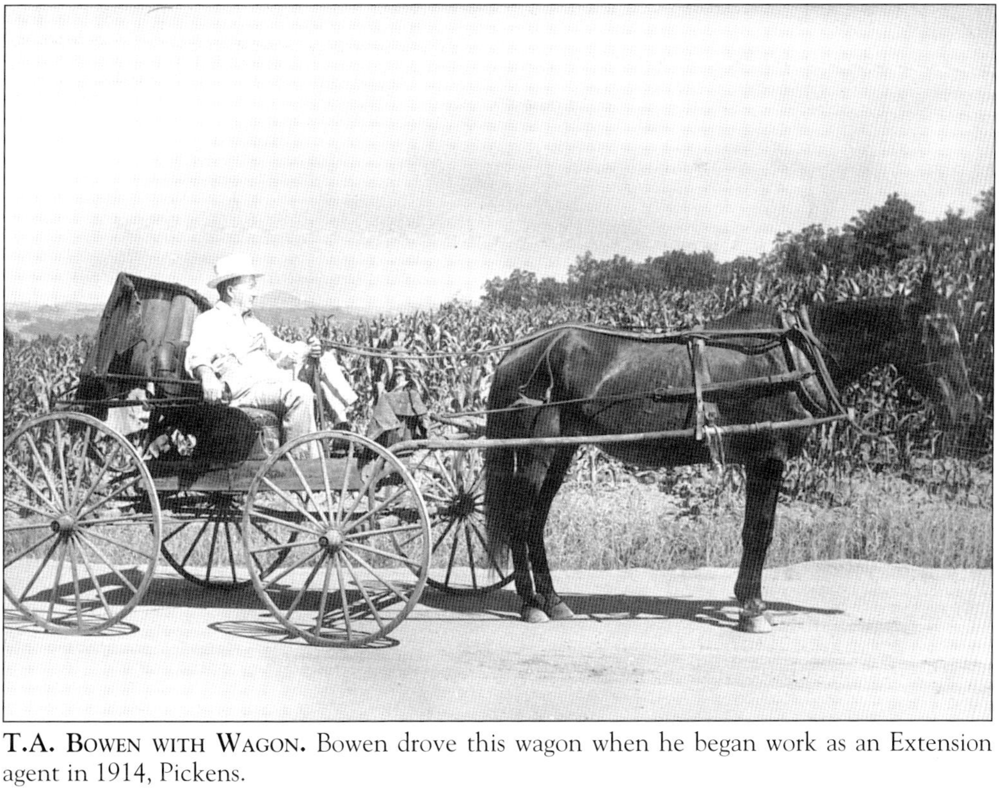

T.A. Bowen with Wagon. Bowen drove this wagon when he began work as an Extension agent in 1914, Pickens.

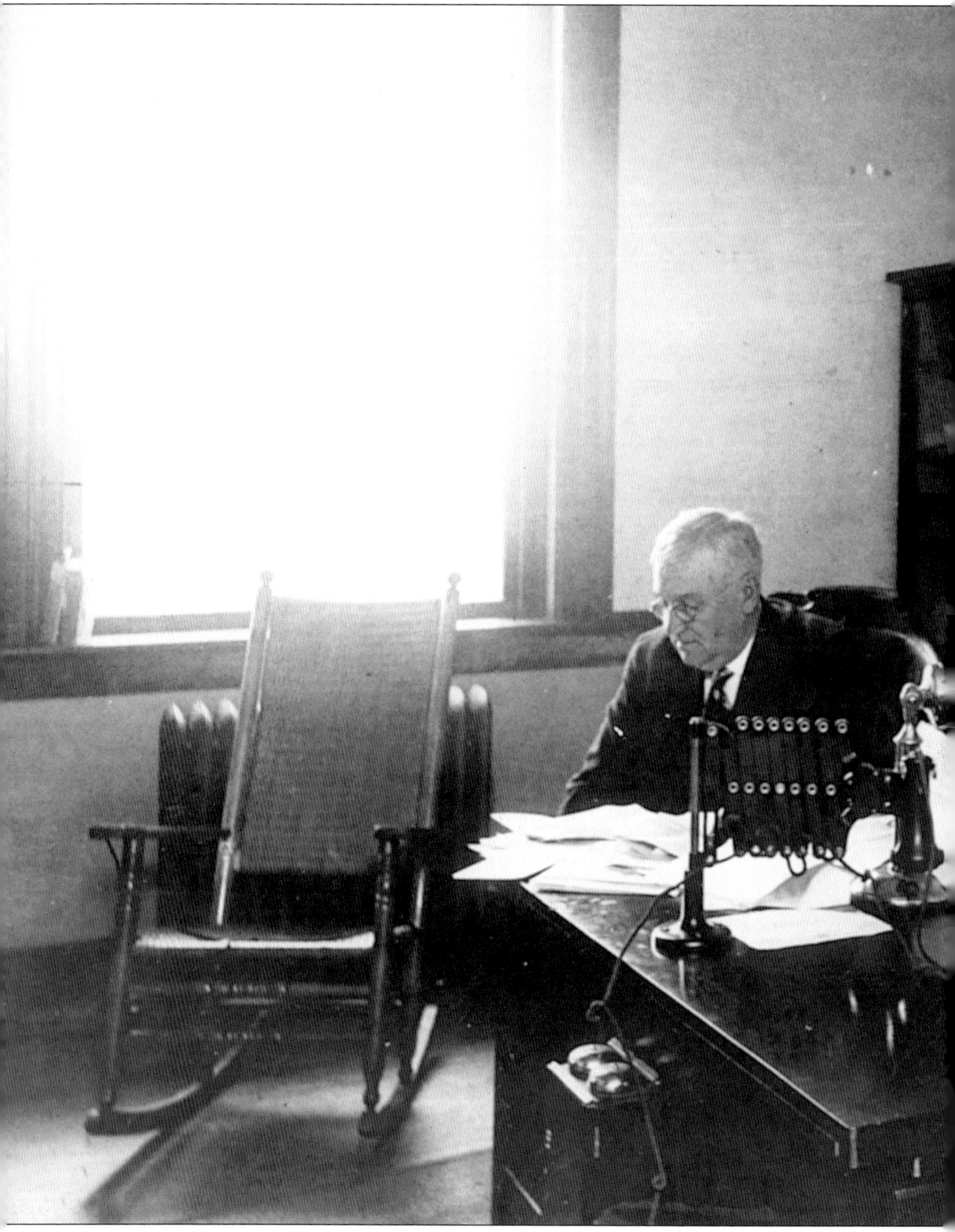

W.W. Long, Director of Cooperative Extension, 1913–1934, Clemson. Long, a native of

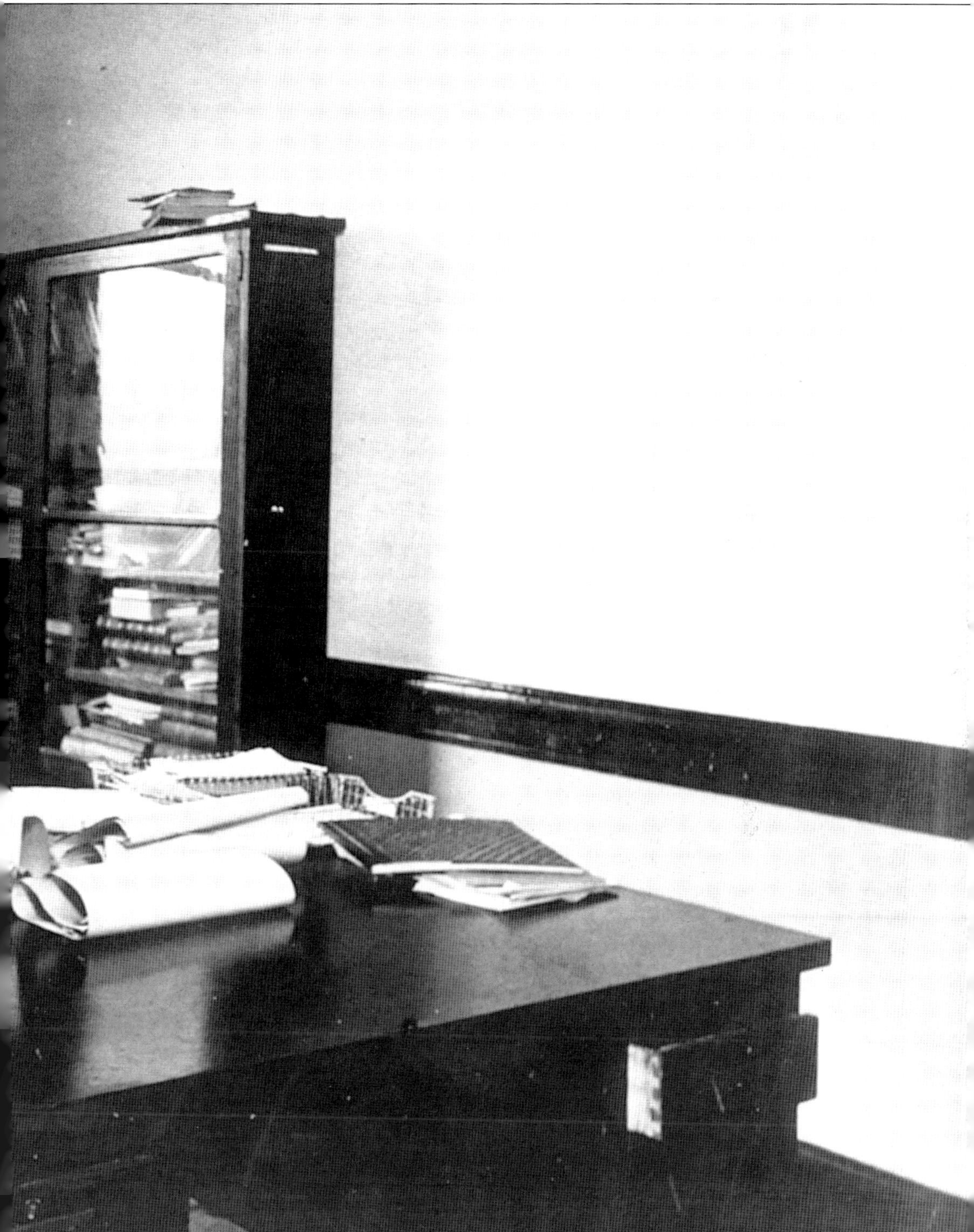

Warrenton, North Carolina, laid the foundation for Extension work in South Carolina.

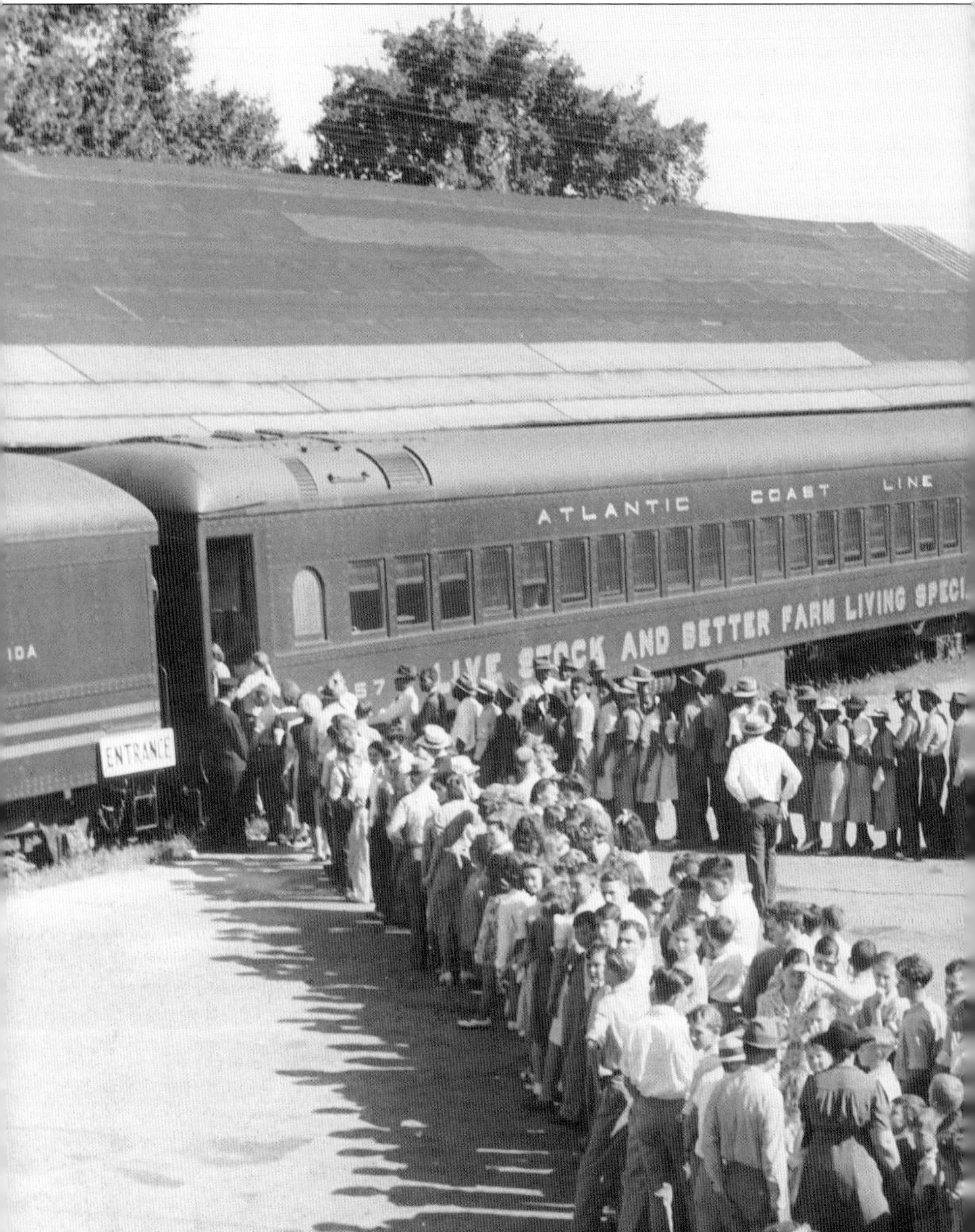

BETTER FARM LIVING TRAIN, 1941, NEWBERRY. The train traveled throughout the state promoting the work of the Extension Service and providing citizens the chance to see new

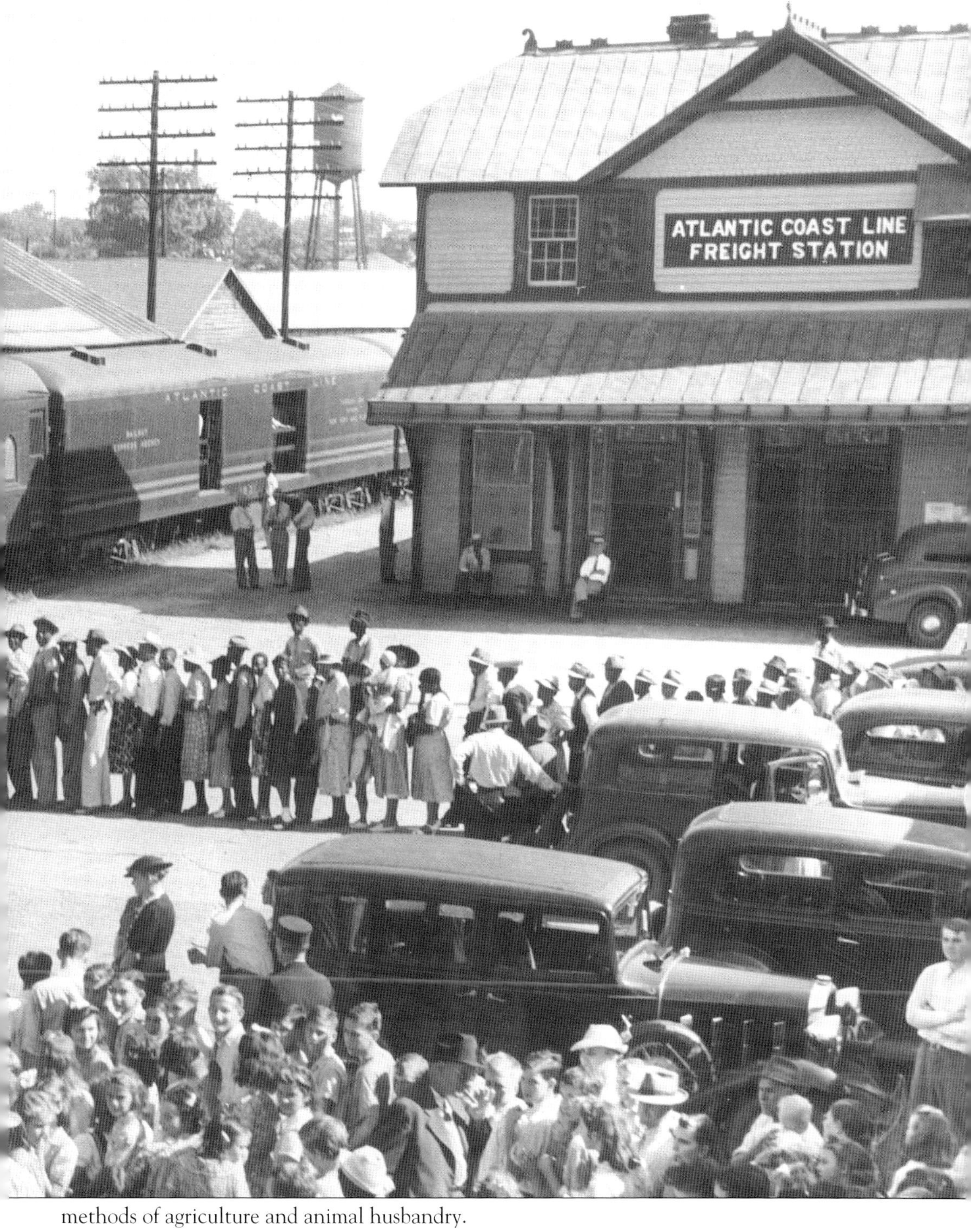

methods of agriculture and animal husbandry.

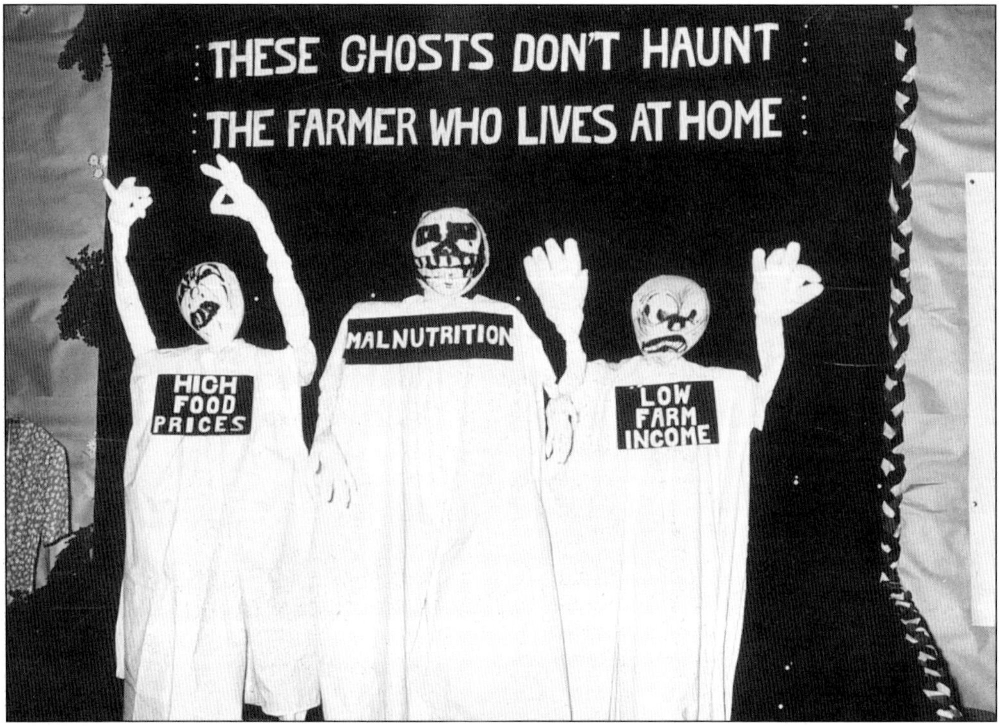

EXHIBIT ON FARM LIVING TRAIN, 1941.

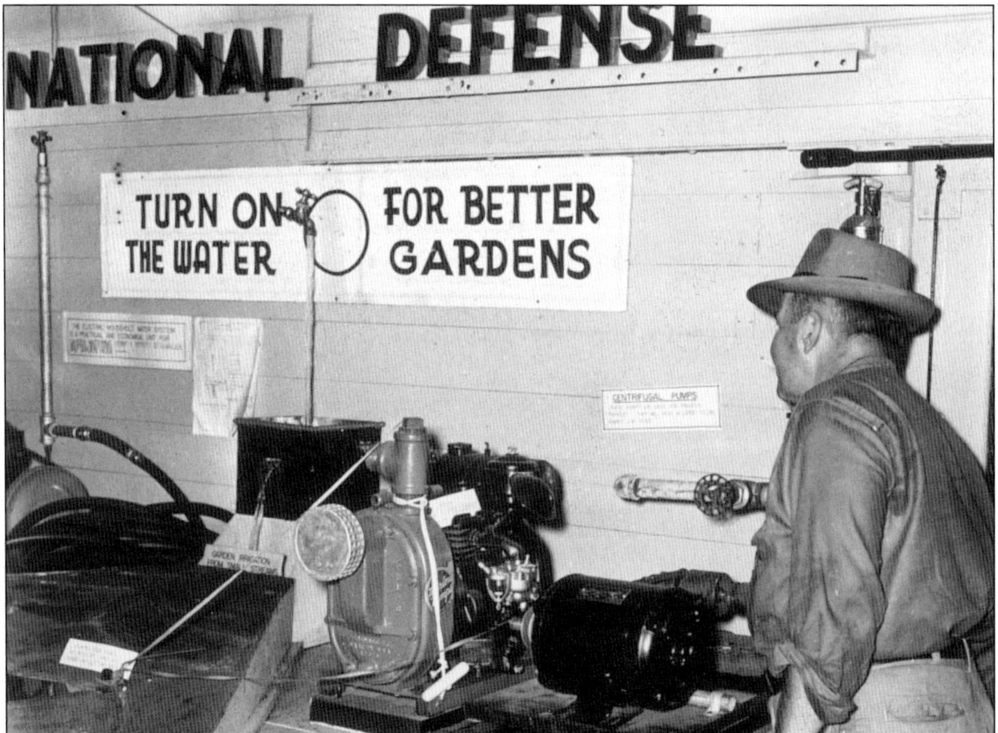

EXHIBIT ON FARM LIVING TRAIN, 1941.

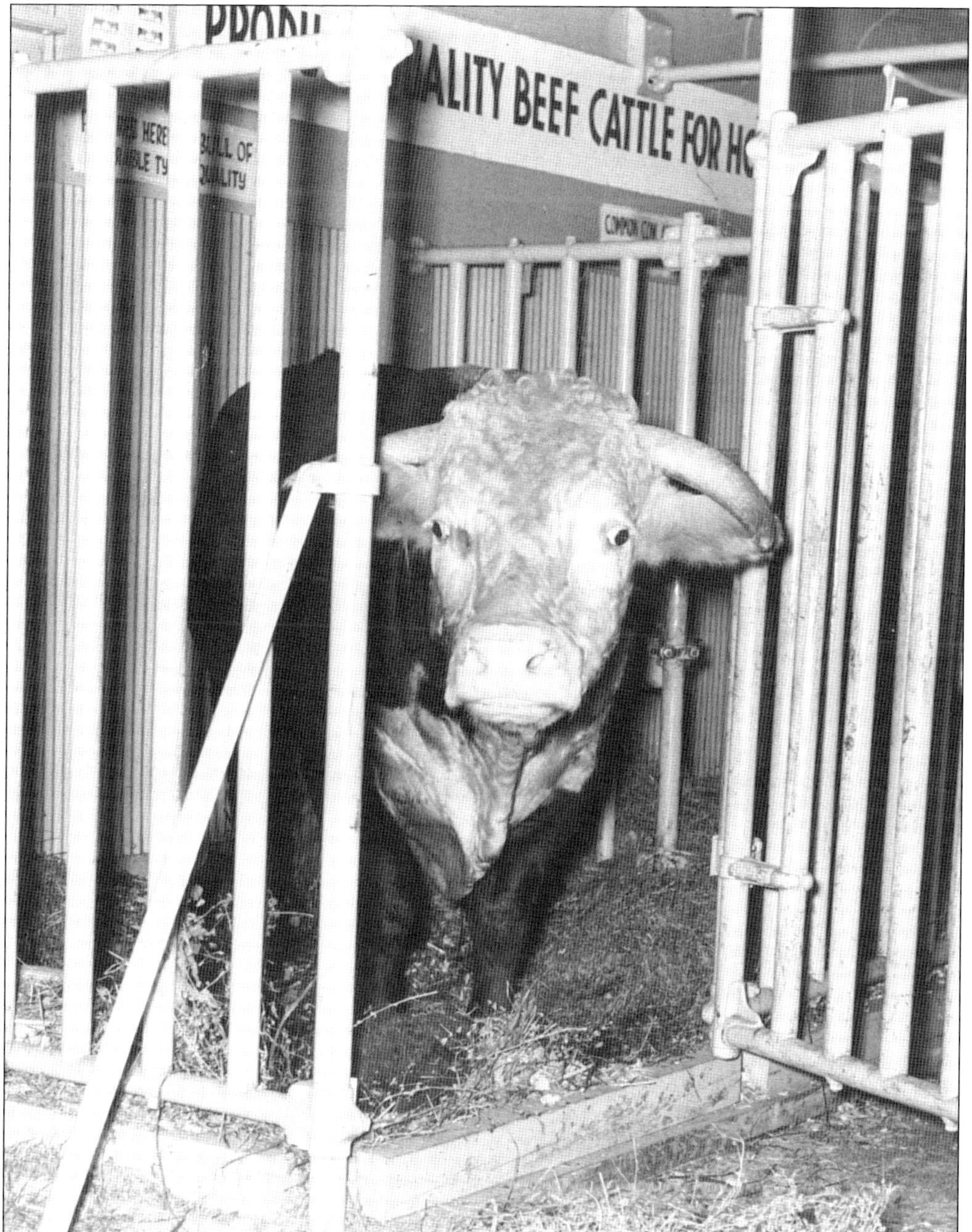

Prize-Winning Hereford steer on Farm Living Train.

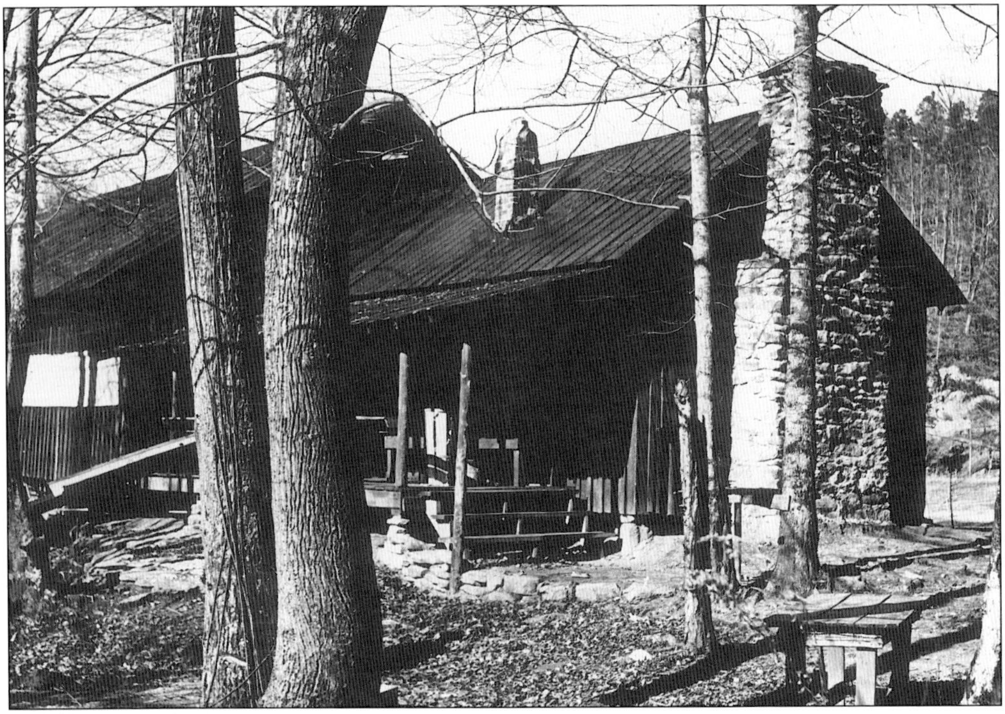

MESS HALL, CAMP ROCKY BOTTOM, C. 1940, PICKENS COUNTY. Camp Rocky Bottom was a summer home to many 4-H camps.

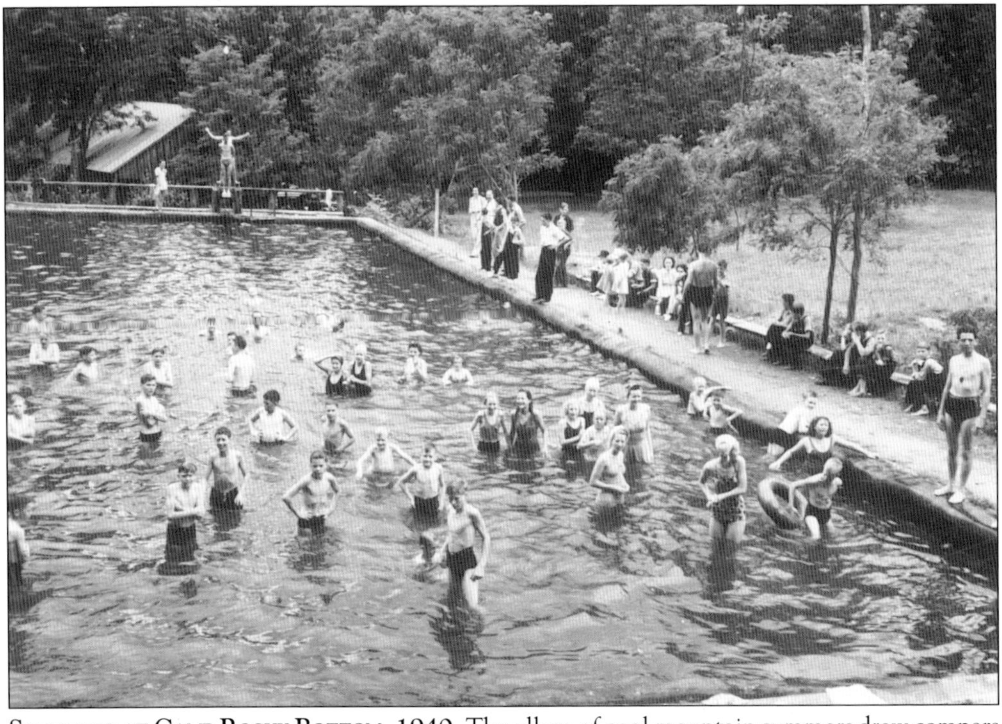

SWIMMING AT CAMP ROCKY BOTTOM, 1940. The allure of cool mountain summers drew campers from throughout the upcountry.

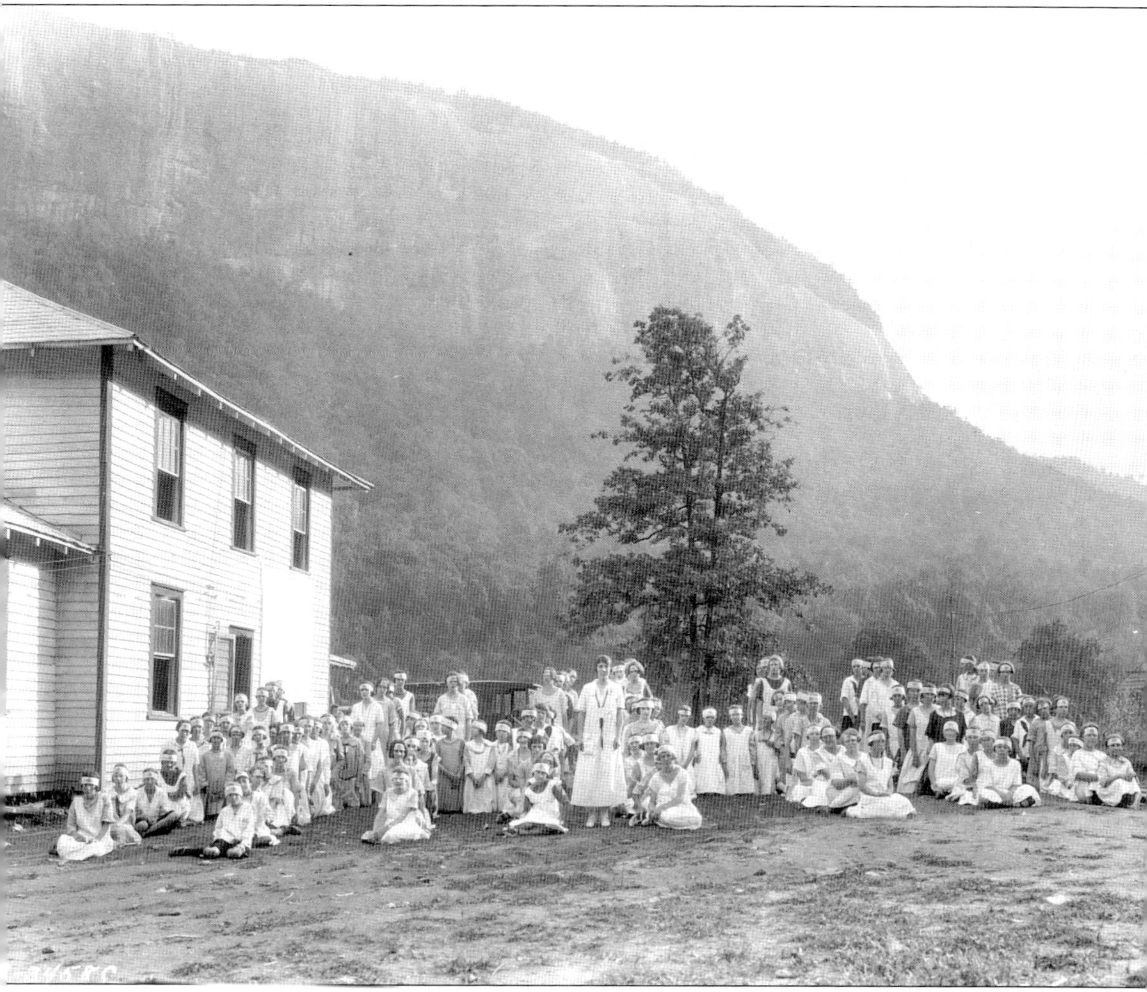

Girls 4-H Camp, Table Rock Park, 1939, Pickens County. The 4-H Club, the Hs standing for "Head, Heart, Hands, Health," afforded girls opportunities that were usually available only to boys. Girls could select project areas traditionally associated with women, for example dress-making or foods, or they could foray into other areas such as cattle, swine, or automobiles.

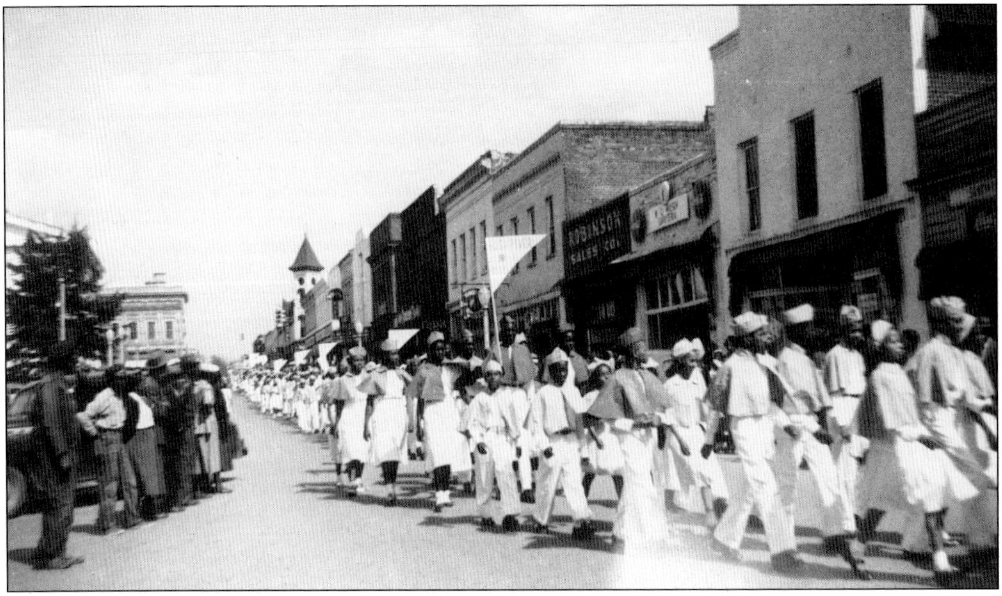

A 4-H Parade, 1951, Anderson.

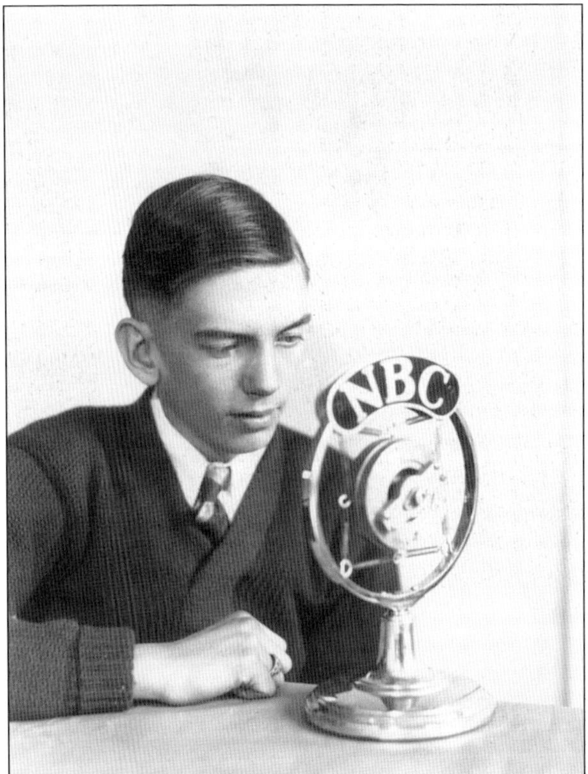

Carol C. Brannon of Spartanburg's 4-H Club. He is pictured here broadcasting a special 4-H program on national radio, February 1, 1930.

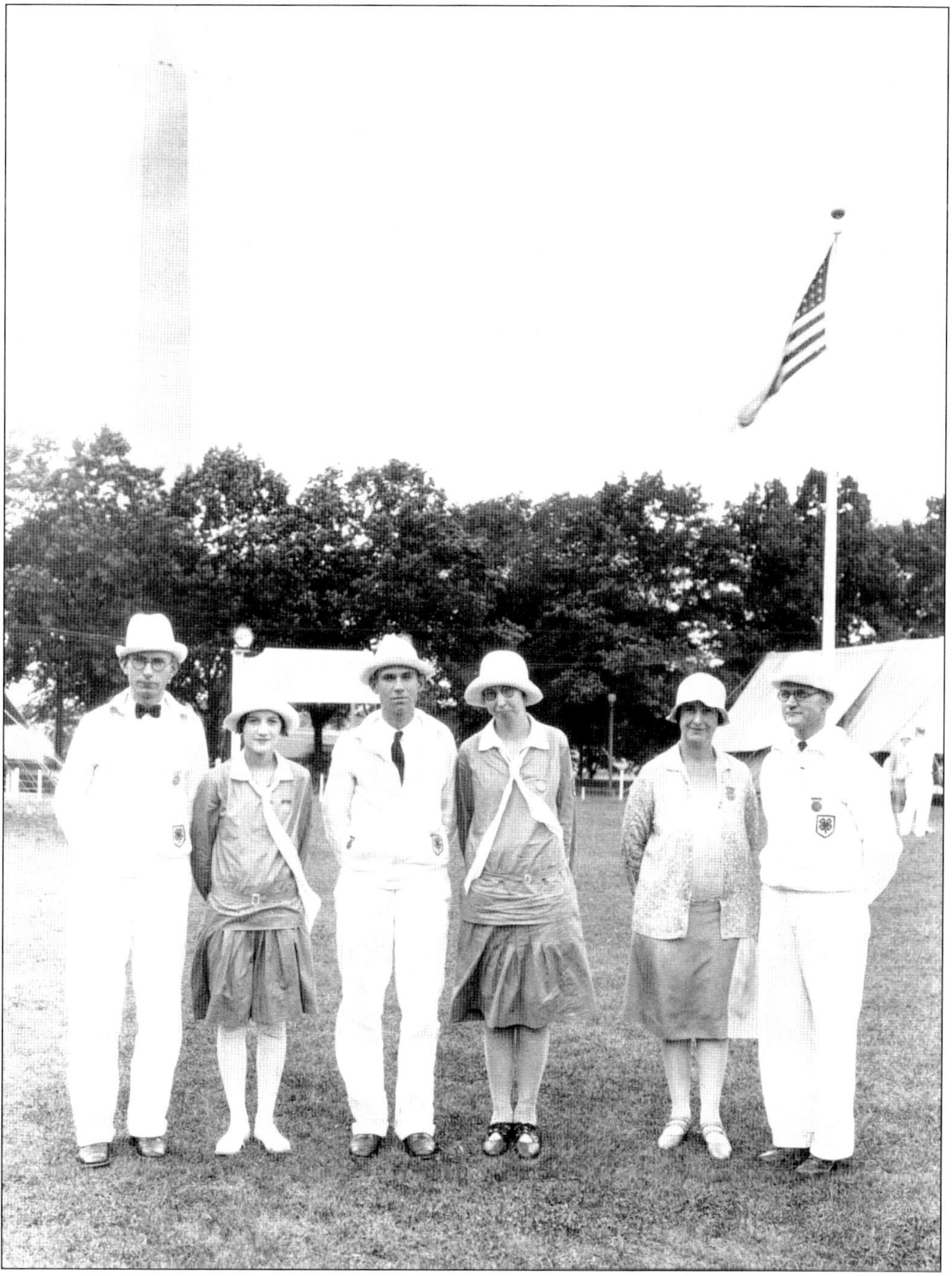

DELEGATES TO NATIONAL 4-H CAMP, 1928.

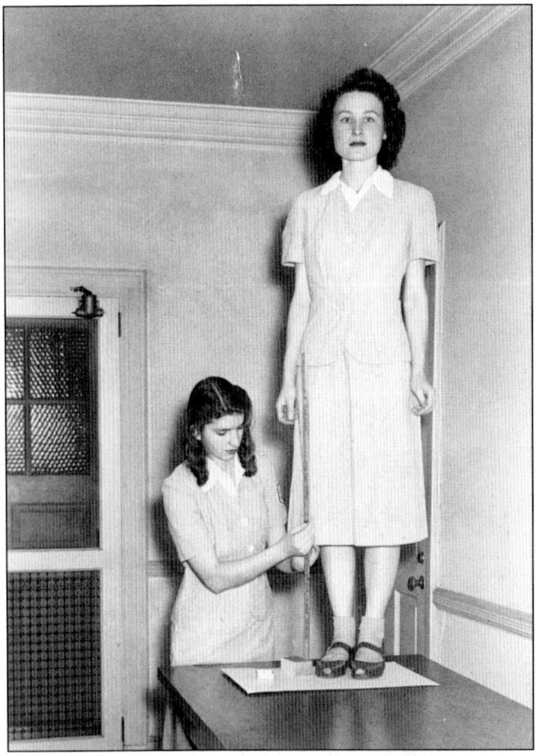

Dressmaking Project, 1946, York.

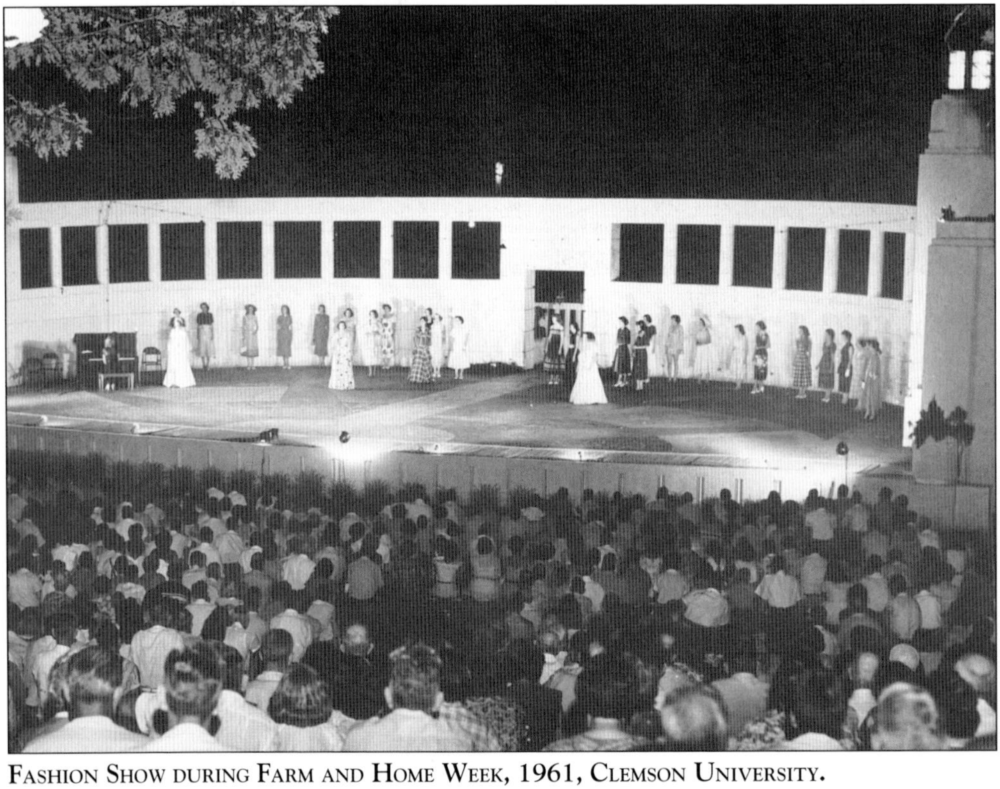

Fashion Show during Farm and Home Week, 1961, Clemson University.

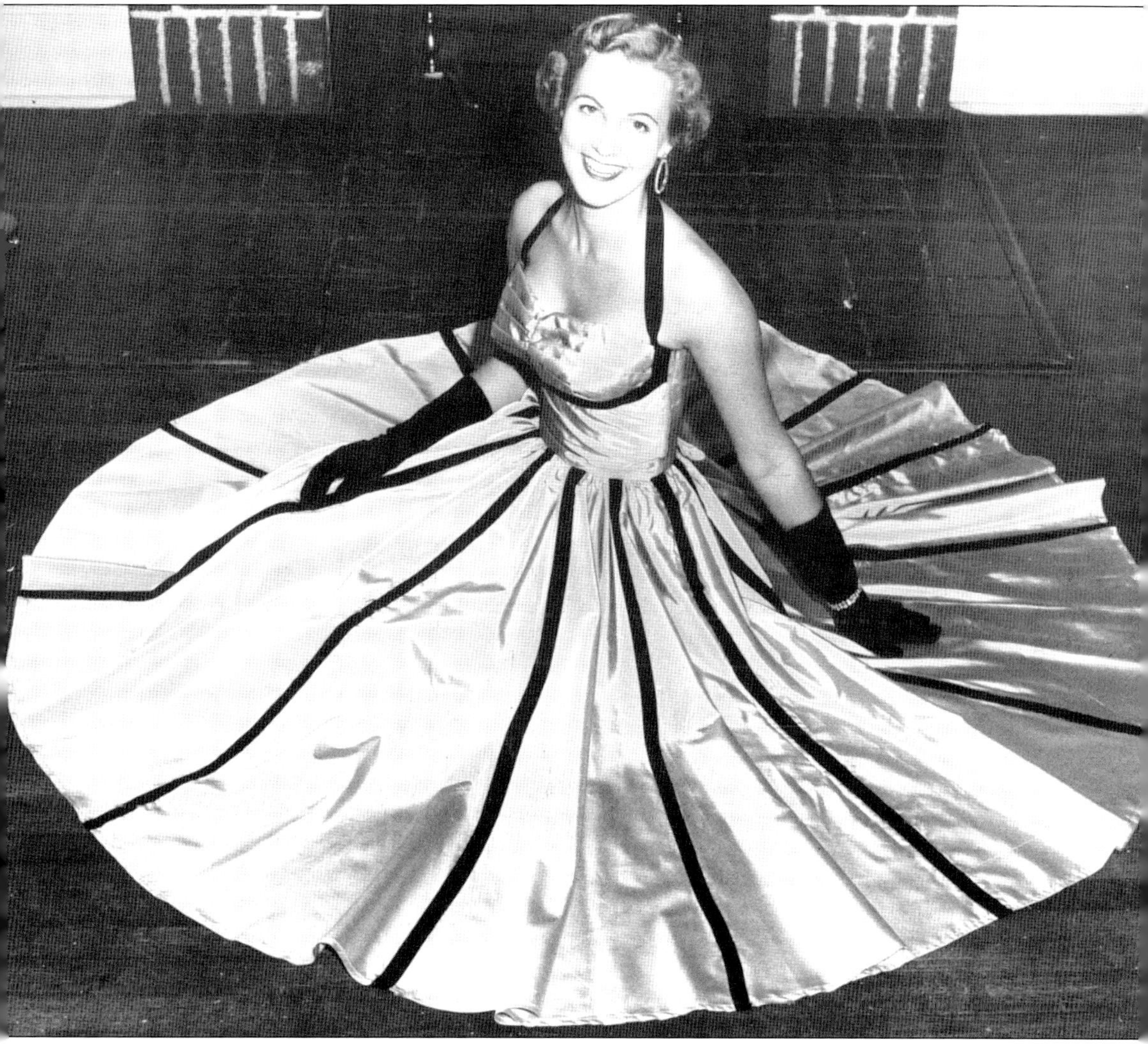

MIRIAM STEVENSON OF GREENWOOD, MISS UNIVERSE WINNER, 1954, AT FARM AND HOME WEEK, IN CLEMSON. She is modeling an evening dress she designed and made herself.

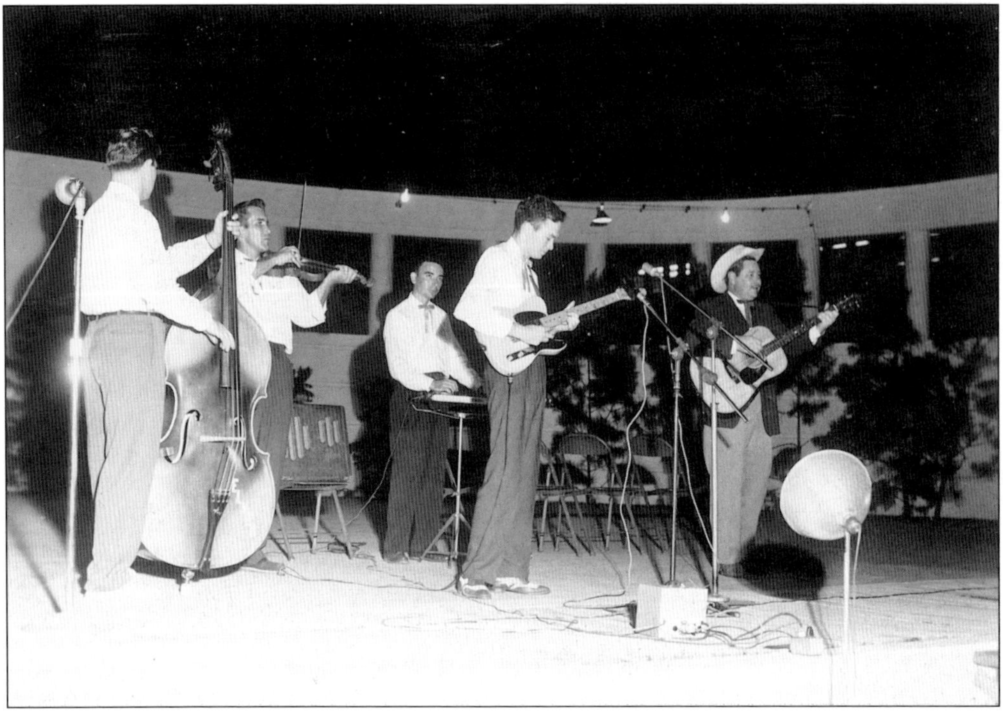

MUSICAL GROUP PERFORMING AT FARM AND HOME WEEK, 1954.

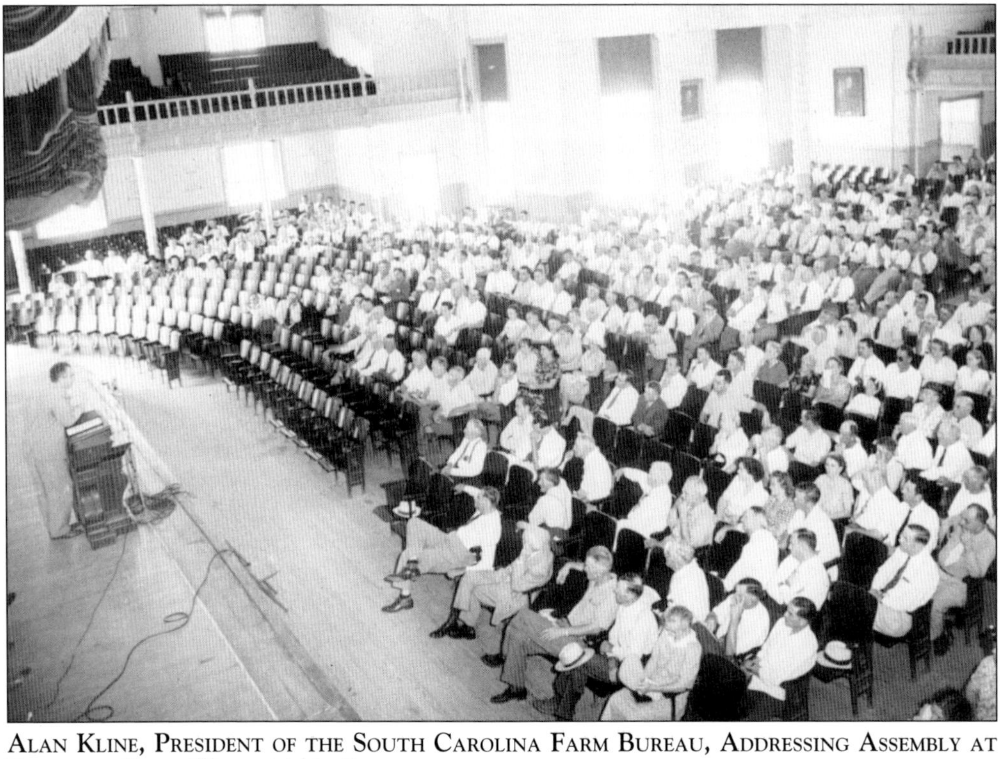

ALAN KLINE, PRESIDENT OF THE SOUTH CAROLINA FARM BUREAU, ADDRESSING ASSEMBLY AT FARM AND HOME WEEK, 1948, CLEMSON.

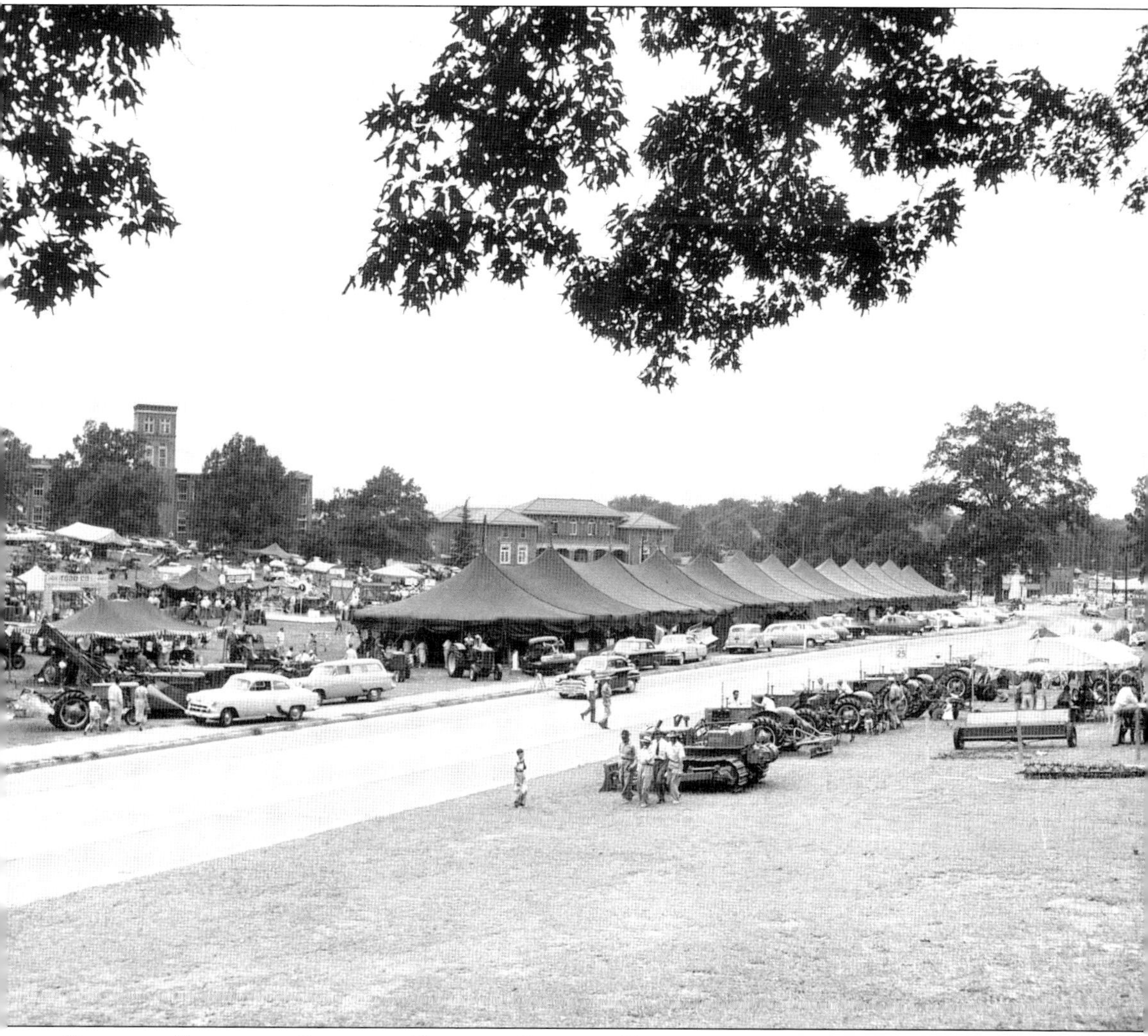

Bowman Field on Clemson Campus, Site of Farm and Home Week for over a Decade, 1957.

INDEX